An Introduction to English Architecture

An Introduction to

English Architecture

Frank Hoar, Ph.D., F.R.I.B.A., A.M.T.P.I.

Evans Brothers Limited : London

First published 1963 by Evans Brothers Limited
Montague House, Russell Square, London W.1

Set in 12 on 13 Walbaum and printed in Great
Britain by Butler and Tanner Ltd., Frome and
London
7/5466

Contents

Preface

I have written and illustrated this book primarily for the layman and the student of architecture. It has been found impossible, in a book of modest size, to include many contemporary buildings of great merit, but an attempt has been made to describe one example of buildings of varying purpose.

My thanks are due to those architects who have given their valuable time and help in compiling this book. My wife has read and corrected proofs with her usual infinite patience, and Mrs. Patricia Fraser has spent many hours and a great deal of effort in research. To all these kind people I wish to record my great appreciation.

H. F. H.

BARTLETT SCHOOL OF ARCHITECTURE,
UNIVERSITY COLLEGE, LONDON

Foreword

In the long history of English architecture there has never before occurred such an intensity of building activity as in the years since 1950. The only other comparable periods were the rebuilding of London after the Great Fire of 1666, which gave Wren his grand opportunity, and the town planning and building developments by the great private landowners and industrialists of the eighteenth and nineteenth centuries.

The situation which now confronts us embraces the whole country, and the reasons are not difficult to find. The damage caused by bombing, although serious and widespread, is only a partial explanation; the increasing concern of local and central government with the appalling housing conditions inherited from the industrial revolution has, over the last thirty years, given the impetus to a tremendous drive to eliminate the slums and the grey areas of depressed and out-dated working-class houses in the great industrial centres. This has resulted in a standard of domestic planning and building which has no rival in the world, and the work of an official body such as the London County Council is the product of some of the best architectural brains in the country.

The increasing tempo of modern life, with its stringent economic conditions, together with the demands of faster forms of traffic, have had an enormous influence on building design, while the increase in population and the necessity for new towns have imposed completely new concepts of town planning and communications in which the problem of the motor vehicle has become all important. This, in turn, has led to new forms of architecture and road engineering, where steel and reinforced concrete have opened new and exciting fields. Speed and cheapness of construction are now vital in order to satisfy economic and sociological pressures, and these can be attained only by the most efficient methods of building organisation and the most simple forms of construction.

The result is a plain and unadorned kind of structure which relies on its function for its shape, and on mass and colour for its effect; the essential supporting skeleton is covered only by the barest necessary cladding, which in turn is determined by its freedom from the expense of maintenance and the ease with which it can be cleaned.

Such new forms of building are not necessarily unattractive. The South Bank Exhibition of 1951, more than anything else, opened the eyes of the public to the force and beauty of well-ordered building designed by first-class artists using new materials and new techniques, and it demonstrated, too, the necessity for good design with its effect on our everyday existence.

In order to assess the appeal of modern architecture, however, it must be judged against the background of all that has gone before, and in this we are singularly fortunate. For interest and variety the architecture of England, since the Norman Conquest, has few rivals, and as a treasure house of fine buildings and works of art this country has a fascination that is unsurpassed.

This book, therefore, aims to help the reader to understand the rapidly changing architectural landscape of our times, and to trace its continuity and the purposes and requirements behind the varying styles of past centuries. The shapes and contours of the great mediaeval castles were dictated by hard military reasons, where comfort barely entered the life within. The message in the great cathedrals was painted in glass and carved in wood and stone, to be understood by a population that was almost entirely illiterate. The advent of more peaceful and settled times in the sixteenth century saw a vast improvement in domestic comforts,

and foreign artists introduced new and surprising standards of culture. An abundance of timber provided material for a type of building that has never lost its charm and appeal, and which may still be seen, unfortunately, in synthetic form in any suburban landscape.

Sea-power and the discovery of new centres of trade brought fabulous wealth to a small and privileged class of people who used it to impressive effect in their palatial homes. In the seventeenth and eighteenth centuries the great Whig families, each one of which exercised autocratic authority in its own domains, introduced the Baroque as a symbol of power and prestige while the accession of William and Mary, with their background of sober domesticity, brought Dutch ideas to a solid middle class. The revival of travel among the richer classes in the eighteenth century brought to their great houses the cream of European painting and works of art, and Rome became the Mecca of European culture with Venice as its playground. Architecture was the rage and the fashion, and aristocratic dilettantes vied with one another in the creation of splendid homes filled with the treasures of the Italian Renaissance. Set in vast parklands whose designs were based on the fantasies of Poussin and Claude Lorraine, their magnificence still remains to charm and enchant us.

The late Renaissance in English architecture continued into the reign of Victoria, although the novels of Scott and the writings of Ruskin inspired a revival of the mediaeval manner against a last desperate stand by the more extreme of the classic designers. The Great Exhibition of 1851 conceived a building whose significance was unrecognised for almost a century, and whose message was buried in the riot and exuberance of the industrial bazaar beneath its roof.

The Crystal Palace was removed to Sydenham and forgotten. The intense insularity of the country, and its innate suspicion of ideas from beyond its safe, encircling moat, discouraged all artistic experiment. Painting, sculpture and architecture, in spite of a few dissentient voices, lapsed into a slavish copying of much that had gone before.

The situation remained almost unchanged until the upheaval of the First World War when England, after a century of undisputed sway, saw the centre of power pass from East to West, and with it her dominant financial position. From Germany, striving to regain her trade and prestige after the Treaty of Versailles, came fresh architectural thinking and clean-cut buildings devoid of all unnecessary ornament. French architects, too, in their search for an architecture more attuned to the scientific basis of modern life, made a significant and logical contribution, and in recent years Italian and Brazilian designers have lent a Latin grace and imagination to the cruder outlines of the early formative years.

All these influences have had their effect in varying degree on the buildings we see around us today, although from time to time the more extreme designs may irritate and disturb us as much as the disasters and anachronisms of the speculative builder. What new wonders and new worlds the space age may show us, what effect if may have on the buildings we live and work in, we can only conjecture, but we can hope that, in time, an increasing interest by the public, a growing awareness of what a building is meant to do, and a keener appreciation of sane planning and fine design will create in England a new architecture that is as essentially English in character as the yeoman's cottage of Tudor times, and blessed with a beauty and a balance that reflect the spirit of what is still one of the most fortunate and envied countries in the world.

11

1

The Feudal period

England at the time of the Norman Conquest was divided and weakened by its separation under the great earldoms of Northumbria and East Anglia, Wessex and Mercia. Experience in the military art was so primitive that after the defeat at Hastings the whole country lay prostrate, and, save for a few minor insurrections, easily suppressed, was quickly and completely subjugated. To subdue a nation of one and a half millions, William of Normandy had at his disposal a force not exceeding 12,000 men and he had in the Pope an ally who, offended at the lethargy and independence of the Anglo-Saxon Church, lent willing aid.

The adventurers who fought under William's banner had no thought but for their own advantage. A tough French aristocracy, ruling from imposing castles, dominated the land and England became a vassal state of the Latin world with its theology, architecture, law, social and political organisation.

Two great Italians, Anselm of Aosta and Lanfranc of Pavia, held in succession the See of Canterbury. The standards of discipline, philosophy and scholarship brought by the conquerors mitigated the cruelty of their conquest, and enormous cathedrals grew side by side with the castles. As early as 1070 Lanfranc started work on the construction of a cathedral at Canterbury based on the Conqueror's own church of St. Stephen at Caen, and nine years later a vast scheme was commenced at Winchester by Bishop Walkelyn.

When the Normans conquered England they found stone churches and a few powerful thanes living in huge barn-like halls of timber and thatch which provided sleeping, living and eating space for a considerable household.

The departing Romans had left them an impressive though decayed system of roads and a few fortified towns such as Chester, London, York, Gloucester and Cirencester at the junctions. Although he imposed a military superstructure the Conqueror had the wisdom to leave England very much as it had always been. For military and taxing purposes the Norman manor was superimposed, but the English village with its strip-divided fields, its hereditary rights of pig-pannage and cattle pasture, its wide variety of tenure and its communal system of cultivation, was allowed to continue unchanged.

The reigns of the Norman kings William I (1066–87), William II (1087–1100), Henry I (1100–35), Stephen (1135–54) and Henry II (1154–89) cover the Norman period of English architecture which is distinguished by a bold and massive appearance, ponderous cylindrical piers, semicircular arches and a coarse but strongly effective decoration in its carving.

London examples of Norman building are the Keep and Chapel of the Tower of London (1086–97), the church of St. Bartholomew at Smithfield (1123–50), the Rotunda of the Temple Church (1185) which was badly damaged in the last war and now restored, and the crypts of St. Mary-le-Bow and St. John, Clerkenwell.

Durham Cathedral is almost entirely Norman, and the cathedrals of Norwich, Gloucester, Peterborough, Hereford, Winchester, St. Albans, Exeter, Ely, Chichester and Oxford are predominantly so. Waltham and Tewkesbury abbeys, and many small churches, mainly in the southern half of England, still retain their sturdy Norman appearance.

Among the castles Windsor has a shell keep of c. 1170 of which the upper half and the windows are nineteenth century, and twelfth-century castles can be seen at Carisbrooke, Isle of Wight (1140–50), Conisborough in Yorkshire, and Launceston, Trematon and Restormel in Cornwall. The fifty or so other examples include Colchester (c. 1090), Castle Rising in Norfolk (1140), Nor-

wich Castle, Rochester (1126–39), Hedingham in Essex (c. 1140) and Orford in Suffolk (1166–72).

The Early English period which followed saw the development of the pointed window and spread over the reigns of Richard I (1189–99), John (1199–1216), Henry III (1216–72) and Edward I (1272–1307). This is the period of English Gothic at its purest, simple in style and pleasing in its proportions. Tall, narrow windows with simple tracery, projecting buttresses, steeply sloping roofs, groups of slender columns and foliated and deeply cut capitals to the shafts are characteristic and may be seen in London in the cloisters of Westminster Abbey (1245–69), the choir, Lady Chapel and nave (restored) of Southwark Cathedral and the Chapel of Lambeth Palace. Salisbury Cathedral was, with the exception of the spire, built in the few years following 1220, and the transepts at York Minster with its nave (1261–1324), the nave and west front of Wells, the nave and chapter house of Lincoln, the choir, transepts and 'Galilee' porch at Ely, the choir at Worcester, the Elder Lady Chapel at Bristol, and Lichfield Cathedral were built during these years.

The Feudal Period, which ended with the more serious deprivations of the Black Death in 1349, included part of the period of the style known as 'Decorated', which comprises the reigns of Edward II (1307–27) and Edward III (1327–77). This style was more ornate than the Early English. Vaults became more complex. The lierne vault, so called from the number of ribs or 'liernes', became a feature, and window tracery became more flowing and geometrical.

Three bays of the east cloister of Westminster Abbey, the chapter houses at Wells (1319), Salisbury (1263–84) and Southwell, three bays east of the octagon at Ely, the nave, chapter house and west front of York

Minster, the twin towers over the north and south transepts at Exeter and the Eleanor Crosses are among the best examples. Figures in canopied niches were frequently added, as at Exeter.

Stokesay Castle is of this time, but by the middle of the fourteenth century the golden age of the mediaeval stronghold had passed. Maxstoke in Warwickshire is a typical defended manor of the period.

Among the abbeys, Westminster was founded in 960 and partly rebuilt (1055–66) by Edward the Confessor. Fountains Abbey appears to have been founded (1135) soon after Rievaulx (1132) and Kirkstall (1152).

At Oxford, University (1249), Balliol (1263), Merton (1264), Exeter (1314), Oriel (1326) and Queen's (1340), and at Cambridge, Peterhouse (1284), Clare (1326), Pembroke (1347) and Gonville and Caius (1348) were the colleges founded before the year of the Black Death.

Thus the architecture of England developed in a matter of three centuries from the ponderous and impressive style of the Conqueror to some of the loveliest in Europe, a tribute to the discipline and the civilising effects of the Normans on a poor and primitive island off the coast of Europe.

The end of the eleventh century saw a country for the most part of waste land, heath and forest, the lonely skyline broken here and there by a feudal keep on its mound or the towers of a great abbey. Sheep walked the uplands of the Cotswolds and Downs, and a few villages, their unfenced strips of earth ploughed by the inhabitants, were the only signs of life in the wild and romantic countryside. The peasantry of this period were housed, much as their forefathers had been in Saxon times and earlier, in rude timber-framed or rammed-earth huts covered with turf or thatch, without chimney or windows, the rain leaking through the sodden roof to the mud below. Huddled together for safety around the larger but equally uncomfortable manor or farm house, they formed the lowly villages which dotted the countryside.

Little Wenham Hall built above an undercroft. Dating from the late 13th century, this is probably the earliest domestic brick building in England
1 Hall
2 Chapel
3 Stairs down to undercroft

These villages were held by the local lord from the king. A powerful noble might hold a number of such communities, each managed by a steward and visited at intervals by the owner. Life in the villages was hard, squalid and rigorous in the extreme, the inhabitants living like the poultry and cattle that shared the same roof.

The Domesday Book reveals manors of all sorts and sizes, inhabited by many, as the Archbishop of Canterbury's great manor at Harrow with land for seventy teams of oxen, or by few, as on the Westminster manor of Cowley, with only two villeins. The Roman law of the Normans treated the serf as a chattel, a thing without rights, and the typical manor was cultivated by such until the time of the Black Death in the fourteenth century. Each villein was allowed the produce of his own 'virgate' of some thirty acres in return for services on the demesne and certain dues in kind. Defence against casual attack was paramount through the centuries until Tudor times, not only against man but against wild animals. Wolves became extinct in England only as late as Henry VII's reign.

By modern standards the manor houses themselves must have been appallingly uncomfortable, but a steady improvement took place in the twelfth and thirteenth centuries, and while security was the first consideration they became gradually more convenient and more commodious. In time the manor houses were rebuilt in stone, the timber hall being retained as the principal room, while chapel and private wing were built in the more permanent material under the same roof of lead or stone slates. This more fire-resisting form of construction has preserved several examples of the period.

In the courtyard of the manor house, farm buildings and workrooms were often ranged together for convenience and added safety.

Next to the hall were the buttery or wine store and the food store or pantry. The kitchen was placed some distance away owing to its incurable habit of catching fire, a constant danger. In time the kitchen, with brewhouse, stables, dovecot and the rest, came together in the courtyard in lean-to buildings ranged against the protecting stone walls.

By degrees, and for still greater safety, the hall was sometimes placed on an upper floor, the ground floor being given over to stables or store rooms, as at Boothby Pagnell near Grantham in Lincolnshire. This manor house, which dates from the second half of the twelfth century, has an undercroft and an upper chamber approached by an outside staircase. It is built solidly of stone, the windows small and round-headed.

Fear of fire dictated stone vaulted storerooms, but where the intervening floor was of timber the solution was to place the fireplace against the wall with a hollow chimney to lead off the smoke, as at Abingdon Abbey, in Berkshire. The bare earth floor, now gradually being covered with rushes, lasted down to the sixteenth century. There was no glass in the windows, which could be closed in cold weather only with shutters. The chapel had many uses other than religious, becoming an office or a guest room if necessary.

The hall was the focal point of the manor, and here lord and servants took their meals, local affairs were settled and a rough justice meted out. Here the retainers slept, while the lord and his family retired to the solar. By the twelfth century the lord's table had come to be placed at the far end of the hall away from the service entrances and their draughts, and set on a dais or low platform, the retainers ranged around the hall at trestle tables.

In the thirteenth century such a manor house might be surrounded, again for safety, by a moat, and beyond the moat would be a small stone church and a village of little hovels. Surrounding all were the fields which were shared out afresh each year among the various households.

Of the manor houses of the period which still remain, Charney-Basset Manor House (c. 1280) in Berkshire, consists of a hall and two transverse wings, with a small chapel on the first floor containing the piscina and a two-light east window. The solar adjoins the chapel to this day and retains its original king-post roof with tee-beam and struts.

Little Wenham Hall in Suffolk (1270) is a rather unusual building of the time. Although only a very small castle-type of building in stone it is elaborately built, the hall and main room at first-floor level for safety, and the windows, in their tracery and carving, almost ecclesiastical in richness. It was obviously built by a person of some consequence. The hall, as at Oakham in Rutlandshire and Stokesay in Shropshire, comprises almost the whole of the living accommodation, and the windows, deep-set in the thick walls, have window seats where the women could see to sew.

Oakham Castle in Rutland was built by Walkelyn de Ferrers about 1180. A double line of pillars with richly carved capitals supported the arches which bore the beams of the roof, now completely renewed as the original timbers had perished. The hall is one of the finest works of the transition from Norman to Early English architecture and measures 65 feet by 43 feet. The lengths of timber available limited the width of the central space and the two aisles covered by roofs leaning against the wall of the nave. Few houses were of a breadth to demand such a method of roof covering, but the simple constructional problem applied to churches which have survived the centuries.

Oakham Castle is really a strongly de-

Oakham Castle, Rutland, 1180: the Hall

fended manor house. The wall surrounding it is now ruined, and was probably at no time guarded by the customary towers. The embankment on which it stands may be extremely ancient and must at one time, with its surmounting wall, have presented a formidable place to attack. Records of the fourteenth century show that the enclosure was once entered by a gatehouse which has now disappeared, and which contained also stables, a store for hay, and a pen for prisoners. The hall, with its extraordinary collection of horse-shoes, is all that now remains and is typical of many others down to the end of the sixteenth century. It was entered through two doors, the kitchens at the lower end and the family rooms at the other. The fire must have been a central hearth with a louvre in the roof for the escape of smoke, but as the roof has since been rebuilt there is no available evidence of this. The original windows were small and gave an inadequate light to the interior, although this has now been rectified by the addition of modern dormers which have increased the light to an appreciable extent.

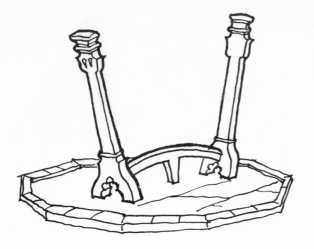

The hearth, Penshurst

Penshurst Place in Kent, built in 1341 just before the first visitation of the Black Death, has been for centuries the home of the Sidneys, and is a typical and well-preserved manor house of the period. The very fine hall, measuring 64 feet by 39 feet, is 48 feet in height with the usual screen at one end and the dais at the other; the central hearth still exists and the roof contained a louvre above it for the escape of smoke. In Elizabeth's reign the original arrangement of dwelling and service rooms was supplemented by additional rooms, and about 1340 pointed windows with graceful tracery were installed.

The vast hall at Winchester, which stands near the old town gate at the top of the picturesque High Street, was commenced in 1222 and completed about twelve years later. It is, by reason of the mediaeval importance of the city, one of the most historic in the country, and it saw the great feast given by William of Wykeham to Richard Cœur de Lion, after the escape of that monarch from captivity, when he returned to Winchester to be crowned. Philip and Mary dined there with Gardiner, and Margaret of Anjou was entertained by Cardi-

nal Beaufort. The hall measures 111 feet by 53 feet in width, the aisles being formed of clusters of slender columns which support pointed arches, a development from the single pillars and round arches of Oakham Castle.

Acton Burnell in Shropshire is perhaps the oldest surviving domestic building in the country planned as the dignified residence of an important man, in this case Bishop Burnell, Chancellor of Edward I and Bishop of Bath and Wells. The licence to crenellate was granted in 1283, but the home was not intended in any serious way for defence, in spite of the military appearance of the four tall towers at each corner of the rectangular plan. Burnell also added to the thirteenth-century palace at Wells a new chapel which, although ruined, is one of the most impressive English buildings of the Middle Ages, with its great hall, which measures 115 feet by 59 feet.

Stokesay Castle (1240–90) in Shropshire is intermediate in type. The big Gothic windows facing outward across the dry moat are in contrast to the grim military façade of Bolton in Yorkshire, while the gatehouse

Crenellation

18

Stokesay Castle, Shropshire, 1240–90: section through the great hall to show the roof

was built later in Elizabeth's reign, when its purely defensive rôle had disappeared. The chief apartment at Stokesay is the hall, about 51 feet by 31 feet, covered by a simply designed open timber roof, with rooms attached at each end. The sturdy three-storeyed tower was probably occupied by retainers, the rooms at the other end by the family. The topmost storey of this part was later altered by the addition of a picturesque half-timbered structure with larger windows, giving a more cheerful aspect to the interior. Early windows were never glazed, the ensuing draughts being kept out by shutters. The central fire was therefore a double necessity in cold weather to give light as well as heat to the hard-living inhabitants.

There is a fine example of a Norman town house known as the Jew's House, on Steep Hill, Lincoln, below the cathedral. St. Mary's Guild, also at Lincoln, and Norman House at Christchurch, Hampshire, are two further houses dating from this period.

Norman House dates from the second half of the twelfth century, and contains a narrow basement lit by slits in the walls. The hall, a large room with windows on three sides and a fireplace surmounted by a circular chimney stack, is on the first floor. The roof was open timbered and the floor has now disappeared.

The mediaeval castle was introduced by the Normans. It was at once the private residence and fortress of its owner, whether king or baron. Artillery transformed the English castles and, in the seventeenth century, finally destroyed them as strong points on which the defeated monarchy could fall back. Their ruins, in the eighteenth and nineteenth centuries, appealed to the more romantic minded and were either restored in some cases or became part of a dwelling house unsuited to military needs.

Before the Norman Conquest the defensive position was a fortified raised earthwork with an enclosure designed for the defence of a whole community, of which there are many examples in the country, although all traces of the original timber palisading have long since vanished. It was surmounted by some kind of stockade formed of tree trunks or by dry stone walls, such as Worlebury in Mendip, where the remains can still be seen. A ditch added to its strength; the excavated

19

earth was thrown downhill and gradually two steep 'scarps' were formed, the biggest of which can be seen at Maiden Castle, near Dorchester.

The Normans developed the idea at Bramber and Dover, and at Ardres near Dieppe, which is probably the finest example we know. In almost every case the fundamental and most important feature of these castles was the mound or motte. All over the country, on strategic hill or vantage point, they rose—little islands of foreign power in a subjected countryside. At the top of the mound was a flat space with an earthen rampart piled round its edge; at the base of the motte was the bailey, a simple enclosure surrounded again by its own earthen rampart and by its own ditch which joined that of the motte, forming what is known as the motte-and-bailey castle. Examples may be seen at Berkhamsted, at Topcliffe in Yorkshire and at Trecastle in South Wales.

The huge stone castle at Sarum has gone and only its foundations remain, but the mound on which it stood can still be seen. At Corfe the mound was carved out of the hill-top. As the mound or motte increased in height it became the more easily defensible, and together with the bailey, the enclosed courtyard which now contained the garrison, its cattle and workshops, it became the plan on which the great Norman castles at Rockingham, Warwick and Huntingdon, and above all Windsor, were planned. Warkworth has a rectangular bailey, but the most popular form was the motte and the circular or oval-shaped bailey. The Bayeux tapestry illustrates mound-castles at Dol, Dinan and Rennes, each a pointed hill with a ring of palisades at the top encircling a large building. London was overawed by the Tower, begun in wood immediately after the Conquest and finished in stone a generation later, but the only surviving part built by the Con-

queror is the White Tower, with its 15-foot thick walls.

The speed with which the early fortifications were built is a tribute to Norman discipline and its dynamic energy. The enormous mound for the Conqueror's castle at York took only eight days to rise at the hands of the sweating Saxon peasantry; a second, begun in the summer, was completed and garrisoned by five hundred men before winter, and the motte at Thetford, which measures 80 feet from the top to the bottom of the great ditch, must have involved many men and a fantastic amount of earth shifting. At Hastings, to cover his disembarkation, William threw up an earthworks of the usual type shown on the Bayeux tapestry with a mound surmounted by a palisade. In the event of a defeat he would have taken refuge there until relieved by ships from Normandy, and this procedure was followed in nearly every case of invasion of new territory.

The motte-and-bailey castle with its palisade and tower, being easy and cheap to construct and efficient in operation, solved to a great extent the problem of subjugating the ever-troublesome islanders. It offered a formidable defence against assault on foot, and against the cavalry and the armoured horsemen who dominated European warfare. These temporary but most effective structures were raised in large numbers during the years following the Conquest, and their green mounds are a not uncommon feature of the English landscape, although all trace of the original buildings which surmounted them have long disappeared. Because of the temporary nature of the defensive materials used it is not easy to describe them in detail, although sufficient information has come down to us to offer a very good idea of their appearance and operation. Crowned with further defensive palisades and a strong

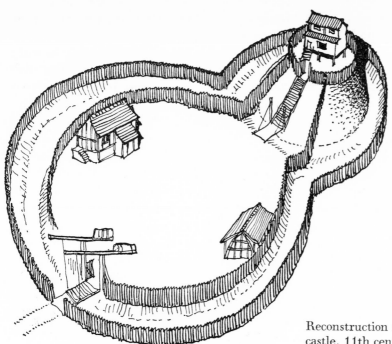

Reconstruction of a Norman motte-and-bailey castle, 11th century

wooden tower as the residence of the owner, which formed the ultimate defence of the castle, there were also buildings to make the castle habitable. Within the bailey was a hall for the retainers, in which they ate and slept, together with stables, storehouses and barns. These wooden palisades and structures had, however, an obvious weakness—they had no defence against fire—so that their replacement by stronger materials was essential, and this was done as soon as labour and stone could be obtained.

The efficient Norman mind was concerned also with economy. Oxford Castle was founded in 1071 by Robert d'Oilli who added a chapel to it in 1074, of which the tower still stands on the bailey wall where he built it, overlooking the entrance from the west, as part of the stone castellum with which he replaced the original wooden palisade. At Earls Barton the line of the castellum was drawn to include the tower of the

neighbouring Saxon church, which thus became a part of the defence instead of a probable menace.

The main entrance to the castle was a gateway into the bailey, often defended by wooden towers built up from the stockade, with an access bridge across the ditch. Between the bailey and the summit of the motte was a sloping bridge or causeway raised on piles, thus rendering the motte a separate entity within the castle. Jean de Colmieu, a twelfth-century chronicler of Northern France, thus described these structures: 'For it is the custom of the nobles of this region, who spend their time for the most part in private war, in order to defend themselves from their enemies, to make a hill of earth, as high as they can, and encircle it with a ditch as broad and deep as possible. They surround the upper edge of this hill with a very strong wall of hewn logs, placing small towers on this circuit,

21

according to their means. Inside this wall they plant their house or keep, which overlooks the whole thing.'

Another French chronicler, Lambert of Ardres, writing about 1194 of the mound at Ardres in Flanders which was raised at the beginning of the twelfth century, described it thus: 'Arnold, Lord of Ardres, built on the motte of Ardres a wooden house, excelling all the houses of Flanders of that period both in material and in carpenters' work. The first storey was on the surface of the ground, where were cellars and granaries, and great boxes, tuns, casks and other domestic utensils. In the storey above were the dwelling and common living rooms of the residents, in which were the larders, the rooms of the bakers and butlers, and the great chamber in which the lord and his wife slept. Adjoining this was a private room, the dormitory of the waiting maids and children. In the inner part of the great chamber was a certain private room, where at early dawn or in the evening or during sickness or at a time of blood letting, or for warming the maids and weaned children, they used to have a fire. . . . In the upper storey of the house were garret rooms, in which on the one side the sons, on the other side the daughters of the lord of the house used to sleep. In this storey also the watchman and the servants appointed to keep the house took their sleep at some time or other. High up on the east side of the house, in a convenient place, was the chapel. . . .'

The use of stone came in after the country had been subjugated and the urgent defensive period had given way to a more ordered way of life. The square and massive stone towers that now arose high over the countryside were of the simplest. Window openings in the lower storeys were small, for protection against missiles and against escalade, and for the further reason that there was no glass. The construction of these buildings was a perpetual exercise and experiment in new methods of defence against an ever-changing theory of assault, of which the most elaborate example is the Tower of London, built about 1077 by Gundulf, Bishop of Rochester, which contains a complete chapel, a basement and main floor, unfortunately divided at a later date. Beneath the chapel are two storeys of vaulted prisons, the lower being the grim and sinister 'Little Ease'.

Other great square keeps were built in the first half of the twelfth century as at Norwich and Castle Hedingham in Essex, but the golden age of the square tower is the reign of Henry II in the second half of the twelfth century, when splendid examples arose at Bamborough, Scarborough, Newcastle-on-Tyne and Dover, where the walls are from 21 to 24 feet thick.

Hard military reasoning governed the development of these castles. In many cases it was found that the plateau formed by the motte was too large to cover with a single massive keep, in which case a stone curtain wall was built, forming a ring of masonry around the keep. This type is found at Berkeley, Cardiff, Usk, Totnes and Launceston.

There are forty-nine castles mentioned in the Domesday Book as existing before 1086; it is thought at least eighty-five were built before 1100, but out of these only six or seven appear to have been built in stone. Of the stone keeps that arose in the reigns of Henry I, Stephen or Henry II, only a few —London, Colchester, Pevensey and Richmond (Yorks)—belong to the Conqueror's period. To overawe the larger centres of population, walled in the old Saxon style with ditch and palisade, the majority of the thirty or so royal castles built before 1100 were erected inside or alongside the walls of the major towns. Such were the castles of London, York, Worcester, Winchester, Old Sarum, Lincoln, Hereford, Gloucester, Exeter, Colchester, Chester and Cambridge. They were erected in many cases against the outer wall of the town as a mark of suspicion, and when placed inside, the citizens' dwellings were ruthlessly destroyed over a wide area so that the fortress was not hemmed in and could not be taken by surprise.

Other castles were built at strategic points of defence, or were designed to hold open the main lines of communication. Dover, Hastings, Pevensey, Dorchester, Southampton and Scarborough were formed to guard the coast, others, defending interior lines of communication, were placed at fords, such as Newcastle-on-Tyne or Wallingford, at the most important crossing on the Thames. The more vital defensive castles were usually confiscated by the King in his own interests, as happened at Newark and Corfe. A chain of strong fortresses extended along the Welsh border at Chester and Shrewsbury, Ludlow, Hereford and Gloucester, and in the north,

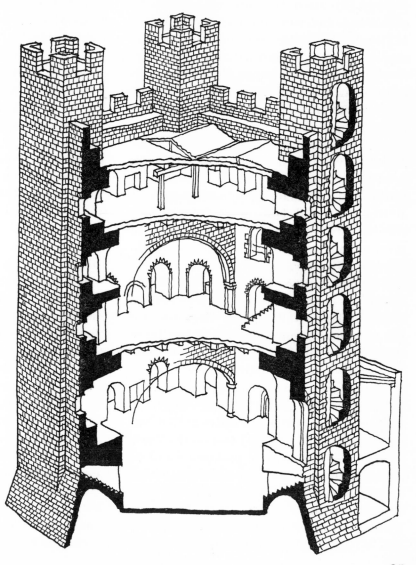

Castle Hedingham,
Essex, 1130–40:
typical Norman square
tower keep

23

Richmond, Bamborough and Scarborough were built in strength in dominating positions.

In dividing the subject land among his followers, William the Conqueror followed a subtle and complicated course. Where strength was needed, as along the frontier with Wales, the estates were large, and were dominated by imposing castles manned by strong garrisons, but elsewhere, the estates were divided, in many cases remote from each other. The border strongholds were strategically sited in military relation to each other, and were built on high cliffs, as at Dunster, or protected by morass or watercourse, as at Kenilworth. Artificial lakes were formed by the damming of streams, as at Leeds in Kent or Caerphilly in Glamorgan, so that mining—one of the most formidable methods of mediaeval siege craft—was impossible. But the owner of the baronial castle was usually satisfied with a height or mound with steeply sloping sides, or with the span of a hill cut off by a deep ditch, as at Chepstow and Hastings, where a deep cutting between the castle and the rest of the hill can be seen. It is particularly obvious from the air.

The great square Norman keeps, whose design was borrowed from France, and from behind whose walls feudal England was governed and organised, were of solid masonry, nearly 100 feet high, with dungeons in the basement, a guard room at a higher level, and big square living room or hall above it, usually with the water-well easily accessible. The roof was for the archers and guards. Walls of 12 to 20 feet in thickness, so that communicating passages could be made in them, were strengthened by flat buttresses and loopholed for archery. The basement with its massive encircling walls, without an opening of any kind, could be entered only by a trapdoor from the first-floor room, the hall of the castle, which contained the sole entrance reached by a ladder or a strongly defended stair. The lord and his family occupied the floor above, with chapel and sleeping quarters in the thickness of the walls, and on the battlemented roof were the kitchen and ovens for the preparation of food in times of peace, and for the heating of missiles in war. Two such examples, the White Tower and Colchester Keep, were built during the lifetime of the Conqueror, but the large majority of the square keeps, such as Norwich, Rochester, Hedingham and Newcastle, arose in the reign of Henry II. Crusaders, fighting in the eastern Mediterranean, learnt new methods of castle building from the Saracens and Byzantines. A curtain wall with round towers at intervals surrounded both keep and bailey, such as the great Krak des Chevaliers in Syria, which in turn influenced Richard I's impregnable fortress at Château Gaillard, rising on steep cliffs above the Seine near Rouen. Château Gaillard was at least twenty years ahead of any other French or English fortress. Here the keep and inner bailey were surrounded by a middle and an outer bailey, and its construction embodied the most advanced ideas of the day. It was the object of the skilled military architect to construct his wall so that the besieger should find no 'dead angles' uncovered by the missiles of the defence.

The cylindrical keep, also borrowed, in essence, from France, appeared late in the twelfth century, and marked a decided advance on the square keep which preceded it, in that its loopholes presented a wide field of fire to the defence; further, it had no angles to be more easily dislodged than the radiating stones of a rounded tower. Again, it had no angles which could not be commanded by loopholes in either face of a square tower, so that defensive missiles could

24

search every part of the surrounding area and put a check to mining operations. Another feature was the spreading base which prevented direct attack from a battering ram.

This form of structure was immensely strong and almost impregnable to the assault weapons of the time, but its strength was static, and it could offer no offensive threat, no sally-ports for a counter-offensive. By the middle of the thirteenth century, therefore, the keep had gone out of fashion and castles were planned as bases for offensive operations. The nature of the site determined the shape of the defensive enclosure, and the form of the structure was built so that the whole garrison could operate simultaneously. This was achieved by raising the inner walls, which were concentric with the outer, thus enabling the inner garrison to shoot over the heads of their comrades. It was so arranged at Caernarvon that three tiers of archers could concentrate a murderous fire on a single target, and besiegers penetrating the outer walls were exposed to a continuous and deadly discharge from archers on every side.

The outer works defending the entrance were treated with much cunning and ingenuity, and approaches were narrow and easily defended. The enemy was deceived by mock entrances and cul-de-sacs down which he might rush to destruction, and double gates, narrow twisting passages and an outer barbican were built. The campaigns of the Crusaders in Asia Minor encouraged a constant and ever-changing development in the art of military architecture which transformed the Conqueror's Tower of London and gave it the shape we know today.

Further developments in defence were the provision of a rampart and battlements along the top of the wall. Overhanging battlements, called machicolations, enabled the defenders to pour down through apertures

Machicolation

boiling pitch, quicklime, oil or tar upon an enemy seeking to breach the walls. As the encircling ditch was insufficient defence against the undermining of the outer walls they were increasingly filled with water and are now, as at Bodiam, Wells, Leeds (Kent) and others, one of the most charming features in the romantic appearance of a ruined castle.

The golden age of castle building extended from 1250 to 1350. At the end of the thirteenth century Edward I built a series of magnificent castles to control the conquered Welsh. The finest of these are Beaumaris in Anglesey and Harlech on the coast of Merionethshire, which were purely fortresses with two concentric rings of towered walls and living rooms in the towers and gatehouse of the inner ring, and no keep at all. Other castles of this period, such as Caernarvon and Caerphilly, having a hall and other rooms

25

Reconstruction of Beaumaris
Castle, Anglesey, 1295–1323:
an example of a
'concentric' castle

within the inner bailey, are examples of an integrated whole and were developed from the theory that the massive keep defended by the comparatively weak defences of the bailey was insufficient if the bailey were overcome and captured, and that both features should therefore be built as strongly as possible. This theory was powerfully vindicated by the fall of Château Gaillard in 1204, where the defenders were driven from court to court and in despair made no attempt to hold the keep. The keep thus became militarily unnecessary and the castle then formed an enclosure adequately defended by its walls, with its flanking towers covering by cross-fire the outer base of the wall. The protected gateway, or barbican, with double doors and portcullis enclosing a space commanded from above, can be seen at Walmgate Bar in the walls of York.

The building of castles reached its culmination at Conway and Caernarvon, at Caerphilly, Beaumaris and Harlech.

Before the end of the eleventh century there were more major churches under construction in England than anywhere else in the world. Winchester and Old St. Paul's

both covered an area of 65,000 square feet as compared with the 54,000 square feet of Cluny, the largest church in Western Europe. The first stones of Rochester Cathedral were laid within a few years of the occupation, and Canterbury was commenced as early as 1070, with Lincoln following soon after. Monastic establishments were founded, in many cases, as at Canterbury, where priory and Cathedral were one. Cathedrals of the monastic foundation include Ely, Norwich,

Canterbury Cathedral, 1096–1107: groined vault

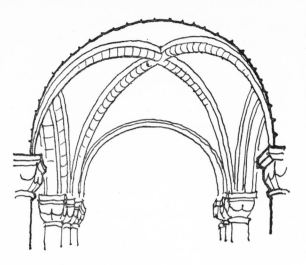

Peterborough Cathedral, c. 1100: ribbed vault

Oxford, Rochester, Peterborough, Winchester, Worcester, Chester, Carlisle and above all Durham; they contain some of the very finest Norman craftsmanship, although this is not by any means confined to the monastic cathedrals. Three enormous crypts at Worcester (1084), Gloucester (1089) and Winchester (1079), lying beneath the whole of the eastern part of these cathedrals and of great interest with their early groined vaults, alone survive from the major church buildings of the eleventh century.

The abbeys of Fountains and Rievaulx in Yorkshire were founded during the Norman period, although they were much enriched at a later date. The abbey church of St. Edmundsbury, which once covered an area of 68,000 square feet, now almost entirely disappeared with the exception of its magnificent tower, was built at this time. Tewkesbury, with another fine tower, and the abbey church of St. Albans were also built, the latter comparable in its ponderous massiveness with Durham. After the Dissolution of the monasteries the huge building was used as a quarry, and fragments have been identified in many of the oldest

houses in the city. Mediaeval paintings in the nave were whitewashed during the Cromwellian dictatorship and came to light again only during restoration in the 1860's.

The most important Norman monument of the eleventh century is Durham Cathedral. Commencing in 1093 from the east, the Norman custom in building a great church, the work had reached the nave by 1099. The vault over the choir at Durham, built in stone and completed as early as 1104, no longer exists but the nave was built about

Durham Cathedral, 1093–**1133:** section through central tower and nave

Durham Cathedral, 1093–1133: single bay in nave showing cylindrical pier. The height to vaulting is 72 feet

1130, and vaulted with stone many years in advance of the other cathedrals. The Normans here overcame one of their greatest difficulties. For smaller churches the barrel vault usually sufficed, but when erected in any large size it exercised terrific outward thrust, necessitating very thick supports. With the development of the ribbed vault the diagonal and transverse ribs transferred the thrust to piers and to flat buttresses at points where the pressure was greatest.

With Durham the general form of the great cathedral church was evolved, and was to remain for several centuries. It was cruciform in plan with a central tower at the crossing supported by massive arches, which in turn were abutted by the nave, choir, and north and south transepts. The setting out of such a huge building was anything but experimental, and must have been carried out by men with long and wide scientific experience, but individual designers before the fourteenth century are unknown. Durham is probably the most impressive of English cathedrals. It rears up mightily on the cliffs above the river and culminates with majesty in the splendid tower. Inside, the enormous cylindrical piers of the nave, with the coarse richness of the arches, are overpowering, and reflect with ponderous emphasis the vigour and strength of the warrior race who created the great church.

The massive and impressive cylindrical Norman pier is found again in Gloucester, Pershore and Tewkesbury, a group of west country churches forming the nearest approach to a regional school of the period. This feature is seen again at Hereford and Malvern, and on a smaller scale at St. John's Chapel in the Tower of London.

About the middle of the twelfth century the pure Norman was showing signs of transition to the pointed arch, and construction became consequently lighter and more scientific. The cylindrical Norman columns gave way to more slender piers, and the massive Norman walling of rubble faced with worked stone was abandoned for walls of more scientific construction and thinner masonry. Before the end of the century Wells Cathedral was substantially under way, and the great Cistercian abbeys of Waverley, in Surrey, and Fountains, Rievaulx, Jervaulx and Kirkstall, in the north, contributed valuable ideas in a time of change and experiment. The choir of Canterbury Cathedral was destroyed by fire in 1174 and the new one was built by a Frenchman, William of Sens, who was seriously injured in a fall from the scaffolding. It was completed by an Englishman but its apse or chevet, with its radiating chapels, is French, and so are the Corinthianesque columns. It influenced even the new choir at far-away Lincoln which was commenced before the end of the century, and it had moreover a significant effect on churches throughout south-east England.

The end of the twelfth century saw the rise of what Sir Christopher Wren called the Gothic period, 'that barbarous and decadent style' which impeded the onset of the Renaissance of the classical Roman style. With that judgment we now profoundly disagree, recognising that both styles are a precious part of the national heritage and that each can achieve buildings as advanced and as perfect in their own way. The significance of the Gothic style with its pointed arch lies in the change over from one of inert stability to one of equilibrium, where the varying thrusts of vault and spire were counterbalanced by a form of construction which altered completely the appearance of the great churches.

English Gothic naves, because of the comparative lowness of the buildings, rarely exceeded 80 feet in height, but in compensation there evolved vaults of extraordinary complexity, culminating in the wonderful lierne vaults of Exeter Cathedral and, later, the marvellous roofs of Henry VII's Chapel

Typical section through an Early English cathedral to show construction, 13th century

1 Arcade
2 Triforium
3 Clerestory
4 Nave
5 Vaulting
6 Roof timbers
7 Flying buttress
8 Buttress
9 Aisle

at Westminster, St. George's Chapel at Windsor and, above all, King's College Chapel at Cambridge. In the soaring height of the big continental churches there is a feeling almost of remoteness, although they are awe-inspiring in the sheer achievement of their daring construction. With the lower English churches there is a more friendly and charming spirit, which is again enhanced by their attractive surroundings. Masonry construction in the thirteenth, fourteenth and fifteenth centuries achieved the realms of exact engineering, and walls between the supporting piers eventually disappeared entirely, to be replaced by huge areas of brilliantly coloured glass.

This first Gothic period is known as Lancet or Early English and depends for effect on simplicity of ornament and pleasing proportion. Openings are tall and narrow, giving an impression of height, and exteriors are marked by projecting buttresses, pinnacles and steeply pitched roofs, with groups of slender shafts, connected by bands to the main piers, replacing the massive Norman columns. In the deeply channelled arch-mouldings are lines of dog-tooth ornament, and capitals and bosses are foliated, the wide naves spanned by pointed rib and panel vaults with diagonal and transverse ribs, bold and graceful, as at Lincoln and Westminster. The arrangement of windows developed from the single window to a composition of three, the tall one in the centre flanked by lower ones, with a small projecting ridge or dripstone running round the head of each to throw off rain from the glass. This grew eventually into a single arched dripstone over all three. The blank space between the heads of the lancets and the surmounting arch was then opened by small circular windows, the origin of tracery in later periods. The curves became more and more complicated throughout the first half

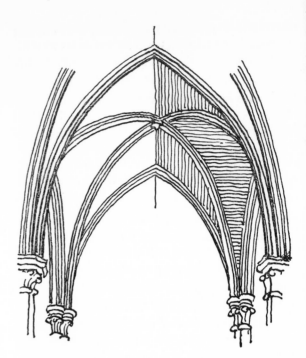

Salisbury Cathedral, 1220: rib and panel vault

of the fourteenth century and exercised the utmost skill of the sculptor-masons who carved them, until in France the style culminated in the writhing and flame-like patterns of the Flamboyant style.

At Canterbury the new cathedral and Benedictine Abbey, commenced in 1070 under Lanfranc, the first Norman archbishop, was based on the design of the Conqueror's Abbey at Caen, but was enlarged and entirely remodelled between 1096 and 1115. Considerable Norman work can still be seen, notably the Norman tower (1096–1115) and the crypt.

Canterbury is a lovely and most successful compromise. The martyrdom of Becket in the cathedral in 1170 brought a continuous stream of pilgrims to the Cathedral for the next three centuries, bringing with them a revenue that ceased only with Henry VIII's famous writ against Becket for 'treason, contumacy, and rebellion' with the inevitable removal of the gold and jewels of the cathedral in twenty-six cartloads to the royal treasury.

The nave of Wells Cathedral was completed by 1190 and the wonderful west front with its numerous statues by 1229. The figure sculpture compares favourably with anything in England, and the west front as a composition is undoubtedly the finest in the country. The cathedral was fortunately spared the depredations of the nineteenth-century restorers and is one of the most picturesque and romantic of the great English churches.

The stone carving at Wells is outstanding. The capitals of the nave and transept columns are marvels of mediaeval craftsmanship and interest, with their representations of every-day life and custom of the time. The detail and the felicity of the whole conception of the building have few rivals in the kingdom, and the mediaeval town and the Bishop's Palace with its encircling castellated walls and moat, the swans moving gracefully on its surface, complete a picture of charm and interest that is unsurpassed in Western Europe.

The sculpture of this period shows a freedom and originality which give it a deservedly high place in the history of art. Certainly it has no superior in England, and preserves much of the severity of form, the dignity of attitude and the treatment of drapery derived from classical tradition. The most complete collection is at Wells, the most graceful consisting of the figures of angels in the spandrels of the arches in the Angel Choir at Lincoln (c. 1270).

In the thirteenth century the sepulchral effigy became important as a form of sculpture, the figures generally being those of ecclesiastics or warriors whose drapery or armour lent itself to grace and nobility of treatment. The earliest royal effigy is that of King John in Worcester Cathedral (1240),

and there are notable collections in the cathedrals of Exeter, Hereford, Salisbury, Wells and Worcester. Contrary to common belief, the warrior with crossed legs has no necessary connection with the Crusades. The Percy tomb (c. 1345) in Beverley Minster and the tomb of Edward II (c. 1337) in Gloucester Cathedral are outstanding.

The most typical example of the English Gothic vernacular is Salisbury, which was commenced in 1220, the same year that saw the beginning of Amiens, its most typically French counterpart. The original Norman cathedral was at Old Sarum, on the spur of the chalk downs some distance to the north of the present city. The site proved unsuitable for many reasons, including lack of water and limitation of space, and work commenced on the cathedral in April 1220 and was completed, save for the spire, and dedicated in September 1258.

There is no grander Gothic conception in England, although it lacks the exquisite detail of Wells. It remains today, with the exception of the spire, almost exactly as when built, and is singularly fortunate in the wide and spacious lawns which surround it, enabling the viewer to see the church from every possible angle. The interior, however, in comparison with Wells is disappointing, and the use of the brown Purbeck marble, surely the most unsuitable material for the Gothic spirit, adds in no way to its attraction. The tower and spire were built towards the middle of the fourteenth century on the inadequate piers of the low central tower, and were reinforced by Wren with bands of wrought iron; latterly the cross and the masonry at the top of the steeple have been renewed. The stability of this magnificent feature, 402 feet in height from ground level, appears to defy all known laws, although it is reinforced by the original timber centering. That it still stands is almost miraculous when it is recalled that the central towers of Lincoln, Peterborough, Ely, Ripon and Winchester all collapsed, and the spire of Norwich blew down, a testimony to the dishonesty of the masons, and the inadequacy of their foundation work.

At Lincoln an earthquake in 1185 did much damage; rebuilding commenced in 1192 and the church as we know it today was almost completed by the early fourteenth century. The glory of the cathedral is the celebrated 'Angel' choir (1255–80) in the purest Early English style, and the 'Galilee' porch in the south transept, with its profusion of 'tooth' ornament.

The character of Westminster Abbey reflects Henry III's enthusiasm for French work, the flying buttresses supporting the south wall of the nave, seen from the famous school, being more reminiscent of the great French cathedrals than in any other English church. The nave at 105 feet is taller than most English naves and the chevet is decidedly French.

Exeter Cathedral was almost entirely rebuilt between 1280 and 1369, the choir between 1280 and 1310 and the nave and west front, with its huge curvilinear window, between 1320 and 1370.

Many of the larger churches extended their buildings in the thirteenth century. Durham built its Chapel of the Nine Altars, and other cathedrals extended their buildings to the east, as at Chichester, Ely, Exeter, Cuckfield, Peterborough, Rochester, St. Albans, Southwell, Wells and Worcester. By the middle of the century the traceried window appeared and later became more elaborate, with quatrefoil and trefoil openings above.

The massive appearance of Norman work is sometimes merely an illusion, and calamity overtook many great buildings. It was a time of mass production, with a vast amount of enthusiastic but unskilled labour working under the supervision of a handful of craftsmen. An outer skin of masonry was filled, sometimes by extremely haphazard methods, with a core of rubble or stone chippings mixed with mortar. It was not to be wondered at that the walls sometimes failed, and at Winchester in 1107 the central tower crashed to the ground. The north-west tower at Gloucester failed in 1170 and the central tower of Lincoln in 1240.

On the night of 12th February 1322 disaster came to Ely Cathedral. The monks had only just left their matin service when the central tower, whose insecurity had long been suspected, crashed to the ground. The fall of the tower destroyed three bays of the choir, but by good fortune the sub-prior of the cathedral was a certain Alan de Walsingham. There was no better qualified man in the kingdom to deal with such a situation, and the originality and skill with which he designed and carried out the reconstruction marks him as an engineer and architect of the highest order. The Lady Chapel in itself would have been sufficient to establish his reputation, without the constructive genius he displayed in the conception of the octagon.

The wreckage of the tower was cleared, and Walsingham was presented with the opportunity of building what has been called the only Gothic dome in the country. Instead of the former four supports, he provided eight by including four of the nave piers, so making the structure immeasurably stronger and in addition enlarging the space at the crossing. The stonework was finished in 1328, and the timberwork of the octagon in 1342. The weight of the lantern is taken on the eight massive oaken angle-posts, each 3 feet 4 inches by 2 feet 8 inches in section. The raising of such enormous timbers with the primitive mediaeval tackle is in itself a matter of wonder, and a tribute to the courage and skill of the mediaeval engineer.

The operations at Winchester to underpin part of the walls revealed that some of the foundations rested only on faggots standing in water, and at Ely, where the thirteenth-century foundations stand on rock 6 feet below ground, the nearby Norman work stops 18 inches above it. But in the main the great Norman buildings have stood up well to the test of time. Foundations as a rule were solid and taken down to firm and stable beds. At Glastonbury they go down 12 feet, at Durham 14 feet.

Art in the English cathedrals reached a high standard about the middle of the thirteenth century, and rose to its culmination during the next hundred years in the carving of foliage and the woodwork of screens and canopied stalls, notably those in Winchester Cathedral.

The evidence, both documentary and actual, of the wide use of colour in mediaeval churches is considerable, and it is much to be regretted that the examples still surviving are insufficient to describe it with any accuracy. It was particularly important in its relation to the churches of the thirteenth century as the simplicity of the architecture was in direct contrast to the brilliant and glowing colours of the decorations. The restorations of the nineteenth century did widespread damage and the repainting of

Ely Cathedral, 1322–40: oak framing to octagon over the crossing

the frescoes at a later age naturally reflected the period in which they were carried out.

Professor Lethaby has left some valuable notes on his researches into the evidence of colour in Westminster Abbey, which may be taken as an example of other churches as there is no reason to suppose that its use was limited to the few. The stonework was first limewashed all over and the joints of the masonry were marked in red lines, sometimes with a small red flower to each rectangle. The diaper work in the choir was gilded on a red ground, and the spandrels of the south-eastern chapels still show evidence of colour in the carving of the foliage. The ironwork of straps and hinges on doors were brilliantly coloured; the magnificent door of Henry III's Chapel at Windsor was covered with scarlet gesso and the pattern of iron scrolls may have been gilded.

The tombs and fittings of Westminster Abbey, recently renewed, were also coloured, in particular the tomb canopies. The figure sculptures of the transepts bore colour, and the draperies were elaborately patterned.

The earliest wall paintings, representing Christ enthroned, and scenes involving the angel Gabriel, still exist in St. Gabriel's Chapel in the crypt at Canterbury. The drawing is in strong line, filled in with colour, and the figure of St. Paul in the upper church is finely drawn.

There are more Norman decorations in the little twelfth-century church at Kempley in Gloucestershire, and at Hardham church in Sussex. None of these can in any sense be termed great art. There was no Norman Giotto. Well-known paintings of this period were the mural decorations of the middle of the thirteenth century in the 'Painted Chamber' of the Palace of Westminster.

The chapter house, or council chamber of a monastic or cathedral establishment, was the most important of the peculiarly monastic buildings, ranking only after the church itself. At Canterbury and Winchester they are similar in size, measuring 90 feet by 40 feet approximately, and are rectangular in plan. Some of the chapter houses of the twelfth century have vaults spanning up to 35 feet, as at Durham and Gloucester. In the monasteries the chapter house was used by the brethren for the daily meeting after breakfast to recite prayers, to listen to that part of the martyrology appropriate for the day, and to hear from the abbot of matters of business affecting the community.

The most interesting chapter houses are polygonal in plan, and are remarkable instances of engineering in stone. They are a peculiarly English development and are nowhere else found in like form. They vary in size from 18 feet diameter at Manchester to 58 and 59 feet at Westminster and Lincoln. The earliest example is at Worcester, a circular building 56 feet in diameter, completed in 1092.

The octagonal chapter house at Wells is one of the most important and successful works of late thirteenth- and early fourteenth-century design. The undercroft can hardly be later than 1220, and the chapter house itself was in use by 1319. The picturesque and celebrated stairs which turn and at the same time continue to the bridge over the main gate date, however, from the fifteenth century. The treatment of the vault is the most astonishing feature of this remarkable building, for no less than thirty-two ribs, giving an extremely sumptuous effect, spring from the central column.

The huge traceried windows of the period lit these enormous chapter houses to brilliant effect. The chapter house at Westminster, 58 feet across, was nearing completion in 1254 and formed the model for Salisbury, which followed ten years later. The two re-

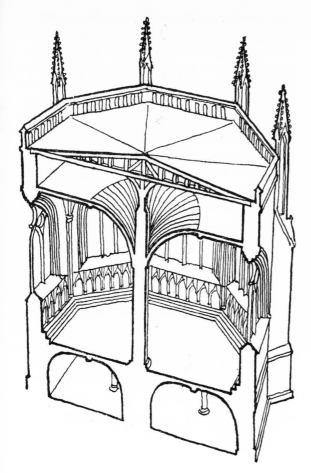

Wells Cathedral: section through octagonal chapter house. The undercroft was completed in 1286

markable chapter houses at York and Southwell were begun in the late thirteenth century, the latter comparatively small, only 31 feet in diameter, and the York example 58 feet across, with an elaborate timber vault.

The larger monuments of architecture during the Middle Ages were based on sound structural principles, reached by a process of trial and error. Many of the more ambitious essays failed, but they provided the experience on which the buildings which followed were erected.

English mediaeval engineers never attained the soaring heights of the continental cathedrals, or the extreme daring of continental engineers, who raised the vaulting to the nave of Amiens to 145 feet and of Beauvais to 156 feet. The tower over the crossing at Beauvais rose to a dizzy 500 feet and then crashed, bearing with it the nave. The soaring choir is all that now remains, and even this was unsuccessfully fired by the departing German army in 1944.

Stone in England was not always readily available, but there was a super-abundance of fine building timber. In the use of this material the English engineer was pre-eminent, and nowhere did he demonstrate his skill more nobly than in the roofing of the chapter house of York Minster, built during the last decade of the thirteenth century, a whole generation before the octagon at Ely. It is unusual in having no central column, as at Wells, to receive the vaulting. The timber roof had therefore to span a distance of 64 feet, but the mediaeval builders found that no timber of that length was available. The main tie-beams had perforce to be made up of two beams each 52 feet long, the remaining distance at each end being covered by single beams secured between the double beams. These two main tie-beams, crossing at right angles, support the central post, 64 feet tall, built up in three stages, firmly wedged at each stage between double tie-beams. The timber vault to the octagon is suspended beneath, as shown in the illustration.

A system of carpenter's marks on the timber proves that the roof was prefabricated and assembled on the ground before being hoisted up over the chapter house. It is not known whether this was done on the site or in the forest where the timber was cut, but it is known that the roof of

35

Westminster Hall was prefabricated at Farnham in Surrey, which was then, in the year 1395, a great forest.

Another typically English feature of the cathedral is the cloister. There are many continental examples, perhaps the best known being at Ratisbon (Regensburg) Cathedral, at S. John Lateran in Rome and at Monreale Cathedral. S. Paolo in Rome has remarkable twisted and coupled columns, S. Trophime at Arles has coupled columns in the Romanesque manner, and the church of the Apostles at Cologne is another Romanesque example. There are others at S. Juan de los Reyes at Toledo and in Rome at S. Maria della Pace, but they are not an essential adjunct to a cathedral as they are, almost without exception, in this country.

From the thirteenth century onwards the great churches of the secular canons also built splendid cloisters in imitation of the monastic churches. At Salisbury they were a favourite subject of J. M. W. Turner and give an effect of great spaciousness. Norwich, Canterbury, Worcester and Gloucester all rebuilt their cloisters during the course of the fourteenth century, and Westminster in the last few years of the thirteenth century. All these are distinguished by the size and splendour of their traceried windows, and by particular features such as the elaborate sculptured bosses at the intersection of the

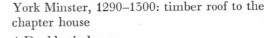

York Minster, 1290–1300: timber roof to the chapter house

1 Double tie-beam
2 Main tie-beam
3 Principal rafters 13 inches by 12 inches

vaulting groins at Norwich, or the fine vaulting at Worcester. The earliest fan vaulting is in the cloisters of Gloucester, and the most remarkably complex lierne vaulting in the cloisters of Canterbury, which may be the work of Henry Yevele himself.

After many early disasters due to faulty foundations, a more proper regard was paid to the support of the buildings. Foundations were dug deep, broken stone was crushed in, wooden piles were driven in as necessary and heavy flat stones were bonded together by lime and sand mortar. Rope and pulley tackle was used to lift stones into position, and scaffolding was constructed of long poles lashed together with withes or with rope made from the flexible inner bark of the lime tree. Hoisting machines called gins, vernes, trace wheels or cranes came into increasing use in the fourteenth and fifteenth centuries, the smaller worked by hand, the larger by treadmill or water power. There was considerable danger in using them but even so they raised the spire of Salisbury and lifted the heavy oak beams, almost 3 feet square and over 60 feet long, which formed the framework of the octagonal tower at Ely.

The methods of construction of the mediaeval monastical establishments are not without interest. The best timber to be found was usually in Royal ownership, and forest laws were extremely strict. The finest oak or chestnut was obtained by a grant; and no less than 90 great oaks were used in the building of the west front at Wells between 1220 and 1225. Stone was as far as possible transported by water. At Norwich and Peterborough it was brought by sea from the Midland quarries and up river to the building sites, while Caen stone was brought across Channel to Chichester, St. Albans and Canterbury, and Purbeck marble by sea from Portland to Durham.

The different guilds of craftsmen first showed signs of definite organisation in the thirteenth century. In the erection of a large building, contracts for fixed sums were made with the varying guilds of craftsmen, who sometimes enjoyed the addition of a bonus if the work was highly approved. They enjoyed also a measure of social distinction, and as early as the middle of the century, sculptors, architects and painters were ranked as esquires. As the Gothic style developed it became a matter of exact engineering, the success and stability of the new system of skeleton construction and balanced abutment depending largely upon their skill.

Members of religious orders in the Middle Ages committed themselves to living on earth as a preparation solely for life in the hereafter. They often fell short of this very ascetic ideal and showed themselves more money-minded than parish priests who had taken no vows of poverty.

Secular life was sufficiently insecure to tempt many to join a religious order, without any vocation, for the sake of tranquillity and an assured livelihood. Monastic standards commenced to decay after the thirteenth century, and respect for learning became no greater than that for austerity.

The monks lived a retired communal life, working hard in the fields or copying manuscripts, carving in wood and stone, and painting. They provided food for the poor, and gave lodging to travellers, but their chief function was the recital of prayers, by day and night, for the living and for the dead.

Monks of the Carthusian Order led a particularly austere existence. Each in his own small house and garden, they lived as hermits, speaking one with the other only once a week and tormented perpetually by a hair shirt. It was the only order that maintained its founder's ideal, as none but the most intent on sanctity could have survived its rigorous demands.

The mendicant friars, on the other hand, journeyed far and wide, preaching and tending the poor. The satire of Chaucer reflects the jealousies of the parish priests and the temptations to which the friars were exposed.

The early fourteenth century saw the population of the religious houses at its peak. The visitations of the Black Death in the middle of the century halved the numbers of monks, and they were never again as numerous.

The few monastic churches that survive served at the Reformation as cathedrals. They were Chichester, Exeter, Hereford, Lichfield, Lincoln, St. Paul's, Salisbury, York and Wells. The other cathedrals—Canterbury, Carlisle, Durham, Ely, Norwich, Rochester, Winchester, Worcester, Peterborough, Chester, Oxford, Bristol and Gloucester—were attached to monasteries.

The chief monastic orders in England were the Benedictine, the Cluniac, the Cistercian, the Augustinian, the Premonstratensian, the Carthusian and the several orders of the Friars and the Knights of St. John. The Benedictine Order was founded during the sixth century by St. Benedict, who encouraged all branches of the arts, and Canterbury, Westminster and all the older English monasteries belonged to this order.

The usual arrangement of these monasteries was a square cloister having on one side an aisled church, the south transept of which bounded one side of the cloister. Parallel to the nave, on the opposite side of the cloister, were the refectory and kitchens, the dormitory on another side connected to the church for night services. Cellars for wine, beer and oil were often under the dormitory. An inner court contained an infirmary, guest house, kitchen, servants' hall and library, and scriptorium for writing and illuminating. A common court contained granaries, bakehouses, servants' rooms, stables, prison and barn, and mills and workshops, gardens and orchards and fishponds completed the monastic settlement. Many monasteries served as inns for travellers, as many continental examples continue to do to this day. At Aylesford Priory, near Maidstone, from whence the Carmelites were evicted in 1539 and to where they have recently returned, there is a guest house over the entrance gate that is still in use. This hospitality was exercised most freely by the big Benedictine monasteries, such as Durham, York, Peterborough and St. Albans, which were on the Great North Road, and at those establishments near bridges on the River Severn at Gloucester, Worcester, Shrewsbury and Tewkesbury. Eynsham, near Oxford, housed students from the university; at St. Albans there was stabling for three hundred horses. Hospitality was given free for two days as a rule, but the custom became open to abuse.

The Cluniac order, with its centre at the abbey of Cluny in Northern France, included Lincoln and Salisbury, both of which churches have double transepts. The Cistercian order founded the magnificent Fountains Abbey, hidden in its lovely green valley on the River Skell near Ripon in Yorkshire. Bristol, Carlisle and Oxford Cathedrals, with the celebrated church of St. Bartholomew the Great in London, were of the Augustinian Order, which differed but little from the Benedictine and was first introduced to this country in 1105.

The monasteries were the chief centres of learning and religion, until they were gradually eclipsed by the rise of the universities at Oxford and Cambridge. In 1070 William deposed the Saxon Archbishop of Canterbury,

Stigand, and installed Lanfranc, one of the first minds of the age and a Lombard of high administrative ability, an act which brought the English monasteries into contact with the broader European stream of Christian life, learning and art. Paul of St. Albans came from Caen, Ingulf of Crowland from St. Wandrille, Walter of Evesham from Cerisy, and his successor Robert from Jumièges. The first three Norman Abbots of Westminster came from Jumièges, Bernay and Bec.

In the social system of the Middle Ages the monasteries played a most important part, the monk following different pursuits, according to the Order to which he belonged. The Benedictine was the chronicler; the Augustinian the preacher, given to disputations; the Cistercian the recluse, interested in agricultural pursuits; the Cluniac the student and artist; and the Carthusian the ascetic.

Fountains Abbey in Yorkshire was, until the Dissolution, one of the finest monastic establishments in the country, and although in a ruined condition, the whole of this

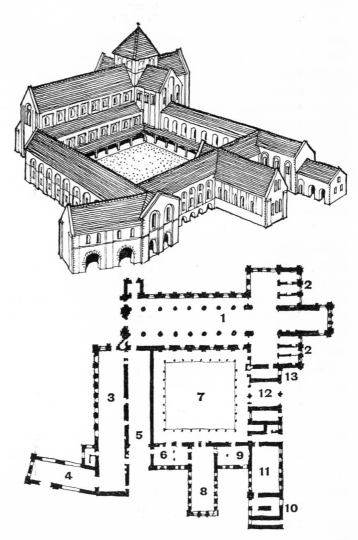

Kirkstall Abbey, 1190

 1 Church
 2 Chapels
 3 Lay brothers' room
 4 Lay brothers' necessaria
 5 Passage
 6 Buttery
 7 Cloister garth
 8 Refectory
 9 Kitchen
10 Necessaria
11 Monks' room
12 Chapter house
13 Sacristy

fascinating monastery is still in a wonderful state of preservation and sufficient remains of the original buildings to give a very clear impression of its pristine glory. After the Dissolution it came into the possession of Sir William Gresham, whose successor pulled down the infirmary and the surrounding wall in order to build Fountains Hall near by, which is still occupied by the Vyner family. To the north the thickly forested cliffs fall steeply to the old Cistercian monastery, which occupies the ground enclosed by the River Skell on the south. A gatehouse to the north-west gives access to an outer courtyard, south of which, and apart from the main buildings, are two guest houses. Next to these is the infirmary of the lay brethren, to the east of which is the huge cellarium, 300 feet in length, the refectory and storehouses of the lay brethren on the ground floor and the main refectory above. From east to west along the north side of the monastery runs the great church, with its very unusual Chapel of the Nine Altars and its magnificent tower, one of the finest in the country, which was built by Bishop Huby between 1494 and 1526. South-west of the church, with the cellarium on the west side, is the cloister, off which is the rectangular chapter house on the east. On the south of the cloister is the monks' refectory with kitchen and calefactory, or warming house, and east of this again the monks' dormitory. Still further east are the punishment cells and the abbot's house, beyond which is the infirmary hall.

An attempt by the present Duke of Norfolk to raise sufficient funds for its restoration as a great Catholic establishment unfortunately came to nothing, although the ruins are maintained in good condition.

The Schools of Oxford, situated between Wessex and Mercia, grew up around the parish church of St. Mary, and apparently originated in one of the frequent migrations of early academic history, in this case from the University of Paris, on the issue of an ordinance by Henry II in 1167 ordering all clerks having English revenues and resident in France to return home 'as they loved their revenues', possibly an early example of a financial crisis. The rivalry between town and gown continued for centuries with frequent deaths and injuries on both sides, reaching its most serious pitch in 1209, when an Oxford townswoman was killed by a clerk and as a result three clerks were put to death by the townspeople. In alarm many clerks migrated at once to Cambridge, whose numbers were further reinforced by migration from Paris, where the college system originated. A famous etching by Charles Meryon shows one of these, the *Collège Henri IV*, as a rectangular arrangement of four courtyards, one with a cloister, the whole dominated by a high square tower.

In the thirteenth century the students congregated in self-governed halls, one of which, Great University Hall, became University College in 1280, and between 1261 and 1266 Sir John de Balliol, by way of a penance, provided for the maintenance of some poor scholars at Oxford. His widow founded Balliol College, and in 1264 Walter de Merton founded the College of that name.

Exeter College dates from 1314, Oriel from 1326, Queen's from 1340 and in 1379 William of Wykeham founded his College of St. Mary of Winchester, which soon became known as New College.

Peterhouse at Cambridge arose in 1284, Clare in 1326, Gonville and Caius in 1348, Trinity Hall in 1350 and Corpus Christi in 1352.

In general equipment and layout, colleges were rather similar to monastic establishments, with hall and rooms grouped around a quadrangle, and many mediaeval houses and manor houses were designed in this way.

The danger to the young universities lay in the numbers of poorly educated youths who wished to study philosophy, and for this reason, and in order to secure a higher standard of education, William of Wykeham founded the famous school at Winchester to feed his foundation of New College. Wykeham's aim was to enlist learned men for the Church, and membership of the New College was limited at first to boys from Winchester. New College, with its chapel, cloisters, its garden and its separate establishment for the Warden, became the model for all future founders and the direct model for future colleges. Lincoln (1427), All Souls (1437) and Magdalen (1458) are all variations on the New College plan.

Few bridges of the Middle Ages survive in their original state. With the development of roads and traffic they were constantly enlarged, widened or altered but the few that remain are not without interest and their history throws a revealing light upon the social and commercial life of the times.

The most famous of the mediaeval Eng-lish bridges was London Bridge, which spanned the Thames on the site of the present structure. It was begun in 1176 by Peter de Colechurch, a priest and a member of an international bridge-building fraternity. The cost was met by the endowment of money or land from the King, the Church, and citizens of the City of London. The Archbishop of Canterbury sent 1,000 marks, and until the sixteenth century the list of subscribers could be seen in the chapel on the bridge. It was not unknown in the Middle Ages for prosperous citizens to bequeath money or gifts for the repair and maintenance of these important structures. These conscientious people were, as a rule, merchants who had benefited in their various trades by the increased safety and convenience of a bridge which obviated the dangers to be met with, for instance, at the fords of rivers, where the lines of pack horse and rude commercial wagons had perforce to halt or slow down, to become a tempting and easy prey for the robber bands which infested the richly wooded countryside. A Newcastle citizen, by name John Cooke, left 20 marks in 1379 to the fortified bridge at Warkworth, and in 1440 Count Neville bequeathed £20

Cringleford Bridge, Norfolk, early 16th century

Bridge with houses, Lincoln,
15th century and earlier

to 'Ulshawe Bridge near Middleham'. Roger
Thornton, of Newcastle, a wealthy merchant, left 100 marks to the bridge over the
Tyne in his native city, and a mean fellow,
one John Danby, left only a beggarly 6s. 8d.
to Warleby Bridge in 1444.

Mediaeval engineering never reached the
level of the Roman science of over a thousand years before, and English bridges rarely
equalled the fine Continental examples. The
Romans had proved that by separating the
arch stones from the spandrils a bridge was
relieved of much wear and tear caused by
the vibrations of a great weight passing over
the structure, but this principle appears to
have been unknown in this country in the
Middle Ages although the celebrated military bridge at Cahors in the south of France
is built on this principle.

A feature of mediaeval bridges was the

number of piers on which they were built
and the limited span of the arches. The reason was economic as well as military. It was
obviously easier to construct a smaller than
a greater arch, but in those unquiet years it
was frequently necessary to destroy a bridge
for defensive reasons, and essential that the
destruction of one arch should not upset the
equilibrium of the structure by the with-
drawal of a counterbalancing thrust from
one side of the pier. Every arch of the military bridge at Cahors is a bow between two
piers that retains its own oscillations without
affecting the remaining arches, and the
bridge must have been constructed with the
possibility of such defensive measures in
view.

Old London Bridge was built on twenty
arches ranging in width from 18 feet to 32
feet 6 inches, on piers varying between 25

42

and 34 feet in breadth. They were built on strong elm piles covered with thick planks bolted together, the whole structure forming a perforated dam that retained a depth of water in the river to the east but seriously disturbed the flow of sewage to the sea, thereby increasing the risks from the plague which descended with such calamitous effect in 1665. The destruction of the bridge by fire in the following year removed a constant danger to the health of the City, however deplorable or otherwise the loss of a romantic but insanitary structure.

As a piece of picturesque building it must have presented a most fascinating sight. The three-storey timber houses which lined the bridge had leaded platforms above them on which the citizens could walk and admire the view. Some were even furnished with small gardens. Fires were not infrequent,

and in 1212 a tremendous fire ravaged the bridge, killing three thousand panic-stricken people. Others occurred in serious manner in 1300, in 1471, in 1632 and finally in 1666.

The revenues from the bridge were considerable, as a toll was imposed on travellers and merchandise for its upkeep. According to M. Jusserand in his book, *English Wayfaring Life in the Middle Ages*, repairs were never carried out until danger was imminent and often after catastrophe had occurred. Henry III made over the revenues of the bridge to his 'beloved wife' who appropriated them while neglecting to use them for their proper purpose. When the bridge in time reached a condition that was almost ruinous collectors were sent out to gather subscriptions from unwilling contributors who were 'piously exhorted' to give all they were able. The money came in late and a 'sudden ruin' occurred when five arches collapsed, with the houses above them, and, presumably, the unfortunate citizens who lived in them, whereupon a further tax was imposed in 1282 on passengers, merchandise and boats. The bridge at Lincoln is a similar kind on a smaller scale.

The bridge at Crowland, built in the fourteenth century, near the abbey in Lincolnshire, survives to this day in almost its original state. It is unique in its shape, triangular

Bridge with chapel,
Bradford-on-Avon,
Wiltshire, 13th century

43

Bridge over the River Medway, Aylesford, Kent,
14th century

in plan to cross the two branches of the
Welland river which have now been diverted
to sewers, and the bridge stands high and
dry in the little town.

The military bridge spanning the Mon-
mow at Monmouth is the sole example of a
fortified bridge in this country, having ribbed arches like the bridge at Warkworth.
An example of a bridge with a chapel can
be seen to this day at Bradford-on-Avon in
Wiltshire.

Other mediaeval bridges can still be found
in various parts of the country. Stopham
Bridge in Sussex is in good preservation,
with the bridge over the Medway at Aylesford, near the old monastery. Wakefield
Bridge is one of the few with a chapel. Two
further good examples are East Farleigh
Bridge, with its ribbed arches of the fourteenth century, and Packhorse Bridge at
Combe Bissett in Wiltshire.

The wretched hovel that served as a dwelling for the peasant throughout the Middle
Ages was built with his own hands, a framework of sticks thatched with willow withes,

the whole structure daubed with mud. A
kind of primitive concrete made of mud and
the droppings of animals was rammed into
a temporary shuttering which could be
raised little by little until the wall was completed.

As the centuries passed the skilled wood-
worker or 'wright' came into his own, using
timber as the universal material to make
ploughs, carts, ships and houses. As the country became more civilised he made furniture
and with advancing techniques he constructed the intricate and magnificent roofs
and stalls of the cathedrals.

His principal tool was the axe, held in
both hands, with which he made short chops.
Few of the tools he used have survived to
this day apart from the axe and the saw, but
it is known that he used a 'celt' or chisel,
and a 'wimble' or auger to drill the holes
through which wooden pegs were driven to
hold joints in position. He used only the
heart of the tree for building, the softer sap-
wood being rejected.

As his skill improved, the wright became

44

more economical in his use of timber. From the 'cruck' construction of a house (the method whereby the 'ridge' timber supporting the rafters of a roof was supported in turn at each end of the building by a pair of sturdy timbers inclining towards each other) was developed the 'framed' house of vertical 'sills' and horizontal studs. Later, the two inward inclining end timbers were arched in Gothic form, giving additional headroom at the sides of the building.

By the thirteenth century these pairs of curved timbers, as 'trusses', eventually developed into the arched roof truss which became the most notable feature of the mediaeval roof. Supporting the roof truss were posts, hewn from oak, mounted upon a foundation formed by a horizontal baulk or 'sleeper' laid along the ground, and buttressed by inclined struts mortised into them. With the use of the 'frame saw', which had a blade held in a horizontal frame with two end members by which the saw was pulled to and fro by two operators, timbers were squared off.

Stone walls were first of all made of rubble of various sizes, the angles of these walls constructed probably of the worked stones from ruined Roman buildings. (Roman bricks were used at St. Albans.) This method was employed until the skilled mason, with his knowledge of the construction of walls of shaped stone, was brought by the Normans to raise the more permanent castles, abbeys and cathedrals. In time he developed into the master-mason on whom rested the responsibility for the design and construction of the whole building. Under him worked the gangs of labourers carrying stones from the stonecutter who moulded them to their proper shape, to the setters who placed them in position. Under him were the wrights who shaped the timbers of the roof, the plumbers who covered it with lead, and the smiths who fashioned the ironwork. Behind all these came the men who quarried the stone, humble labourers who by reason of their trade were called upon, in the assault of a stronghold, to dig the mines by which the walls were breached. There were the limestone burners making the lime used in mixing mortar, the transport men driving the pack-ponies and the horses bringing materials to the site, and the seamen guiding the ships and barges bringing stone from far-away places.

So complicated did the erection of a large building become that a complete building organisation was set up by Henry III, involving an engineer who later became known as the 'Clerk of Works', a 'comptroller' who supervised building accounts, and a 'purveyor' to find labour and materials. On the permanent staff were a master mason and master carpenter, a smith, a plumber and a glazier. The end of the twelfth century saw the beginning of a period of intense building activity in which the masons took an ever-increasing part until the time came when they were called upon to be responsible also for the actual design of a building. Drawings on deal boards were prepared, and models of certain features of the building were made. 'Forms' or 'templates' were made by the designers for the use of the mason. These were passed from hand to hand in much the same way as, later on, life studies by the great painters of the Renaissance were used for instruction.

A responsible official, in charge of funds, was answerable to the chapter for the building of a cathedral. An administrator arranged the purchase of materials, the issue of contracts and the hire of builders. An experienced master mason, the equivalent of the present-day architect, was put in charge of actual operations, and he it was who designed and supervised the work. As a rule he lived

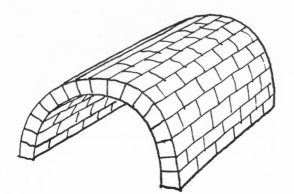

Barrel vault

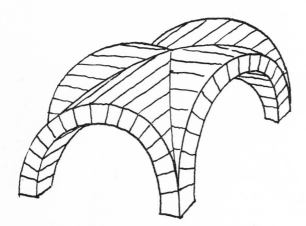

Barrel vault with intersecting vault

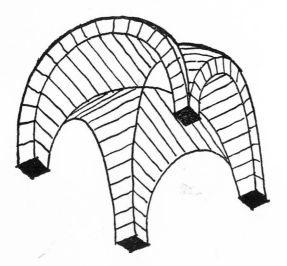

Intersecting vaults from below

46

on the job, but later in the thirteenth century a warden was appointed to act in the absence of the master mason, who may have been employed on more than one work. The warden had charge of the masons who cut the stones in the stone-yard, nowadays a permanent appendage of any large church.

A master carpenter headed a staff of carpenters providing scaffolding, centering, roofs, choir fittings and doors. Windows were made on the site or contracted out to guilds in the neighbouring town. There were draughtsmen to set out the right size and design of window openings, and at Wells a plaster floor in a room over the north porch still survives, covered with incised lines over a long period of use. Smiths were in constant attendance, providing necessary metal work or sharpening and maintaining tools, and making heavy wrought-iron bars for tie-bars or reinforcement. The rate of work varied enormously, but Gothic construction on the whole is very sound. Direct hits by heavy bombs on Cologne Cathedral, whose nave soars to 150 feet, as well as many near misses on other great churches, appear to have affected the stability of the construction in no serious manner, and most by now have been repaired by modern methods and are sounder than ever.

Transport by water reached a high pitch of efficiency after the Conquest, making available the quarries of fine Caen stone to the whole of the south of England. As time went on the devices for raising stone improved until from small stones and low courses the mason was able to build with much larger stones in courses of much greater height.

Until the middle of the twelfth century each stone was squared with an axe on a bench known as a 'banker'. Each mason adopted his own sign or mark by which his work was known. After the Conquest the 'bolster' or wide chisel came into use in

England, used particularly for circular work on shafts and mouldings, and in the twelfth century a bolster with a serrated edge called a 'claw-tool' was used to remove the rougher parts of the stone before the tooling proper was commenced. The deep Gothic mouldings were roughly formed with a heavy axe, worked with claw and bolster, and finished with a comb or 'drag', a scraper held in the hand to remove the marks of tooling. The more skilled masons were the carvers, and the turners who turned the columns and the slender shafts with a heavy stone lathe.

In the setting-out of a building the standard unit of measurement differed from place to place, and no fixed standard came into use until the time of Elizabeth. Smaller buildings were limited in width by the span of the roof. Large buildings were planned in 'bays' of similar dimensions so that the same timbering could be used in the construction of the vaults.

English builders in the eleventh century discovered the method of building an arch and using it as a centering for a slightly wider arch above it, and again if necessary for a wider arch above that. The next development shows the plan of the pier following the section through the arch. The introduction of slender shafts into the angles thus formed softened the harsh contours, and in the last quarter of the thirteenth century these compound piers are seen at Wells in clusters of shafts which continue vertically down the rich mouldings of the pointed arches they support.

The stone vaults of the earlier large buildings first of all took the simple form of the 'barrel' vault, the semi-circular tunnel-like variety which is simply a long stone arch. This type of vault called for very massive stone supporting walls, with the added disadvantage of being unable to provide space for windows unless placed in the wall below

Intersecting Gothic vault

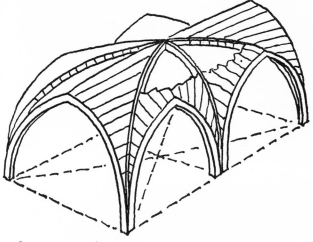

Sexpartite vault

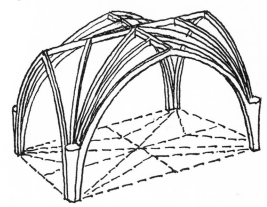

Gothic vault over oblong compartment

47

the 'springing' of the vault. This problem was overcome by dividing the building into bays, each roughly equal in width to its span, each bay covered with a transverse vault at right angles to the axis of the building. The result is a cross-vault, the sharp intersecting edges of the two vaults being known as groins. Once the lines of these groins were constructed in narrow stone arches, they formed the supporting ribs for the intersecting tunnel arches and obviated the considerable amount of wood centering which would otherwise have had to be used.

By the beginning of the twelfth century this type of vaulting was commonly used over the aisles of a large church. The invention of the vaulting rib resolved so many difficulties of vaulting over wide spaces that by the middle of the twelfth century the whole of Durham Cathedral had been covered in this way. This invention also had the added advantage of carrying the weight of the vault to four points instead of, as hitherto, to a continuous wall, which, now that its structural use was gone, could be dispensed with entirely and replaced with glass. The introduction of further ribs reduced the area of unsupported 'web' (the area of vault extending between the ribs), until the vault became a mass of short structural ribs or liernes, seen to their best advantage at

Gloucester and Tewkesbury. By the end of the fifteenth century elongated voussoirs, drooping towards the floor and ending in elaborately carved finials, supported a multitude of vaulting ribs rising up to meet others springing from the walls. Thus evolved the 'fan' vaults of Henry VII's Chapel, St. George's Chapel, Windsor and King's College Chapel.

With the discovery of the rib and the concentration of thrust at a definite point instead of continuously along a wall, the provision of some means of counter-thrust had to be devised. This was done by thickening the walls at the points of thrust, and expressing also the bay layout of the building. As their function became more clearly understood buttresses were given a greater projection in their lower courses, and weathered or sloping set-offs marked each change of face. To give added stability the buttress was topped by a heavy pinnacle, which became a very notable feature of the Gothic skyline.

As churches rose higher buttresses became deeper, and as such would have presented a solid wall obstructing the aisles. The flying buttresses transferred the thrust of a tall vault over the aisles to a buttress supporting the aisle walls and these are best seen in England on the walls of the nave at Westminster Abbey.

Boothby Pagnell, Lincolnshire, c. 1180. The hall is on the upper floor for defence

2

The English period 1349–1485

In that slowly-moving age the transition through which England passed from a feudal to a national society was gradual, but the event which emphasised this change more than any other was the Black Death of 1348–50, and its subsequent visitations in 1360–1, 1364 and 1375.

These four attacks of bubonic plague surpassed in horror any comparable event of mediaeval times. Their effect on the country was so calamitous and on such a scale that they marked finally the end of the feudal period, and England passed from a society bound together by relationships between king and baron, lord and man, to a society or order of groups, the king, nobles, country gentlemen, citizens and townsfolk. The pithy German expression, *von Lehnstaat zum Ständestaat* (from the feudal state to the state composed of estates or orders of society), summarises the situation.

Examples of depopulation occasioned by

the plague are frequent throughout the country, and have been recognised and described with the aid of aerial photography and local records. The village of Tusmore in north-east Oxfordshire, about five miles north of Bicester, is one such example. It was completely depopulated by the disease. In 1279 it comprised sixteen villein families, three cottars and four freemen, twenty-three households in all. The village was not wealthy, even by the very moderate standards of the time, and when taxed in 1334 paid only half the local average, but in 1355 it paid nothing at all—it had been completely wiped out by the Black Death. A licence, granted in 1357 to Roger de Cotesford, Lord of the Manor, gives him leave to 'enclose his hamlet of Toresmere and the highway from Cotesford to Sylthorne passing through it, the hamlet having been inhabited entirely by Roger's bondsmen, but now void of inhabitants since their death in the pestilence. Roger is to make a new road in the north of the hamlet.' The earthworks of the village, and the outlines of the streets can today be seen from the air.

There were other reasons for depopulation not attributable to the Black Death. There are a score of abandoned village sites on the crown of the Yorkshire wolds to testify to their depopulation following the change-over from arable to grazing land. The economic consequences of the plague were equally devastating, and prices rose sharply, with an inevitable rise in wages. The old order of lord and labourer came to an end when landowners had no alternative but to let land at a rent to tenants who, having no money to find stock, were provided by the owner with stock and seed, for which the tenant had to provide an equivalent at the end of his term. Thus began the modern farm, with the familiar triple division of landlord, farmer and labourer.

This solution to the problem of limited labour was, however, by no means final. The peasantry, anxious to profit by higher wages offered in defiance of the 'Statutes of Labourers', passed to keep down wages and prices, often ran away from their employers in spite of the ferocious penalties. The general discontent culminated in the Peasant Revolts of 1381, but although burnings, murders, robberies and executions took place before order was restored, the villeins had won a complete victory. Serfdom decayed completely, and the cost of labour rose to unprecedented heights.

The economic remedy to the land-owning classes was found in sheep farming, with ready markets in Flanders and the Netherlands to take the wool which was shipped to Calais. Arable land, on which the now better-paid peasantry was employed, was converted to grazing land and the peasants lost their employment. This island, with its moister climate and unlimited pastures, produced the best wool in Europe, with the Cotswold wool as the finest in England. The great sheep-owning barons counted their flocks by thousands and tens of thousands, but the end of the reign of Edward III saw the proportion of sheep reared by the peasants increasing over the number reared by lay and ecclesiastical landlords. Cottagers began to eke out a living by setting the women to spin, and thus began an alliance between agriculture and weaving which prospered abundantly and was broken only by machinery and steam power in the nineteenth century.

From records of the Spencer family at Althorp we have another glimpse of rural life at Wormleighton, some twelve miles southeast of Warwick. John Spencer, a grazier from the parish of Hodnell near by, bought the estate with its moated manor house, from William Cope, cofferer to Henry VII, in 1506, with a view to converting the arable land of some 240 acres to pasture. As a result sixty villagers lost their employment, the village was abandoned and Spencer was prosecuted in 1517 by Wolsey's Commissioners for causing the depopulation. Spencer pleaded that in building his new manor he had kept workmen busy for three years and that in any case he was employing almost as many as Cope had expelled in 1496. The site of the village may still be seen from the air.

The Essex villages of Coggeshall, Shalford, Dedham, Bocking, Braintree, and above all Colchester, were famous for cloth making. Nearly every cottage had its spinning wheel and loom, and the hum of the spinning wheel mingled with the clattering hooves of packhorses bringing wool to be worked, or taking away cloth for sale in Colchester. The famous cloth merchant, Thomas Paycocke, lived in Coggeshall, where his fine

Stoneacre, Otham, Kent, 1480: timber-framed hall house of a well-to-do yeoman

house with carved timbers now belongs to the National Trust.

The demand for wool in the Netherlands increased sheep farming, and the consequent prosperity in the hands of farmers led to the erection of large parish churches in the sheep-rearing counties. A growing home trade, the development of foreign commerce and the change from villeinage after the Black Death enhanced the importance of the Guilds which controlled craftsmanship. All this local activity promoted the building of houses for the prosperous yeomanry and merchant classes as well as market halls, moot halls, guildhalls, barns and bridges, and towns developed in size and importance.

The distribution of wealth, following the decline of the clergy, saw the rise of successful medical men, merchants and lawyers, and encouraged the growth of a national type of domestic architecture. This is above all the English period of architecture in England, when it was almost entirely free from foreign influence, and buildings which rose naturally from the needs of the builders and the materials available appeared over the land. Now arose the splendid 'wool'

churches, with their lofty, dominating towers, pinnacled and battlemented, such as at Lavenham in Suffolk and Thaxted in Essex, Tenterden in Kent and Cirencester in Gloucestershire.

This period comprises part of the reign of Edward III (1327–77) and the reigns of Richard II (1377–99), Henry IV (1399–1413), Henry V (1413–22), Henry VI (1422–1461), Edward IV (1461–83), Edward V (1483) and Richard III (1483–5). It embraces the Perpendicular style of English architecture, derived from the vertical lines of the window tracery and the panelling covering both internal and external walls and even buttresses. Windows were crowned with four-centred arches, often of great size, and the fan vault, the supreme structural and decorative feature of this period, was evolved.

The principal examples in London of this era are the south and west cloisters of Westminster Abbey, the Savoy Chapel in the Strand, Westminster Hall, Crosby Hall, Chelsea, and the Great Hall of Lambeth Palace. Outside London, King's College Chapel, Cambridge (1512–1515) and St.

51

Cruck house, 14th century

George's Chapel, Windsor (1473–1516) are entirely of this period, and also considerable parts of the cathedrals at York (choir), Canterbury (nave), Gloucester (transepts, choir and cloisters) and Winchester (nave) and the towers at Gloucester and Canterbury. Of this period at Oxford are New College (1379), Lincoln (1427), All Souls' (1437) and Magdalen (1458); and at Cambridge, Gonville and Caius (1348), Trinity Hall (1350), Corpus Christi (1352), King's (1441), Queens' (1448) and St. Catherine's (1473). Castles include Herstmonceux (1441) in Sussex, Raglan (1430–69) in Monmouthshire, Wingfield (1441–55), Ashby-de-la-Zouche (1474), in Leicestershire, Warkworth (1400) in Northumberland and Tattershall (1436–46) in Lincolnshire. Manor houses include Ightham Mote in Kent, Sutton Courtenay in Berkshire, Baguley in Cheshire, Smithills near Bolton in Lancashire, Great Chalfield Manor House in Wiltshire, Oxburgh Hall, Norfolk and the chapel and centre portions of Haddon Hall.

This era saw the foundation of Winchester College (1382) and Eton (1440–1) and other schools such as Durham (1414) and the City of London (1442). The Guildhall at York (1448–80), severely damaged by bombing in 1942, had a low-pitched roof supported on tall oak columns of this period. The Abbot's Barn at Glastonbury in Somerset, the Old Barn at Fullstone near Sittingbourne in Kent, and the huge barn at Bradford-on-Avon date from this time, and hospitals are found at Ewelme in Oxfordshire (1436), St. John's Hospital, Sherborne (1437) and Christ's Hospital, Abingdon (1553).

It was, above all, the golden age of the English manor house, although the times were not so settled that they could be built without some form of defence. Murder, rape and robbery with violence were common, but any licence to 'embattle, crenellate, and machicolate' any large dwelling house had still to be obtained from the king, ever fearful of the power of the barons. At Bodiam, in 1386, such licence was interpreted by Sir Edward Dalyngrigge in the widest possible terms, where an almost impregnable castle rose from its moat.

With the growing importance of the towns, secular buildings became more common. The 'Angel' at Grantham and the 'New Inn' at Gloucester still survive, and guildhalls were built at London, Lincoln and Coventry. Towns retained their defensive walls, with towers at intervals and barbicans over the gateways, still to be seen on a considerable and picturesque scale at York and Chester. Churches, too, sometimes formed part of the defences—the footway under St. James's Chapel at Warwick, where the massive substructure of the church arches over the narrow and easily defended entry is a favourite subject for transatlantic cameras. There is, however, nothing now to compare with old German towns such as Rothenburg or Ravensburg, or Carcassonne in France and Avila in Spain, the reason being that the city-state of the continent lasted until the nineteenth century and was forced to retain its defences long after the need for English towns to do so had disappeared.

It is difficult to overestimate the psychological effect of the walls of a town on a mediaeval traveller, for they not only guaranteed the best personal safety but they provided opportunity for access to market places where people had goods to sell or money to buy. To traders and craftsmen they were essential; within them trades and crafts could flourish. There was a concentration of walled towns in the south and east, as the coasts were more subject to invasion or to attack from pirates, and again on the Welsh and Scottish borders, but in the Midlands as a rule only the county town was walled.

Most towns, even without walls, had substantial defences, the burgesses meeting the cost of repair and maintenance either from the common chest or in proportion to their individual wealth. London, Canterbury, Lincoln, Southampton, Chepstow, Winchester and Gloucester still retain parts of their mediaeval gateways and walls in varying conditions; Chester has about two miles of wall in fine preservation, to a height of 12 feet, strengthened at intervals by towers, of which King Charles' Tower and the Pemberton Tower are preserved, with a path behind the parapet along which the guard kept watch.

York has probably the finest city walls in the country. Many of the great gates are in good preservation, dating principally from the reign of Edward III, and the six imposing defensive gateways, which date from Edward I, each possess portcullis, turrets and barbicans, the cross loopholes crowned by battlements.

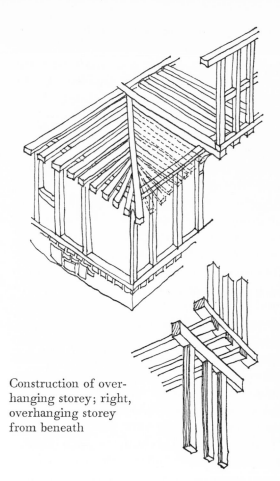

Construction of overhanging storey; right, overhanging storey from beneath

The charming timber-framed mediaeval houses, still to be found in quantity in the older towns throughout the country, were usually built to overhang the footway, thus making fuller use of their sites and affording a certain protection from the weather to pedestrians. The reason, however, was structural; the thick timber beams supporting the floors were always laid with the deeper side beneath: to counteract the whip in the floor the walls were built to overhang the supporting walls to make a counter-balance, and thus the style grew in the form we know today.

London, in the fifteenth century, was the largest town in the country, with 120 parish churches, numerous monastic foundations, as well as the great Cathedral of St. Paul. Norwich, centre of the wool trade with the Low Countries, climbed rapidly to the second place followed by a declining York, with Chichester, Colchester and Chester not far behind in size and importance.

Few mediaeval guildhalls have survived. The Norwich guildhall, with its finely executed flint exterior, is characteristic of the fifteenth century. London's guildhall was burnt out in the Second World War as well as that of York, but the Lincoln guildhall, over the Stonebow gate, was built in the fifteenth century and still remains, although much altered at a later date.

The beginning of the sixteenth century saw the decay of the mediaeval town walls, no longer a defence against Tudor cannon. Civic pride had declined before a wider national fervour, and large towns such as London, Oxford and Bristol had already started suburbs and development along the approaching roads.

The fourteenth-century manor house, under the new social conditions, now assumed the plan it retained for the next three hundred years. The hall, as at Penshurst, with the central hearth open to the roof, with its characteristic and magnificent timber structure, was entered through doors on either side of a decorated wooden screen, over which was the music gallery. On the other side of the passage formed by the screen were the kitchen quarters, and at the far end of the hall was a raised dais, on which the owner's family took their places for meals. From the dais one entered the bower, a withdrawing room for the ladies of the house, and above the bower was the solar, used as a bedchamber. The hall attained a place of great importance in this century. Here the Lord of the Manor continued to dispense justice, and, strewn with

rushes, it still provided a sleeping place for the family retainers.

Few mediaeval timber halls remain to this day; the dangerous method of heating them by a central hearth placed among the years-old rushes on the floor, as well as their inflammable construction, were the cause of their all too frequent destruction.

Manor house, barns, outhouses and dovecots were usually, with protection still in mind, castellated and grouped around a courtyard entered by a gatehouse and protected by a moat and drawbridge. Windows facing outward remained small against the possibility of escalading, but those facing the courtyard became larger. The latter part of the century saw the development of the oriel window, a form of bay window (see the illustration on page 94), which lit the dais and is one of the most charming features of the English manor house.

Timber was plentiful throughout the country, and the half-timbered style predominated in Essex and East Anglia, the Weald of Sussex and Kent, in Cheshire and Shropshire and Herefordshire. Villages like Weobley on the Welsh marshes and the arcades of Chester still retain their enchantment. Rye in Sussex, Warwick, Winchester, Norwich, Gloucester and Salisbury and others among the older cathedral towns preserve the diminishing numbers of mediaeval houses.

Good building stone is confined to a belt passing across the country from Dorset to Yorkshire, which includes such villages as Broadway and Moreton-in-Marsh, and others in Gloucestershire and Oxfordshire, and Stamford in Yorkshire, all built of the mellow golden stone. Granite was used in Devon and Cornwall, where the hard stone was worked to an extraordinary richness at Launceston Church. The dark grey stone of the Lake District and the Pennine chain, with the flints of Norwich, all play their part in the development and treatment of local styles dependent on, and controlled by, the use of local materials.

Not many of those manor houses still left incorporate any substantial mediaeval architecture, as the increasing prosperity of the owners led them to extend or rebuild their homes in contemporary styles, replacing timber with brick or stone, and building with durable materials in a manner which suited the way of life for the next three or even four hundred years.

Moated manor houses are quite common in those parts of the country where the necessary water was easily obtained and a clay soil helped to hold it. These manors continued to be surrounded by a moat long after the need for defence had gone and most are still in occupation or are preserved by the National Trust.

The life of the manor continued to centre in the hall and, until comparatively late in mediaeval times, the whole of the house-hold used this room for eating, sleeping and living. It was furnished in the simplest manner, the only chairs being on the dais at one end on which the lord and his family ate with guests at a trestle table, which was dismantled when not in use and propped against the wall. Before the introduction of separate rooms for sleeping, the owner's bed was also placed on the dais, beside the table. As a refuge from the colds of winter the bed was hung with tapestry or velvet, and in it the owner received visitors, a custom which lasted to the end of the eighteenth century.

Much of the mediaeval furniture was painted in bright colours, and although not comfortable by any standards it gave a gay and lively appearance. Hunting trophies and weapons hung on the walls, but the only real ornaments were the dishes and wine-cups of silver and gold which were displayed on special occasions. The mediaeval 'salt' stood on the dais table with the 'nef' or ship in richly decorated metal, such as silver.

Furniture at the end of the fourteenth century was still primitive, although eating and drinking vessels had reached a good standard. The high table was covered with a linen cloth, and platters of pewter and wood were used. In the wealthiest households, plate of silver or gold was not unknown, but their state of cleanliness is open to grave suspicion, although hands were usually washed before meals as cutlery had not yet arrived and the fingers remained the usual means of eating. In the larger households music accompanied meals with an occasional divertissement by 'fools, jester and mimics' to add to the entertainment.

The Normans introduced two meals a day, a practice which lasted until the fifteenth century, when four became general. Breakfast was at 7, dinner at 10, supper at 4, and

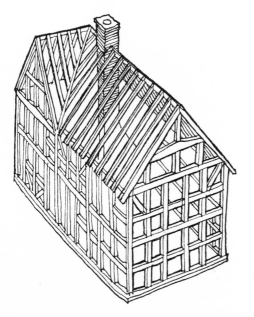

Timber framing of typical 16th-century house

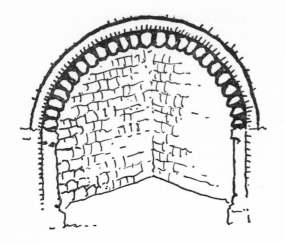

Norman fireplace

the heavy evening meal eaten in bed about 8 or 9 o'clock, depending on the season of the year. The feeding and clothing of the inhabitants of a manor house called for a high degree of organisation. What could not be supplied from the estate had to be ordered some months in advance from the merchants of London, or from the local county town, with French wines, spices, dates, oranges and sugar. The mistress of the house supervised the dairy, the brew-house and the kitchen, the curing and storing of meal, meat and game from the estate, and the spinning and weaving of the household cloth.

In the fourteenth century for the first time the gentleman's family retired from the great hall to eat their more fashionable meals in private. Just as, at the height of the Roman Empire, the tribute and plunder of conquered countries undermined the austerity of Camillus and Cato, so the spoils of France during the early successful years of the Hundred Years War increased the comfort of the English feudal family. Noble prisoners, awaiting ransom, lived as guests of their captors and introduced cosmopolitan manners and ideas, luxury and refinement.

At the beginning of the fifteenth century tapestry and hangings increased in popularity until a stage was reached, as at Hardwick Hall, when the household needlework became a matter of wonder. Beds were freely hung with tapestry, walls were hung with cloth, the hall and chief rooms with Arras depicting hunting scenes or allegorical or religious subjects. The walls of lesser rooms were often painted, sometimes with mural paintings.

Later buildings were warmed from a great fireplace in the wall, as at Sherborne Abbey, although there was no fireplace at Deene Hall in Northamptonshire (home of the family of Lord Cardigan, of Balaclava fame) until one was constructed in the nineteenth century. In one of the roof bays the absence of cross braces marks where the course for the escape of smoke used to be.

Although rushes were used to cover the floors, which were commonly of clay, they

Boothby Pagnell, Lincolnshire: 12th-century canopied fireplace

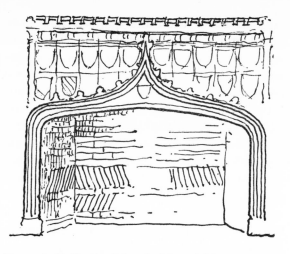

Tattershall Castle, Lincolnshire: 15th-century

were sometimes left unchanged for years, together with a noisesome accretion of fragments of food and the more unpleasant household rubbish. This lack of hygiene encouraged the frequent plagues that visited the country, although some attempt was made to improve the situation by the use of carpets. Eleanor of Castile, wife of Edward I, is given the credit for their introduction, and she it was who covered the walls of her rooms with tapestries from Arras or Paris, and later from London. Heraldic tapestries became popular, as well as a worsted substitute manufactured in Norfolk.

The practice of placing the hall above an undercroft (see the illustration on page 15), which can be traced back to early mediaeval times, continued into the fourteenth and fifteenth centuries when the hall on the ground floor became customary. The reason was partly military and defensive, for the times were still unsettled, and the more remote parts of the country were open to foray and attack. Examples of main apartments at first-floor level are at Woodford Castle in South Dorset, Nunney near Frome in Somerset and Wardour Castle in Wiltshire. It was as well, even in the later Middle Ages, to be

able to defend one's house against wandering bad characters, but none of these houses, except possibly Nunney, would have stood against a siege.

The fifteenth century saw an improvement in social conditions and increasing commercial prosperity, in spite of the Wars of the Roses. The hall remained the principal feature with its fine open timber roof, oriel and fireplace surmounted by a canopy to carry off smoke and fumes. A greater concern with good food and cooking was reflected by buttery, pantry and larder with the addition of scullery, bakehouse, brewhouse and dairy. Granaries, stables and corn mills became more numerous. The assurance of safety under the Tudors saw the rise of the unfortified manor house, although the memory of the dangerous days of former years was still vivid and many of the features of the castle were retained.

Later halls are marked by the elimination of intermediate columns, the roof covering all from wall to wall. Windows became larger, with an oriel to light the dais and a porch over the entrance door. The solar grew into a suite of rooms and the servants

Sherborne Abbey, Dorset, 1470: fireplace

57

were provided with their own rooms apart from the family. An example of a late hall is at Cothele House in Cornwall, built in the time of Henry VII. Its somewhat earlier appearance may be explained by its remote position and the time it would take for new ideas to travel. The oriel and the fireplace may still be seen, but the dais has disappeared.

Kirby Muxloe Castle, built in Leicestershire in 1480–4, has come down to us. A great rectangular moat was excavated and the nearby stream was dammed and diverted. By the spring of the following year eleven ditchers were working four days a week, and hundreds of cubic yards of soil were removed. Wagons made by local craftsmen brought the raw materials for the building, freestone from the monastic quarry at Alton Hall, eleven miles away, and lime from Barrow on Soar, nine miles away. Sand and clay for bricks, with timber and straw, were found on the estate, and lead for the roof came from Wirksworth by way of the Derwent river.

The manor was built with an eye to defence, and superficially it resembles the solid castles of earlier years. The gatehouse and west tower had gun-ports, but the house would never have held out against determined assault. Careful consideration was given to display and decoration, the brick courses forming patterns which culminated in an heraldic design over the main gate. The building was well advanced, carpenters and bricklayers, free-masons, rough-masons and plumbers were busily employed, when all came to a sudden and tragic stop. A new king, Richard III, had ascended the throne, and in 1483 the unlucky owner of the manor, whose sympathies had lain with the opposition, lost his head on the block. After a necessary delay, work was again resumed, and the building accounts of 1484 show that just under a thousand pounds had been spent and 1,342,500 bricks laid. The moat has now silted up but the mediaeval appearance of the manor has been retained by a careful restoration under the National Trust. In its symmetry the manor with its sturdy gatehouse is reminiscent of Bodiam.

Haddon Hall in Derbyshire, which dates from Norman times and which now belongs to the National Trust, includes most of the domestic features of this period, and the old kitchen arrangements can still be seen with the fourteenth-century banqueting hall and its oriel window. Its romantic situation and its furnishing in the sparse mediaeval manner mark the building as an outstanding example of its kind, although very much larger than most manor houses of the time. South Wingfield (c. 1440), also in Derbyshire, and Cothay (c. 1480) in Somerset, are others, both built of stone, the former around two courtyards. There are two courts at Haddon Hall, the main hall itself being placed in the dividing wing, with the protection afforded by the outside wings as the reason for its comparatively large windows, while the exterior windows of these wings, facing outward over the open and sometimes hostile countryside, are small and easily defended. Much of the west wall portions of the chapel, the lower parts of the east and south wall and the Peverel or Eagle tower are of the twelfth century, but the bulk of the building as we know it today is fourteenth century and shows the desire for increased comfort. The plan of the house is revealing, the external walls much thicker than those inside, the windows on the outside few and small, showing the necessity for perpetual watch against casual and unexpected attack.

Bolton Castle, in Yorkshire, on the north side of Wensleydale, built deep in the Pennines at the end of the fourteenth century,

Athelhampton, Dorset, showing oriel window to hall: battlemented section, 1485, left wing, 1500

is unusual in the massive elaboration of its fortifications, and looks as grim and effective as any of its Norman forebears. It dominates the village of High Bolton, each gate protected by a portcullis, the outward facing windows small and the protective walls and turrets strongly built, the striving towards added comfort reflected in the greater elegance of the interior rooms. Well lit by windows opening on to the courtyard, the hall occupies the whole of the first floor on the northern side, with a separate hall for the family and guests on the south side.

Ockwells (1460), near Bray in Berkshire, has finely carved timber gables, with large windows in patterned lead 'cames' coloured with heraldic devices. It is one of the few timber and brick buildings of the period. The hall measures 40 feet by 20 feet wide and is 36 feet in height, the walls are timber framed with brick infilling, and there is a boldly projecting oriel window.

Cothay Manor House, in Somerset (1480), another stone composition of houses, outhouses and dovecots, is arranged in picturesque manner around a courtyard. It contains a typical hall of the period, with double pierced screen and massive open timber roof, with a fine Great Chamber also with an open timber roof.

One of the loveliest battlemented houses of the mediaeval period is at Athelhampton in Dorset. Built in 1485 by Sir William Martyn, of mellow local stone, its original rafters still span the fifteenth-century hall which has a finely designed oriel window. The south-west wing, built in 1500, contains the Great Chamber with a secret staircase leading up to the Long Gallery or Library above. In the gardens the original fifteenth-century dovecot is in a state of perfect preservation.

The site of the manor of Maxstoke overlooking the valley of the Blythe near its junction with the Tame and Cole, east of Coleshill in Warwickshire, is entirely surrounded by a moat and is built of sandstone, 170 feet square, with a gatehouse at the east front and octagonal towers at the corners. The builder was Sir William Clinton, Earl of Huntingdon, who commenced it in about 1345. It was remodelled in part by Sir

Humfrey Stafford, Duke of Buckingham, in 1445.

Sir William Clinton was Lord of the Manor of Maxstoke, a well-wooded parish in the northern part of the old Forest of Arden, where he undertook two building projects, an Augustinian Priory, adjacent to the village and a mile and a half south-east of the manor house, and Maxstoke Castle, with its surrounding moat. He gave the canons the site of his old manor house and the southern half of the parish as an endowment.

The plan of Queens' College, Cambridge, founded by Henry VI's queen, Margaret of Anjou, is an early example of the standard layout of the greater houses of the late fifteenth and early sixteenth centuries, the solid brick cloisters connecting the scattered parts of the house.

Bodiam, in east Sussex, was partially destroyed by order of Cromwell. Its strongest point is the gatehouse, once protected by three portcullises, the vaulted roof pierced with holes through which defenders could pour molten metal on an attacking force. It was built late in the fourteenth century to guard the countryside against French marauders and is surrounded by a moat fed by a tributary of the Rother. In its dismantled state it is one of the most picturesque ruins in the south of England.

Great Chalfield Manor House near Melksham in Wiltshire (c. 1450) is a very picturesque composition of house, church and stables, built of stone and surrounded by a moat. It has no fortifications, as the fortunate county in which it stands escaped the troubles of mediaeval times, although the one entry into the manor was across an easily defended bridge under a gateway. There is a typical mediaeval hall, about 36 feet by 20 feet and 20 feet high, with a bay window high up in the walls and a panelled ceiling.

Oxburgh Hall, near Swaffham, in Norfolk,

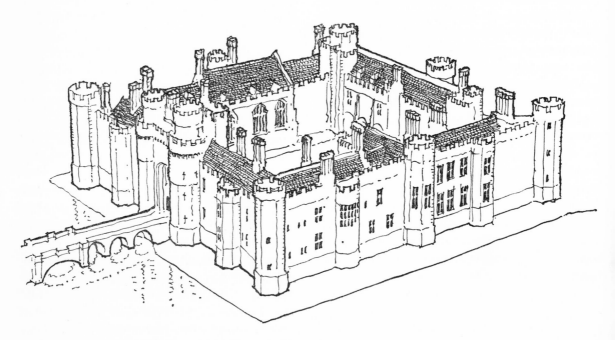

Herstmonceux, Sussex, commenced 1440

built in 1482 of the lovely East Anglian brick by Sir Edmund Bedingfeld, is square in plan around a great courtyard, which is entered by a bridge spanning the surrounding moat under the high gateway, seven storeys in height. The stepped gables reflect the Dutch fashion. The house has come down in direct male descent in the Bedingfeld family for over four hundred and fifty years and was given to the National Trust in 1952.

At Old Wardour, in Wiltshire, the traditional keep-and-bailey plan was retained although the building was erected at the end of the fourteenth century. The wall around the bailey is not notable for strength and the windows of the great tower house within the bailey give no serious intention of defence. At Thornbury in Gloucestershire, built as late as 1511, the two-court plan of Wingfield (1384) in Suffolk is followed. Other fortified manors are at Sherburn (c. 1380) in Oxfordshire and Hever (1462) in Kent, which has a castellated gatehouse, drawbridge, portcullis and moat, and is a square built residence, half house and half fortification, occupied now by a branch of the Astor family.

Herstmonceux, in Sussex, now the headquarters of Greenwich Observatory, was built in 1441, and was restored in this century. Built of brick, its whole appearance is imposing and romantic in the extreme but its defence was never meant to be taken seriously although the gatehouse, as in most examples of this period, is a fairly formidable military feature. There is a remarkable nineteenth-century castle at Peckforton in Cheshire, built (1846–50) by Salvin for the first Lord Tollemache, who had as much reason to fear attack as the original owners of Herstmonceux.

From Herstmonceux and Oxburgh there is a short step only to the purely residential

Prestbury Old Hall, Cheshire, 15th century

Tudor country houses which retained in some cases the quadrangular form, like Castle Ashby in Northamptonshire (completed 1642) and in others the moat, like Playford and Helmingham in Suffolk.

Herstmonceux, with its elaborately fortified wall and its fine gatehouse, is a notable example of a great house of the first half of the century. Tattershall Castle in Lincolnshire is another, where Lord Treasurer Cromwell remodelled an earlier house in the years 1431–9. The house was surrounded by elaborate water defences, enclosing a great hall with a five-storey tower adjoining it which contains a series of splendid state apartments. Cromwell built another large house at South Wingfield in Derbyshire, where the arrangements are more like those of a normal manor house but include on one side of the courtyard a strong tower, which it is suggested may have formed a kind of barracks for the hired gangs of tough mercenary soldiers guarding the house, whom it was safer and more convenient to house away from the private apartments. There are other examples of this kind of partition,

61

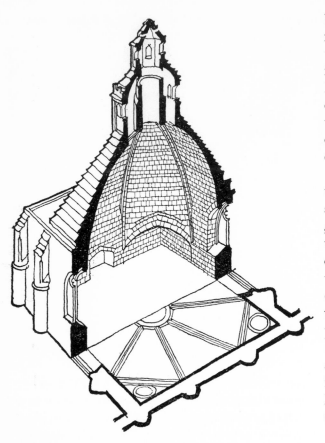

The Abbot's Kitchen, Glastonbury, c. 1400

notably at Bodiam, although these towers may have been built as strong rooms for valuables.

In early times the kitchen was detached from the house, but few examples have survived as the construction was usually of a temporary nature. Later it became more permanent and was substantially built. The Abbot's Kitchen, at Glastonbury (c. 1400), is a most interesting building and is still in a fair state of preservation. There are others to be seen at Stanton Harcourt in Oxfordshire (c. 1470) and at Raby Castle in Durham.

At Glastonbury the kitchen is octagonal, 34 feet from side to side, the four corners being occupied by fireplaces. The octagon rises to a height of 20 feet and is then vaulted on eight stone ribs up to a ventilating shaft which reaches a height of 41 feet. It is an unique building, the design arising out of the particular function for which it was intended, and it was obviously capable of coping with the needs of a great number of guests.

The kitchen at Stanton Harcourt is smaller than Glastonbury, about 25 feet 6 inches square, although the height is nearly as great. The height of these kitchens enabled the escape to the upper heights of steam and cooking smells, and of smoke. The timber work in the roof at Stanton is extremely elaborate and picturesque, with ovens in the thickness of the wall on one side and fireplaces on the other.

Further mediaeval kitchens may be seen at the older colleges of Oxford or Cambridge, in the huge vaulted kitchen at Burghley House near Stamford, and at Durham Cathedral Priory.

In the fifteenth century the development of domestic building showed an increasing awareness of comfort and amenity, although this country remained a very long way behind the standards of culture enjoyed in more southern countries. Amongst the Greek and Roman literature brought to light about this time was the *Treatise on Architecture* by Vitruvius which was written in the time of Augustus and was printed in Latin in Rome in 1486. Erasmus (1467–1536) directed attention to the original text of the New Testament and the Greek classics, superceding the writings of the mediaeval philosophers, and in Italy, which saw the rise of the Renaissance, the arts were in the hands of such as Benvenuto Cellini, Brunelleschi, Donatello and Ghiberti.

All this new development in the arts of the southern countries affected England to

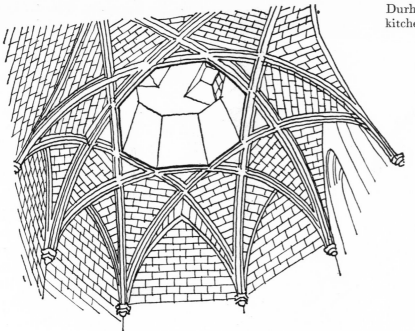

Durham Cathedral Priory, 1366:
kitchen vault

no appreciable extent, the main reason, apart from the difficulties of travel, being the difference in sociological structure. England was a thinly-populated agricultural country, its limited wealth based on the production of wool. Money was more evenly distributed. There were no great fortunes to compare with those of the Medicis of Florence, the Fuggers of Augsburg, or the great Lombard and German banking families. There were consequently no enormously wealthy patrons of the arts to encourage the genius of a Michelangelo, a Cellini or a Raphael, even had the talent been available. There were no sovereign city states to compare with those of Italy, whose concern with artistic prestige did so much to encourage the art and architecture of the period.

Building in England remained indigenous and almost purely functional, although a greater concern with comfort became increasingly apparent with the lessening need for military defence. The different apartments were usually entered from outside as it had not yet occurred to anyone to provide covered access. Furniture was still sparse, the tables and benches of rough trestles, with a dresser, a few stools and a chair for the master of the house. Wall hangings were not considered essential, but beds became very elaborate, with rich hangings to keep out the cold. Panelling began to make an appearance and gained in richness and complexity with the years. Brick came into increasing use and timberwork reached its culmination as at Lavenham in Suffolk, or Rye in Sussex. The timbers of the framework were placed close together, the voids filled with plaster, wattle and daub, or sometimes with brick. In Lancashire and Cheshire the timberwork reached an unrivalled elaboration at Rufford and Moreton Old Hall. Every district used the material available on the spot, the local brick, stone, timber or flint being used honestly and usually with

63

the most fortunate results. Travel being
slow and communications bad there was
little interchange of ideas and each individual district developed its own traditions
with appropriate detail, often forming quite
independent schools of design.

The inns of the period are well known.
The 'Mermaid' at Rye, the 'Angel' at Grantham, the 'George' at Glastonbury, the
'Star' at Alfriston, the 'Swan' at Lavenham,
the 'George' at Norton St. Philip, Somerset,
and the 'Dolphin' Inn at Norwich, which
has recently been remodelled, are in use to
this day, not least among the attractions
this country has to offer to tourists from
abroad.

The hospitals, almshouses and bede houses
of the time are still to be seen in full and
useful employment. Probably the oldest
almshouse in the country (c. 1136) is the
Hospital of St. Cross at Winchester, founded
by Bishop Henry of Blois for thirteen poor
and aged men. The whole forms an attractive group of late Norman church, gatehouse
(where free beer and bread may be had for
the asking), Master's house, refectory and
dwellings around the ancient quadrangle.
The hospital at Ewelme in Oxfordshire
(1436), on the side of a hill, with an entrance from the village street, was built by
the Duke of Suffolk as a charity. The rooms
for the old people are placed around a quadrangle with a cloister lit by dormers with
carved barge boards to the gables. Higher
up is the church, with school buildings in
fine patterned brickwork.

The timber houses of the peasantry have
almost entirely disappeared, though there
still exist many examples of the small yeoman's cottage, such as at Wardless and
Otham in Kent. The 'cruck' house (see illustration on page 52) of the peasant may still
be seen at 'Teapot Hall' near Screwelsby, in
Lincolnshire, where the roof of this tent-
like structure comes down to the ground.
The house is thatched and a loft, which

64

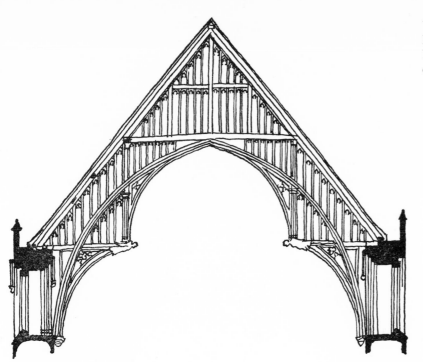

Westminster Hall, 1397–9; hammer-beam roof built by Hugh Herland, master carpenter

served as a bedroom or bower, is reached by a ladder.

One stone arch divided the twelfth-century hall into two fairly narrow rectangles which were spanned by timbers. As the size of the hall increased in the thirteenth century, becoming oblong in contrast to the almost square shape of the previous century, it was no longer possible to divide it suitably with one stone arch. This led to the development of the tie-beam timber roof. These beams ran from wall to wall where they rested on timbers called wall-plates running along the top of the walls. Some of the weight of the roof was transferred to the walls through vertical beams running down the wall some 5 or 6 feet to a stone corbel. The tie-beams were also supported by a curved brace joining the beam to the lower end of the vertical wall-beam. Smoke from the fire in the middle of the floor escaped through a louvre in the roof.

During this period tithes were often paid in kind and some of the barns where the tithes were stored in winter, owing to difficulties of transport, are of imposing dimensions. The Abbot's Barn at Glastonbury, in Somerset, is 86 feet long by 30 feet wide and 30 feet high, with two central transepts,

The Abbot's Barn, Glastonbury, 14th century: construction of timber roof

Westminster Hall, 1399, showing the hammer-
beam roof

and walls of stone with a great open roof of massive timber. It dates from the thirteenth century. Great barns may also be seen at Ashleworth in Gloucestershire, at Bradford-on-Avon (1350), at Great Coxwell in Berkshire and one measuring 94 feet by 35 feet near Sittingbourne in Kent. These buildings are a triumph of timber engineering.

Greatest and most historic of all is Westminster Hall in London. It was originally built by William Rufus in 1099 but fell into a state of ruin in the following century. It was repaired by Thomas à Becket and used subsequently as a banqueting hall, and from 1244 onward as a court of law by order of Henry III, the last court moving to the Strand only as recently as 1882. No other walls have seen so much of the history of the nation, for here every important state trial was held during seven centuries.

In 1394 Richard II decided to reconstruct the hall. Hugh Herland, one of the king's master carpenters, was probably the architect and builder of the unique hammer-beam roof, the first and greatest of its kind, which spans the Norman walls to a width of $67\frac{1}{2}$ feet without any intermediate supports. The huge oak timbers were cut in the forests near Farnham, Surrey, and prefabricated on the spot. The tie-beam of previous centuries was cut away leaving the hammer-beams at each side, which are braced in a most ingenious way by curved struts and arched ribs conveying the weight from the principal rafters well down the walls. The roof covers an area of nearly half an acre, one of the largest roofs supported by timbers in the world. Herland, by doing away with tie-beams, thus exposing the full beauty of the roof, solved an architectural problem which had never been tackled before.

The method of raising the money to pay for the reconstruction is of particular interest and has a mediaeval flavour. Certain Englishmen exiled on the continent were allowed, on payment of a substantial sum to the Treasury, to return home. The money was then donated to the building fund.

Early in the nineteenth century, rotted rafters were removed and replaced by great timbers from men-of-war then in the process of being broken up in Portsmouth Dockyard.

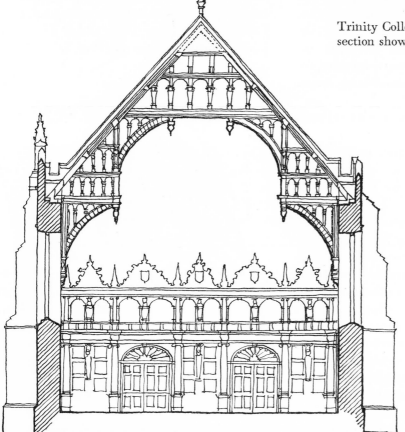

Trinity College Hall, Cambridge, 1604–5: section showing hammer-beam roof

Second only to Westminster in interest come the magnificent halls of the universities of Oxford and Cambridge. The Hall of Trinity, begun in 1604, was modelled on the Middle Temple in London, built thirty years earlier. Both halls measure $40\frac{1}{2}$ by $101\frac{1}{4}$ feet, including the screens.

Unfortunately, the Hall of the Middle Temple received a direct hit during the blitz on London and the magnificent screen was blown to pieces. With Sir Edward Maufe as architect, a fantastic piece of reconstruction was performed; each tiny fragment of the screen found among the ruins was collected and pieced together, the missing pieces replaced and the whole rebuilt in the reconstructed Hall.

At Trinity the hammer-beam trusses support the original double-framed timber roof with three collars. The now familiar arched braces have taken on a Jacobean look; they are lighter and rusticated but lack the powerful simplicity of the earlier examples. The screen and gallery show fine ornate Jacobean carving.

The Guildhalls of Cirencester (1500), Lavenham in Suffolk (1529), and the half-timbered Butchers' Guildhall in Hereford (1621), are particularly fine examples, to mention only a few of the halls of this period.

English Gothic architecture is divided roughly into five periods: the Norman (1066–1189), which comprised the reigns of William I, Henry I, Stephen and Henry II; the Early English (1189–1307), comprising the reigns of Richard I, John, Henry III and Edward I; the Decorated (1307–77), comprising the reigns of Edward II and Edward III; the Perpendicular (1377–1485), comprising the reigns of Richard II, Henry IV, Henry V, Henry VI, Edward IV, Edward V and Richard III; and the Tudor Period (1485–1558), which comprised the reigns of Henry VII, Henry VIII, Edward VI and Mary.

At the time of the visitations of the Black Death the development of Gothic architecture had reached the period known as 'Decorated', which extended roughly from about 1307 to 1377. The style is more ornate than the Early English from which it derived, and the decoration is more elaborate. Tracery became more flowing and geometrical, and vaulting ribs reached an astonishing complexity, as in the nave of Exeter Cathedral. Previously each rib, or 'lierne', marked a change in the direction of the surface of the vault, but now otherwise quite simple vaults were given an appearance of intricacy and richness by the number of liernes adhering to them. A star-shaped pattern of liernes lent the name 'stellar' to vaults at Gloucester (1337–77), Canterbury (1379–1400), Tewkesbury, Winchester, Bristol and Wells, and the choir of Ely. Carved bosses,

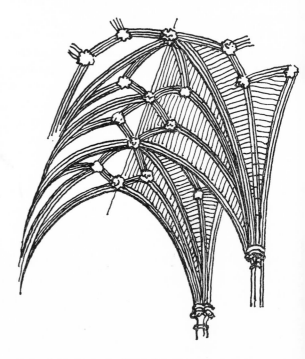

Bristol Cathedral, 1306–32: lierne vault

often of extreme richness, covered the sometimes awkward mitres at which the ribs abutted. Decorated with heraldic shields, grotesques, heads of angels, or foliage in brilliant colour, they lent a blaze of richness to the grey background.

The cathedral in the Middle Ages held a position in the national life incomparably more significant than that of the present day. As few could read, the message of religion was conveyed vividly in painting, in glass, and in sculpture. The cathedral combined the functions of the modern library, museum, community centre, concert hall or free school and in its craftsmanship crudely pointed the moral for the warning or encouragement of the masses which thronged within its walls. The Last Judgement in gay colour, Paradise opening to receive the just, and gibbering devils tormenting the lost souls in a flaming hell—the scene itself was both noisy and colourful and the vaults of the great church were painted in bright fragments.

From the Luttrell Psalter and other illustrated manuscripts of the period we have a lively glimpse of the crowds, the appearance of which, gathered to gossip and do business, was gay in the extreme. The prosperous burghers clothed in dark gaberdine, flat velvet cap, broad leather belt and dangling pouch; peasants in tunics with the front slit to the skirt, long, tight, buttoned sleeves, the hoods with pendant tails on their heads falling over their shoulders; women in flowing kirtles and hoods; the unmarried girls in little bright skull caps; the coats and hosen of the younger men blazing with colour, one leg in one bright colour and the other in joyous contrast. The men no less than the women flashed in jewels and costly stuffs; shoes with toe-points chained to the waist prevented the wearer from kneeling to say his prayers. The man of wealth wore a rich gown trailing behind on the ground, and both men and women of fashion wore enormous head-dresses of fantastic shape, like horns, turbans or towers. The grovelling beggar, filthy in his rags, added plaintive cries to the general din and the shouts of hawkers and hucksters clashed merrily with the chants and psalms of the struggling choir. The churches were, in fact, the community centres of the Middle Ages.

The Bishop of Exeter in 1330 complained that during divine service certain clergy 'fear not to exercise irreverently and damnably certain disorders, laughings, gigglings, and other breaches of discipline'. For instance, 'those who stand at the upper stalls in the choir, throw drippings from the candles upon the heads or the hair of such as stand at the lower stalls'. William of Wykeham made regulations against wrestling and slinging stones in chapel.

The plans of English churches are generally in the form of a Latin cross, but the origin of the plan is conjectural. The crossing of nave and transepts (the arms of the cross) is usually marked externally by a tower, as at Lincoln, York or Durham, or by a spire, as at Salisbury. Continental examples as a rule emphasise the west front, and there is nothing in this country to compare with the magnificence of the great western portals of Chartres, Bourges, Rheims, Amiens or Notre Dame in Paris. On the other hand the unity of the typical English cathedral that culminates centrally in a great tower as at Canterbury or in a soaring spire as at Salisbury is far more balanced and, as an architectural composition, possibly more satisfying to the eye.

The arms of the cross are divided into the nave with side aisles as the main body of the church, and north and south transepts as the arms of the cross plan. Vertically, the nave is divided into nave arcades, triforium, and clerestory, with the windows of the last named rising to the level of the ridge of the nave vault by means of cross vaults (see the illustration on page 47).

'Gothic' architecture was first brought to what may be described as an integrally fresh style, in the domain of the French king around Paris. From there the new art spread over Europe, although in England Gothic in pure form, freed from survivals of Romanesque detail, was first seen in the choir of Lincoln and the nave of Wells before 1200. With the exception of Salisbury there is no complete English Gothic cathedral built as an entity and the work of one architect, such as St. Paul's in London. Even the spire of Salisbury is a later addition. As a rule the typical cathedral includes every style from the earliest to the latest, a supreme example of the English habit of muddling through, but few can be described as decadent to any extent. Inspiration may at times be lacking, but there is no marked retrogression. By the fourteenth century the great period of cathedral building had passed, but substantial improvements were made at this time to Gloucester, Winchester, Canterbury, Salisbury, Ely, Hereford, Exeter, Lincoln, Norwich, Ripon, Wells, Westminster and York Minster, where most of the stained glass dates from this time.

The grandest feature of the English Cathedral is the great central tower, in which the whole building conception reaches its culmination. It was achieved in spite of vast expense and intricate and daring problems of construction. Second in interest is the square east end (with exceptions at Canterbury, which is French, and Wells and Lichfield), and third the peculiarity of placing the two western towers outside the width of the aisles, which occurs at Wells and adds breadth to what is probably the finest of the English west fronts.

These towers were intended to carry spires, but few retain them. The church spire had been developed with conspicuous success by the mediaeval builder and possessed a national significance. The three spires of Lichfield still remain, and other central spires of stone are at Norwich, Salisbury and Oxford. The small spires at Peterborough still stand, but the central spire of Lincoln, which was blown down in 1584, was said to have been over 520 feet in height. A water-colour by de Wint shows the two western towers crowned with miniature spires. The central spire at Ripon fell in 1660 and that of old St. Paul's, reputedly 520 feet high, was struck by lightning and crashed in 1561.

Rivalry in the building of towers led to the rise of the fine examples of Lincoln, Worcester and Canterbury, and the magnificent collegiate chapels at St. George's, Windsor, and King's College, Cambridge, were completed at this time. The towers of Chester, York and Durham are also of this period, and the extraordinary west front of Exeter with its sculptured screen.

The construction of a great cathedral presented a problem of finance and administration to daunt any builder. Funds were collected in a multitude of ways. Cathedrals offering powerful attractions in the way of relics or shrines were fortunate, and contributions at the shrine of Thomas à Becket reached an astronomic sum. The shrine of Edward II at Gloucester was also a source of great benefit, and the story of its foundation is not without interest.

Funds for rebuilding or extending the cathedral were low without a sufficiently compelling attraction in the way of a shrine or relics, until Bishop Thokey accepted from Berkeley Castle the body of the murdered Edward II, slaughtered by red-hot irons passed into his body. Against the threat of trouble from the faction then in power, the bishop fetched the body in his coach and was amply repaid forthwith by a series of miracles of a highly remunerative nature, aided further by the skill and adventure of the Gloucester masons, who produced the Perpendicular style twenty years before its time. By 1337 they had constructed one of the earliest known lierne vaults over the south transept, went on to the extremely complicated choir vault and then built, over the cloister, before the end of the century, the earliest fan-vault in the country.

The period of English Gothic architecture known as Perpendicular is peculiar to this country, and no development similar to this thoroughly English style is found abroad. It reached its culmination in the second half of the fifteenth century. The passion for height produced a style of vertical

St. Andrew's, Heckington, Lincolnshire, 1345–80: a typical parish church, height of spire 175 feet

71

lines which, suddenly and abruptly curving inwards, give to the resulting arch a flattened form. Vaulting became more complex, the number of liernes of the Decorated period were multiplied to a fantastic number and finally the system of vaulting known as fan-vaulting was evolved. The buttressing to support the spreading vaulting reached an astounding pitch of ingenuity.

Windows of the period are of immense size and are crowned for the most part with four-centred arches, strengthened by horizontal transoms and by primary and secondary mullions.

Building in stone had now reached into the realms of exact engineering; the reduction of supporting piers emphasised the space in a great church, the decrease in wall area let in the flooding light. The east window at Gloucester is 38 feet wide and 72 feet high, approximately the area of a tennis court.

Among the very impressive works in the early Perpendicular manner are the naves

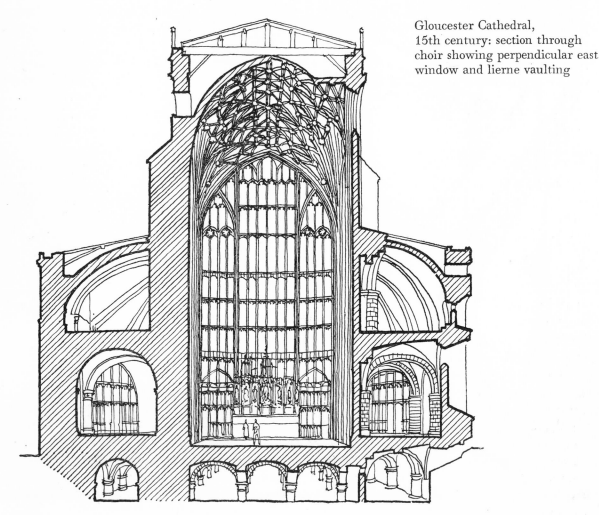

Gloucester Cathedral,
15th century: section through
choir showing perpendicular east
window and lierne vaulting

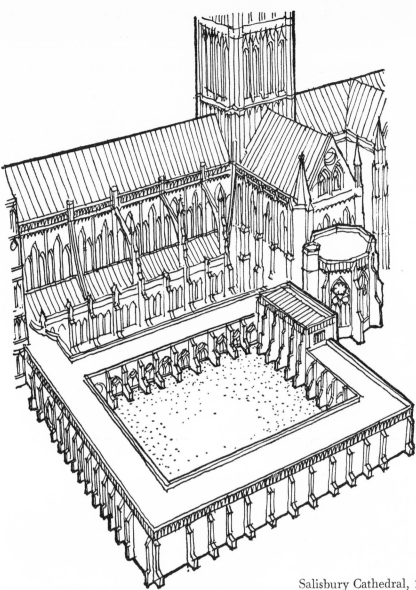

Salisbury Cathedral, 1220: the cloister

and west fronts of Canterbury Cathedral and Westminster Abbey, the rebuilt great halls at Westminster, New College, Oxford, and Winchester College. Also begun was the transformation of the nave of Winchester Cathedral, and the completion of the nave of Worcester with its great dominating central tower.

The other characteristics of the English cathedral are its length, its chapter houses and its cloisters. The cloister, that unique feature of English cathedrals, is placed usually south of the nave and west of the transepts, serving as a means of communication between the different parts of the buildings and as a general meeting place. Those at Salisbury and Gloucester are among the finest, but others almost as

73

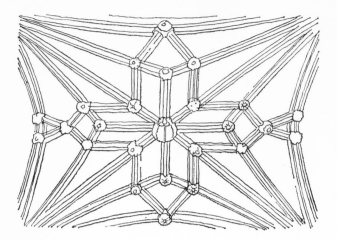

Queens' College, Cambridge, 1448: lierne vault to gatehouse

at Gloucester (1337–77) with the roofs at Canterbury, Wells, Ely, Bristol, Winchester and Tewkesbury Abbey not many years later. The vault of the choir in Gloucester Cathedral (illustrated on page 72) is a particularly impressive example of this Decorated period. Here the multiplicity of ribs and the carved 'bosses' or keystones at their intersection gives a most elaborate and rich effect, exceeded only by the next step in vaulting from lierne to fan, which for sheer technique and magnificence is unequalled in any continental church.

Fan-vaulting reached its culmination at King's College Chapel, Cambridge, and in the lovely chapel at Westminster Abbey which houses Torrigiano's magnificent mausoleum (1512–18) of Henry VII and his queen, Elizabeth of York. Here the fan-vault is constructed of half-concealed transverse arches of which the apparently unsupported pendants are merely elongated voussoirs, and on the pendants (a daring example of stone in tension) the fan-vaulting rests. This roof is a masterpiece of English masonry and as such is without rival.

The earliest of the pendant vaults is at the

lovely can be seen at Wells, Worcester, Hereford, Lincoln, Norwich, Durham, Chester, Chichester, Canterbury and Bristol. One of the few continental examples is at Regensburg on the Danube in Southern Bavaria, where the cloisters are as romantic as anything in Germany, but they are late Gothic, and show strong Italian influence.

Probably the earliest examples of the richer form of vaulting known as lierne are

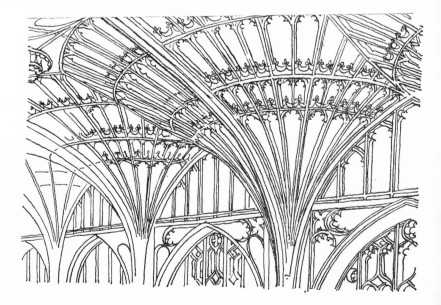

King's College Chapel, Cambridge: detail of main vault

King's College Chapel,
Cambridge, 1512–15: the
pattern of the main
vault—John Wastell,
master mason

Divinity School at Oxford (1479) and the vault of Henry VII's Chapel at Westminster is a development of this. These amazing technical and engineering accomplishments are related to the pendant type of hammerbeam truss that appears at Crosby Hall and Eltham, at Christ Church and Corpus Christi, Oxford, and at Hampton Court, where the arches of the truss are supported on pendants hanging from the truss. The ceiling of the chapel at Hampton Court has a most interesting timber vault which gives the effect of stone, and is one of the most notable achievements of the art of carpentry in existence.

With the completion of the roof, the masons and carpenters had still to carve the decoration on capitals and arches, finish the stone tracery and erect the choir stalls and screens which had been fashioned in the carpenter's shop. Then came the turn of the tilers, glaziers, plasterers and painters.

75

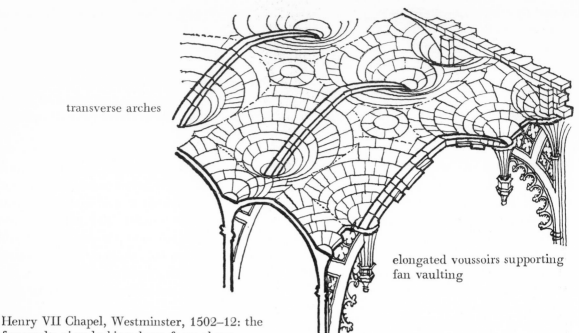

transverse arches

elongated voussoirs supporting
fan vaulting

Henry VII Chapel, Westminster, 1502–12: the
fan vault; view looking down from above

Glazed tiles decorated in greens and yellows were used for more important buildings. Coloured glass was imported from the Rhineland or Normandy as English glaziers could not compete in price with the foreign commodity, although the fourteenth- and fifteenth-century glass of York Minster, notably the Five Sisters window and the Bell-Founders window, was made in nearby Stonegate.

Colour was used in churches and cathedrals from Norman times, when the great cylindrical piers at Durham, Waltham and Lindisfarne were patterned in diamonds, chevrons and spirals. Glass mosaic, glass and enamelling were used throughout the mediaeval period in the decoration of roofs, vaults and furniture. Walls were usually coloured a parchment white and on this a decoration of gold and vermilion was arranged in lines like masonry. The rebuilt vault of the choir at Ely was covered with vermilion and gold.

Bright colour delighted the unsophisticated mediaeval eye. Coloured hangings enlivened the churches, and men and women dressed as colourfully as they could afford. Statues, bosses, corbels, columns, decorative ironwork and hammer-beams were gilded or silvered and painted bright red, blue or yellow. Tempera paintings covered the plastered walls and the large sums of money paid out to painters on a mediaeval building project emphasise their importance in its decoration.

The abundance of timber as a building material saw the rise of the carpenter, whose technique and craftsmanship reached an astonishing quality. East Anglia is the home of the hammer-beam roof which first appeared in the fourteenth century. Like the fan-vault, it is a purely English invention and has no parallel on the continent. The timber arch braces, rising to the ridge or to a collar, spring from brackets projecting from the top of the wall, in turn sus-

76

tained by curved struts springing from wall posts resting on corbels. The earliest known example is the magnificent roof of Westminster Hall, begun in 1394, of which a detailed description is given on page 66.

Probably the finest example, with the exception of Westminster, is at Cilcain in Flintshire. At Dartington Hall in Devon the original hammer-beam roof, which spans 45 feet, has been replaced by a modern truss. In the fifteenth century this form of roof attained to an extraordinary development, notably in East Anglian churches, where the projecting hammer-beams are frequently adorned with figures of angels with spreading wings, as in the splendid north transept roof at Ely, and at Necton, Cawston, Swaffham and Trunch, the most striking probably being at March (1500) in the Isle of Ely. Double hammer roofs are found at Rattlesden, Grundsburgh, Woolpit and Worlingworth in Suffolk, and a late angel roof can be seen over the Suffolk chapel at Ewelme in Oxfordshire, where the triple group of hospital, school and church, founded as a hospital in 1436 by the Duke of Suffolk, is one of the most picturesque in the country. The vault of Warmington in Northamptonshire (c. 1370) is of wood. The roof of Framlingham in Suffolk (c. 1520) is another elaborate timber truss, with that at Knapton only a little less so. Lavenham is richly panelled and supported by flat four-centred timber arches above the celebrated perpendicular nave. The hammer-beam roofs of the great halls at Eltham Palace and Hampton Court were constructed by the royal carpenters in the late fifteenth and sixteenth centuries. Other notable timber roofs are at Needham Market (c. 1480) in Suffolk and Chartham in Kent.

The best of the mediaeval masons were virtuosi in the art of stone carving. William of Wykeham's Chantry at Winchester, which is early fifteenth century, and the Neville screen at Durham are wonderful examples, the latter made in London and transported in boxes to the North. It is probably the finest screen of its age and one of the most remarkable pieces of carving in the country.

Building in stone in the Middle Ages was so expensive that none but the richest could afford to do so. Castles were of necessity built in the strongest materials but churches, monastic houses and colleges were erected piecemeal, and less important buildings were of timber, built on stone footings and roofed with tile or stone flags, so that while the masons had to travel where their

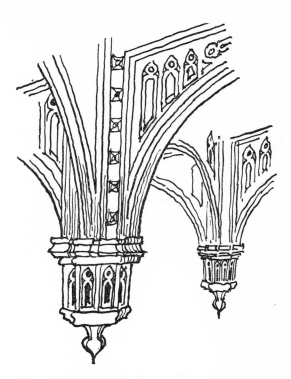

Crosby Hall, Chelsea, 1466: long moulded pendants ending in hollow octagonal finials hang from the intersections of the principal roof beams. Each finial forms the starting point of four arches with traceried spandrels, in the same way as fanvaulting springs from an elongated voussoir

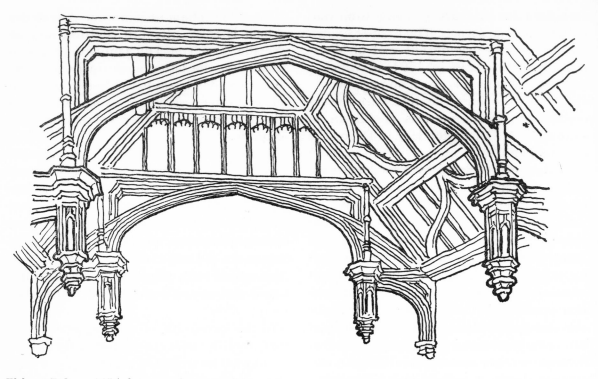

Eltham Palace, 1475: hammer-beam roof

work led them, every town and village had its own tilers, thatchers, carpenters, plasterers and daubers.

Being itinerant, masons could not fit into the local guild system, but formed lodges on each building site. The lodge provided tools, sleeping and eating quarters, and enforced a satisfactory rate of pay for a good standard of workmanship for these very essential craftsmen, who began work at dawn and continued until the light faded, although Sunday and the principal Saints' days were holidays. The status of the masons increased with their skill until Henry Yevele, the King's Master Mason under Edward III and Richard II, designed the new nave and cloister of Canterbury Cathedral, helped in the rebuilding of Westminster Abbey, and supervised the erection of the city wall around Canterbury, as well as carrying on his official work of maintaining the Tower of London and Westminster Palace.

Working drawings came into general use during the fourteenth and fifteenth centuries. Local stone was used as far as possible to reduce the difficulty and cost of transport. King's College Chapel, however, used Yorkshire stone, and ten carts carried alabaster with considerable difficulty from Nottingham to Windsor for the reredos in St. George's Chapel. Water transport, being the cheaper method, was used as much as possible, and stone was shaped and cut where practicable at the quarry with wooden and canvas templates. In the quarries at Burton, Corfe and York, workshops were set up to produce standard patterns for shafts, images and tombs, and, to reduce the risk of damage in transport, the more delicate work was sent out rough-dressed. Axes

78

were used for this preliminary work, and mallet and chisel for the final cutting. Tools were shod with steel and blunted easily, requiring constant maintenance by the blacksmith, but even with these somewhat makeshift instruments the mediaeval mason produced the miracles of carving in Southwell and York Chapter Houses, and the capitals at Wells.

Standard patterns were usual in the earlier examples of tomb construction, in which the mason could show his skill as sculptor. Later figures were made as actual portraits taken from a drawing. In the Beauchamp Chapel (1443–64), Warwick, the figure of the Earl, Richard Beauchamp, Governor of Calais and Regent for Henry VI, is taken from a portrait.

In the clay lowlands of East Anglia the local brick gives colour and warmth and the fifteenth century saw the revival of brick building. Little Wenham Hall in Suffolk, dating from the later thirteenth century, is a lone example of its employment in domestic building of that date, but with the rise of the wool trade to Flanders and Netherlands brick became ballast in the returning ships and was used for building in East Anglia. East Barsham Manor House, Norfolk (1500–15), with its picturesque detached gatehouse, is a good example.

The earliest instance of the use of brick is found at Coggeshall in Essex. Fourteenth- and fifteenth-century work survives in the gatehouses at Thornton Abbey and at Herstmonceux, at Tattershall Castle in Lincolnshire and Queens' College, Cambridge. Details in terra-cotta were made for Sutton Place near Guildford, the home of Paul Getty, the American oil magnate, and in East Anglia at Great Shoring and East Barsham in Norfolk. One side of Wessingham, another Norfolk house, is entirely faced with enriched terra-cotta.

The 'English' period saw the rise of the greater public schools and the founding of colleges at Oxford and Cambridge. When William of Wykeham built New College, Oxford, he founded Winchester College in 1382 to feed it and his example was followed in 1442 by Henry VI at Eton. Westminster originated in 1560 on the model of other grammar schools, of which there were between three and four hundred, free and open to all classes, before 1535. Other schools kept by the priests of newly endowed chantries were commenced at Oswestry (1406), Middleton (1412), Durham (1414), Sevenoaks (1418), City of London (1442), Aldwick (1448), Hull (1482), Chipping Camden (1487), Macclesfield (1502) and St. Paul's (1509).

In the latter half of the fourteenth century English mediaeval art reached its highest form. The traceried window gave a new character to buildings, and the carving of foliage and other ornaments was carried to the extreme, but always within the limits of a fine sense of taste and proportion. Carved screens and stalls, of which the most notable are in the choir of Winchester Cathedral, are unsurpassed in excellence, and lend an emphasis and richness to a great church, often in direct contrast to the simplicity of the stonework.

The canopied tombs, which now became an important feature of English churches, are often so much finer as works of art than the recumbent effigies, usually stiff and awkward, they surmount.

It was the age of the monumental brass, the best examples of which are to be seen in Felbrigge Church in Norfolk, depicting Sir Simon Felbrigge (standard bearer to Richard II) and his wife Margaret (cousin to Anne of Bohemia), but no English work approaches the fine Flemish examples in St. Margaret's Church, King's Lynn, which commemorate the Walsoken and Braunche families. These are the best in England.

The fifteenth century was a period of decline, and although building activity remained continuous and in fact more voluminous than in any century since the Conquest, Gothic art lost much of its freshness. This can in part be attributed to the Black Death, which may have made serious inroads on the few craftsmen of the time, although the carving of woodwork does not appear to have suffered in any way. Chancel and rood screens may be seen in considerable numbers in Norfolk, Devonshire and Somerset, some retaining more than a trace of the colour and gilding with which they were once completely covered.

Sculpture was carved in abundance and there are good examples in the chantry chapel of Henry V in Westminster, but the best work is not of the fifteenth century.

Heraldic sculpture of the period also flourished and was treated with skill and vigour as in the examples in King's College Chapel.

Another material was alabaster, which was extensively used, but the best effigies of the time are in gilt metal. That of the Black Prince in Canterbury Cathedral, and of Richard Beauchamp, Earl of Warwick, are the most impressive; the latter may

have been carried out by a German craftsman.

The angel roofs of Norfolk have been mentioned, but the choicest artistry of this period was reserved for the stained glass. The increasing technological knowledge of masonry construction enabled windows to be erected of immense size, giving wide scope for the display of large single figures in light and transparent colours, the brightness and clearness of the effect enhanced by a generous use of white and yellow glass. The vast windows in the north and south windows of the eastern transepts at York Minster are particularly noteworthy, and were made between 1405 and 1430. The contract for the great east window of the choir is still preserved together with the name of the maker, John Thornton of Coventry, and the date, 1405.

Mural paintings in churches were widespread and popular. Many were covered by whitewash during the Reformation and owe their preservation to this fact, although in somewhat damaged state. The best examples are in the north transept of St. Albans Cathedral, c. 1425, in the scenes from the Apocalypse in the Chapter House at Westminster Abbey, c. 1475, and the 'Miracles of the Virgin' in Eton College Chapel, 1479–88.

Paycocks, Coggeshall, Essex, c. 1500

3

The Early Renaissance 1485–1625

The long predominance of Gothic architecture came to an end in a final magnificent flourish at Henry VII's chapel at Westminster (1502–12), at St. George's Chapel at Windsor (1473–1516) and, more grandly than all, at King's College Chapel, Cambridge (1512–15). This splendid chapel has probably the most inspiring of all Gothic interiors, and although it lacks the scale of Chartres or Milan, the sheer technical accomplishment, the huge stained-glass windows, and the lightness of the structural masonry soaring upward to the lace-like tracery of the fan-vaulting, give an effect of space and grandeur that even the larger cathedrals fail to surpass. The Perpendicular style here reached the apex of construction in stone but the Gothic style was not dead. It was capable of much further and more fanciful development, and it is fascinating to speculate on its future had there been no change of architectural fashion. There was no recession in church building activity. Bath Abbey was being rebuilt at this time, and the nave of Cirencester and Rochester Lady Chapel, together with many other screens, tombs and chantries.

The Renaissance of classical architecture had commenced to seep into the country, and the quadrangle of Wolsey's great palace at Hampton Court was decorated with terracotta busts of Roman Emperors, carried out by Italian workmen. The marvellous stalls of King's College Chapel, also, were carved by craftsmen from over the Alps.

It was a time of tremendous change; gunpowder had revolutionised warfare, and in particular Galileo's (1564–1642) discovery that the earth was merely a small planet in the solar system and not, as had always been thought, the centre of the universe had changed the intellectual perspective of the times. With the invention of the mariners'

Salisbury
Cathedral, 1520:
the Audley
Chantry

compass Diaz, in 1486, discovered the Cape of Good Hope and opened up the east to the trade routes which had been blocked when the Turks took Constantinople in 1453 and conquered Syria and Egypt. Columbus, seeking new allies for Christendom against the Turkish onrush, discovered America in 1498.

This is the era which saw a gradual and at first very tentative acceptance of ideas from abroad, although in Italy it was the period of the High Renaissance. It embraced the reigns of Henry VII (1485–1509), Henry VIII (1509–47), Edward VI (1547–53), Mary (1553–58), Elizabeth (1558–1603) and James I (1603–25).

The principal examples in London are Henry VII's Chapel in Westminster Abbey (1502–12) and the gateway of St. James Palace; the main provincial examples are Sutton Place, Guildford (1523–5), parts of Hampton Court (1515–30), Compton Wynyates in Derbyshire (1520), Layer Marney in Essex (1500–25), Horham Hall, Essex (1502–20), Barrington Court, Somerset (1514–48) and Little Moreton, Cheshire (1550–9).

St. John's College, Cambridge (1511) has probably the most typical of the plans of Oxford or Cambridge colleges. The great brick and stone gateway bears the arms of the founder, Lady Margaret Beaufort, mother of Henry VII, and opens on to the first of three courts, which is flanked on one side by the chapel with kitchen and hall with large bay windows on the side facing the gateway. The second court (1598) contains the Master's Lodge and the third court (1623) the Library and Chambers, with a Renaissance Loggia (1669). The students' rooms occupy the rest of the buildings around the three courts.

At Oxford, the new colleges were Brasenose (1509), Corpus Christi (1516), Christ Church (1546), Trinity (1554), St. John's (1555) and Jesus (1571); and at Cambridge, Jesus (1497), Christ's (1505), St. John's (1511), Magdalene (1542) and Trinity (1546).

Elizabethan mansions include Charlecote in Warwickshire (1558), Losely near Guildford in Surrey (1562–8), Longleat near Warminster in Wiltshire (1567–80), Kirby Hall, Northamptonshire (1570–5), Burghley House, Northamptonshire (1577–87), Montacute in Somerset (1580–1601), Wol-

laton near Nottingham (1580–8), Longford Castle, Wiltshire (1580), Westwood Park, Worcester (1590), Bramhall in Cheshire (additions 1590–1600), Sizergh Castle in Westmorland (1558–75) and Lower Walterstone in Dorset (1568).

Schools of the period include Berkhamsted (1541), Sherborne (1550), Shrewsbury (1552), Bedford (1552) and Christ's Hospital (1552), Repton (1557), Merchant

King's College Chapel, Cambridge: carved figure on the Provost's stall. The swirl and movement anticipate the Baroque by two hundred years

83

Taylors (1561), Highgate (1565), Rugby (1567), Harrow (1571), Uppingham (1584), Charterhouse (1611) and Dulwich (1619).

Mansions built during the reign of James I include Hatfield, Hertfordshire (1607–11), Holland House, Kensington (1607) (destroyed in the last war), Bramshill in Hampshire (1605–12), Blickling Hall in Norfolk (1616–1620), Chastleton in Oxfordshire (1603–14), Audley End in Essex (1603–16), Knole, near Sevenoaks in Kent (1605), Charlton House, Wiltshire (1607), Stockton House, Wiltshire (1610), Aston Hall, near Birmingham (1618–35), Bolsover Castle, Derbyshire (1612) and Charlton House in Kent (1607–1612).

The Bodleian Library at Oxford (1613–1636) is typical of the period, and Fountains Hall near Ripon in Yorkshire (1611) was built largely of materials from the ruined abbey. Hospitals include Ford's Hospital, Coventry (1529), the Whitgift at Croydon (1596–9), Sackville College, East Grinstead (1619), Chipping Campden (1612), Trinity Hospital, Greenwich (1613), Eyres Hospital, Salisbury (1617) and the well-preserved Abbot's Hospital (1619) in the High Street, Guildford. Almshouses of the period are to be found at Cobham, Kent (1598).

During the mediaeval period the greater buildings had been constructed by guilds of craftsmen of whom the names of one or two masons or designers of outstanding merit have come down to us. The temples and palaces of the Renaissance were now the products of individual architects, who, more often than not, combined the talents of engineer, sculptor and painter—Brunelleschi, engineer and sculptor, Bramante, architect and painter, Raphael, painter and architect, Michelangelo, the transcendent genius of painting, poetry, architecture, sculpture and engineering, Leonardo da Vinci and others.

The English artists were now becoming known. The mason at St. George's, Windsor, was Henry Jaynes and the designer and master mason of the fine vaulted roof was William Vertue, who with his brother Robert also worked in Bath Abbey. At King's College Chapel there were Reginald Ely and John Wastell, who built the splendid vault. The screen was undoubtedly carved by Italian craftsmen (1562–4).

The development of the new architecture was shaped, however, by the vagaries and uncertainties of Tudor foreign policy, controlled by tyrant rulers such as Henry VIII, and the unpredictable Elizabeth, which policy, tending towards closer ties with the Netherlands, maintained a very varying attitude towards France, and after 1558 barred all contact with Rome. The period before this was too brief for the assimilation of any mature Italian influence, and Flemish mannerisms took over and for a century remained paramount. We owe the coarse detail at Wollaton, for instance, to craftsmen from the Low Countries.

Wollaton Hall, near Nottingham (1580–1588), was designed by Smithson, who had worked at Longleat, near Warminster, but the refinement and restraint of Longleat has given place here to the over-richness and over-emphasis of the Flemish influence. Wollaton was built for Sir Hugh Willoughby, who had vast industrial and commercial interests, and his tastes were reflected in the opulence and the affected mediaevalism of the mansion, which might have been built for a Victorian plutocrat.

This period of the early Renaissance in English architecture was also one of transition; with the Dissolution of the Monasteries in 1539 the great age of church building came to an end, and architecture became almost exclusively domestic and secular. The transition, however, was too

Wollaton Hall, Nottinghamshire, 1580–8: Renaissance detail misunderstood and misapplied

rapid to be absorbed with any thoroughness, and the flood of architectural literature and books from the Netherlands, filled with so-called classical details and designs only too uncertainly understood, served merely to confuse and bewilder the designers of the new buildings arising throughout the land, financed by the distribution of wealth following the monastic suppression. Houses increased vastly in size although not necessarily in beauty, and were embellished with a riot of cornices, pilasters and details which were at times in anything but the best of taste. The grandiose pile of Wollaton Hall is probably the most vulgar example of these houses, and when, in the reign of Queen Victoria, the mansions of the merchant princes of Liverpool, Birmingham, Sheffield and Leeds arose over the countryside they almost invariably and unfortunately reproduced all that was worst in the houses of the successful Elizabethan adventurers. Time, of course, has dealt kindly with these Tudor curiosities of architecture, giving them a patina and a texture that endows them with a charm and an atmosphere that goes far to remedy their defi-

ciencies; but when the native and attractive English architecture was influenced by foreign styles that arose out of conditions peculiar to their own land of origin, as happens in some of our contemporary building, it lost not only its integrity, but it became meaningless and, in some cases, almost repulsive.

The most significant event of the reign of Henry VIII, in so far as it influenced architecture, was the Dissolution of the Monasteries. The vandalism accompanying this drastic event was wanton and horrifying. More than any single event it marked the end of mediaeval society in England, and made possible the division of the vast estates which had belonged to the Church. The great monasteries and their works of art were in most cases destroyed, but some of the abbeys have become parish churches, as at Tewkesbury, Wimborne, Romsey and Selby.

For a while the sale of the monastic lands replenished the royal treasury, thus saving the King the embarrassment of levying further taxes on his obstinate subjects, who were liable to show their disapproval in no

uncertain manner. In the event, some good came out of the destruction. Henry VIII founded Trinity College, on a scale larger than that of any other at Cambridge, following the example of Cardinal Wolsey, who had founded Christ Church College at Oxford.

The greater part of the monastic lands and tithes were sold. A large proportion was distributed gratis to the families near the throne, and some remained in the hands of the Crown for several generations, their dispersal being occasioned, only through dire financial necessity, by their royal owners up to the time of Charles I. The Durham and Northumberland coal-fields, for instance, had been ecclesiastical property, and after Stuart times they were developed on an immense scale and founded the fortunes of many noble families.

The destruction of the monasteries reduced the wealth and importance of many towns depending on them and their pilgrims for their revenues, although other towns, such as St. Albans and Bury St. Edmunds, were released from the bondage of their ecclesiastic landlords who, in many cases, were no novices in the arts of financial extortion.

At the time of the Dissolution, the Middle Ages were indeed passing away. It is, of course, difficult to name any particular date, or even period, when it can safely be said that the Middle Ages came to an end, but the year 1485, in which Henry Tudor overthrew Richard III at Bosworth and ended the Wars of the Roses, is probably as nearly accurate as it is possible to be, although English society continued for the next half-century as it had done for the previous two hundred years. The proud and ancient castles had outlived their use and were everywhere crumbling into ruin. Many of them, indeed, had been adapted to the domestic uses of a later age and had centuries of splendour still before them, but many more had been abandoned or had served as quarries for the poor hovels built against their walls.

Such towns as London, Bristol, Gloucester and Oxford were prospering and thrusting out beyond the confines of their mediaeval walls. The less prosperous towns, on the other hand, were shrinking and could no longer afford to maintain their surrounding fortifications. The lead and stone of the abbeys were now used for the great houses that took their place, and the peace of Tudor rule encouraged houses that looked outwards, with larger and more spacious rooms, wide lattice windows and oriels and well-lighted galleries.

Many of the famous names of England are heard for the first time, among them the families of Cavendish, Cecil, Russell, Thynne and Herbert. The ultimate criterion of success was a house big enough to entertain the King and a large retinue, and vast palaces arose in all the southern parts of the country. The most popular form of plan showed a central courtyard surrounded by ranges of rooms, one room in depth, the one leading into the other. The courtyard was entered through a towered gateway with a large central oriel, as at Hampton Court. Such features as fortified gateways and battlemented parapets were retained rather more for ornament than for defence, and the addition of the numerous and fantastically ornamented chimneys was new evidence of the increased comfort within. The great hall had now declined in importance, but it remained a feature on which much decoration was still lavished, in particular on screens such as that at Audley End, and on the fireplaces, which were surrounded by carvings of coats of arms, pilasters, columns, and other devices, gilded and coloured, in a profusion that was more robust and grandiose than tasteful. The

widely held theory that Elizabethan E-shaped houses were so planned in honour of the queen is quite without foundation. The familiar long rectangle with projecting porch and wings at each end is the logical modification of the mediaeval manor house or castle. With the disappearance of the gatehouse to the manor house, following the more peaceful Tudor years, the court inside went also, with the two wings, which gradually diminished and retracted leaving only the rectangular shape.

A feature of the houses of this time was the long gallery, frequently occupying the whole length of the top floor, a peculiarly English feature, which was particularly noticed by foreign travellers. The longest of all, now destroyed, was at Audley End,

Typical fireplace c. 1560

87

and measured 226 feet in length. There are also huge galleries at Hardwick Hall and Montacute. Their purpose is not known, but that they were used in winter is surmised from the number of fireplaces in them, sometimes two or three. They were probably used for indoor exercise, and almost certainly for music, for this was the golden age of English music, and madrigals and the songs of Dowland would be sung, during the long winter evenings, in the flickering candlelight.

The best music in Europe could be heard in the Chapel Royal, for Henry VII in his youth had provided the impulse by composing musical tunes and the verses which accompanied them. His court followed the fashion, and from the times of the Wars of the Roses to the reign of Elizabeth the art and the scholarship of the Italian Courts of the Renaissance had great influence on the gentlemen of England, planting within them the seeds of scholarship and culture which they took back with them to their country homes.

During the early and middle Tudor periods the standard of living rose slowly but significantly not only among the wealthier classes but also, as a writer of 1577

has it, among the 'lowest' sort. 'Our fathers,' he writes, 'yea and we ourselves have lien full oft upon straw pallets, covered only with a sheet, under coverlets made of dagswain or hop harlots and a good round log under their heads instead of a bolster. If it were so that our fathers or the good man of the house had a mattress or flockbed and thereto a sack of chaff to rest his head upon, he thought himself to be as well lodged as the lord of the town, that peradventure lay seldom in a bed of down or whole feathers. Pillows were thought meet only for women in childbed. As for servants, if they had any sheet above them, it was well, for seldom had they any under their bodies, to keep them from the pricking straws that ran oft through the canvas of the pallet and razed their hardened hides.'

With the improvements in the standards of living in the early and middle Tudor period, chimneys became general even in cottages. Old men recalled that 'in their young days there were not above two or three chimneys, if so many, in uplandish towns, the religious houses and manor places of their lords always excepted, but each one made his fire against a reredos in the hall where he dined and dressed his meat'. The increasing use of brick made for easier building of chimneys and the increasing use of coal instead of wood for the domestic hearth made it essential, as well as less disagreeable, to discharge the smoke.

At this time the crafts of the carver and plasterer were displayed in a variety of designs, some simple, others most elaborate, in a diversity of motifs. There was little decorative work in plaster before 1500, because before that date the joists carrying the floor-boards had been left uncovered. After that date, in a large room where the floor above was carried on one or two large beams across the breadth of the room, the smaller beams carrying the floor-boards were tenoned into them. If the appearance from below was not considered decorative, the joists were covered on the underside and the large beams were moulded. The ceiling thus became divided into compartments, and then into sub-compartments or panels decorated by small wood ribs in geometrical patterns. The next step was to make the ceilings in plaster, and the plasterers' work became second to none among the decorative crafts.

Most ornate ceilings can be seen in Cardinal Wolsey's suite of rooms at Hampton Court (1525), and in the Abbot's Room at Thame Park, Oxfordshire (1529). There is early plaster decoration of a very elaborate kind at Corpus Christi College, Oxford, and at Yanwath Hall in Westmorland. In the breakfast room at Gwydir Castle, Caernarvonshire (1597), there is an extraordinary chimney piece of coarse, strongly handled and extremely picturesque plaster, a bold heraldic design flanked by figures of Julius Caesar and Augustus decked out as Elizabethan warriors. Sizergh Castle in Westmorland (1565), South Wraxall Manor in Wiltshire (1590) and Levens Hall (1570), also in Westmorland, have fine ceilings. Haddon Hall and Dene Park, in Northamp-

tonshire, have outstanding plaster ceilings, and Stockton House, in Wiltshire (1610), has many examples. Mention also must be made of the coloured plasterwork at Hardwick Hall (1590), near Chesterfield. At Knole (1620), near Sevenoaks in Kent, is some of the best plasterwork on ceiling and mantelpiece in the whole country, and the ceiling of the great chamber of Herringstone in Dorset is an extraordinary design of mermaids, fishes, pelicans and swans, moulded in panels, with three great hanging pendants and a frieze below with elephants and trees.

The Palace at Hampton Court (1515–30) was built by Cardinal Wolsey a few years before the Dissolution of the Monasteries. It belongs, however, with Henry VII's chapel at Westminster, to the period of the Early Renaissance in England as the influence of Italy and the Netherlands on this luxurious building is very marked indeed. Busts and medallions of terra cotta by Giovanni da Majano are incorporated in the brickwork and are northern Italian by influence. The best of them are decorated by the arms of Wolsey and the Cardinal's hat.

Wolsey maintained the standard of living befitting a great prince of the Church, keeping a household of nearly a thousand persons and marching in state with silver pillars and pole-axes borne before him. He was almost as wealthy as the King himself and drew the vast revenues, while neglecting the duties, of Archbishop of York, Bishop of Durham, and Abbot of St. Albans. His arrogance and his attitude towards the lay nobles and gentlemen were no small factors in the anti-clerical revolution which followed his fall from power.

The rank and position of such a man demanded, of course, a background of comparable splendour, and it is to this essential background that we owe most of our great collections of art. The cult of magnificence reached its culmination in the eighteenth-century period known as Baroque, when enormous buildings, built without thought of cost and decorated in gorgeous fashion by the finest artists of the age, proclaimed the power and prestige of the autocrat. Wolsey was such an autocrat, and only he could have carried through to triumphant conclusion a project which must have taxed unbearably the economy of a poverty-stricken country whose total population was hardly more than that of a major city today.

Much of Wolsey's palace at Hampton Court remains as it was built, and became the model on which the Tudor colleges at Oxford and Cambridge were planned. Over a bridge spanning a moat we enter the Base Court under a battlemented gatehouse, and pass under another gatehouse with an oriel window and a curious gable designed in two separate slopes. To the right the front is broken up by octagonal battlemented turrets thrusting boldly against the sky, a feature of Tudor buildings, which generally flank the gateways and are roofed with charming cupolas of lead. The shafts of the chimney stacks, placed in groups, built of brickwork in varied patterns with octagonal bases and caps, are another feature of the palace. The broken and romantic silhouettes of the buildings of this period are not the least of their attractions.

The Great Hall at Hampton Court, like the rest of the Palace, is of brick with stone dressings, the windows, battlements, angles and string courses in the latter material. Tudor bricks are from 9 to 11 inches in length and rarely exceed 2 inches in height, which gives a texture to a wall surface and, with a patina of the centuries on it, a charm that is typically English. Throughout this Early Renaissance period brickwork was laid generally in what is called 'old English

bond' with alternate courses placed lengthwise and endwise. The brick surface was broken up by diapers, or intersecting lines, of darker colour, and being easily cut and moulded it was particularly suitable for the tall, moulded chimney stacks, turrets and battlements which lend such enchantment to the style.

The interior of the Great Hall, 106 feet long, 40 feet wide and 60 feet high, surmounted by the elaborate timber hammer-beam roof and hung around with tapestries, is one of the noblest in the country. The influence is still Gothic, and the upper part of the timber roof is filled with rich Gothic tracery, although the pendants are carved with Renaissance detail.

Knole, 1610: inlaid marble fireplace

Wood framed panelling, another feature of Tudor interiors, is introduced at Hampton Court, adorned with the 'linen' pattern, a treatment suggesting folds of linen. Cardinal Wolsey's Closet is panelled in this way, and hung with tapestry above. This type of panelling reached a stage of great richness, as may be seen in the panelling from the Abbots' Parlour, Waltham, now in the Victoria and Albert Museum; these panels are long and narrow, carved with medallions encircling heads in low relief, the spaces above and below filled with carving very Italian in style.

Probably the most remarkable building of this early period was Henry VIII's Palace of Nonesuch, begun in 1538, which has now completely disappeared. Henry was an enthusiastic builder and erected no less than ten royal residences, although none of them remain today. Nonesuch 'built with so great sumpteousnesse and rare workmanship that it aspireth to the very top of ostentation for show' stood near Sutton in Surrey, and was built by a very diverse crowd of craftsmen, architects, sculptors and decorators from Italy, France and the Netherlands. The decoration was mainly by Italians. Pepys and Evelyn saw this extraordinary building only a few years before Charles II gave it to his mistress, the bold and handsome Barbara, Countess of Castlemaine, who had it dismantled in the 1680's and pulled down. The two diarists have left descriptions of the buildings. The ground storey was of stone, the upper of half-timber, richly gilded and painted. Two great towers, five storeys in height, faced the garden, which was walled and laid out in formal patterns. The architecture of the fantastic inner court was the most astonishing and original of the period.

After Hampton Court came the country palaces of the great families who rose to eminence at this time: Hatfield and Burghley, of the Cecil family, Knole of the Sackvilles, Longleat, home of the Thynne family, Wilton and others. Some of the architects are known. Both Wollaton Hall and Longleat were designed by Huntingdon Smithson, whose more imaginative son designed the romantic Bolsover Castle in Derbyshire. The Countess of Shrewsbury (Bess of Hardwick) in 1551 paid twenty shillings to Robert Watson, master mason, for a plan of Chatsworth. John Shute, painter and architect, published the first English book on architecture in 1563—*The first and chief Groundes of Architecture*. Best known of all was John Thorpe, the designer of the earlier part of Kirby Hall in Northamptonshire, which was commenced in 1570. An album of old drawings, in the possession of Lord Warwick, was found by Horace Walpole; it contained drawings of plans and elevations by Thorpe for Audley End, Burghley, Ampthill, Wollaton, Holland House, Kirby, Longford and others, besides designs for other buildings which were never executed. Thorpe had been to Paris, and may have carried out alterations for a house for the Queen Mother, Marie de Medici.

Not all the great houses of this period, as I have said, are necessarily things of beauty, but among them are many which for picturesque character, and for the magnificence of the works of art they contain, can compare with, and at their best are superior to, anything in Europe. Burghley House, near Stamford in Lincolnshire, is vast and imposing, a fitting background to William Cecil, Lord Burghley, Lord High Treasurer to Queen Elizabeth. Chief Minister to Edward VI, he conformed to Catholicism under Mary and to Protestantism under Elizabeth. He married twice, founding two lines of Cecils, the Earls of Exeter and the Earls of Salisbury. The latter branch built Hatfield,

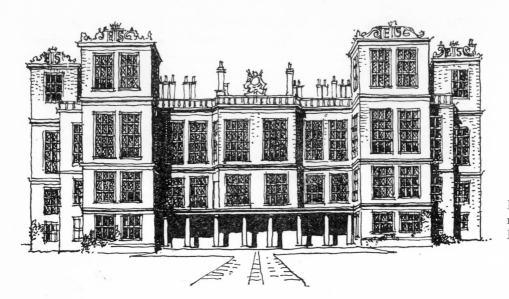

Hardwick Hall,
near Chesterfield,
Derbyshire, 1590

which contains the State papers of Lord Burghley.

There is reason to believe that Burghley was his own architect, although his inspiration was from France and, through one of the chief masons, Henryk, from the Netherlands. Burghley House was commenced in 1577 but was not finished until 1587, and in the interval Burghley's other great house at Theobalds, in Hertfordshire, was completed. Little of the original Elizabethan interior of Burghley now remains, as the main rooms were entirely redecorated by the 5th Earl of Exeter in the last quarter of the seventeenth century. The furnishings and decorations are on a grand and impressive scale. The altar-piece in the chapel is by Paul Veronese, the Georgian state-rooms were painted by Verrio and the magnificent old ballroom by Laguerre. There is carving by Grinling Gibbons, and paintings by Rembrandt and other European masters. Perhaps the finest painted room in England is the Heaven Room, with Verrio's frescoes depicting the forge of the Cyclops, and the great drawing room and the painted staircase are also decorated by the same artist.

Longleat (1567–80), the property of the Marquess of Bath, who now lives in a very much smaller house some ten miles from the mansion, was designed by Huntingdon Smithson. It is, from a distance, a large and imposing mansion with the original hall intact, but so much of the interior was decorated in the Renaissance manner in 1860 that little remains of the sixteenth century.

One of the most remarkable houses in the country is Hardwick Hall (1576–97), near Chesterfield in Derbyshire, built by Bess of Hardwick, who was married to no less than four husbands, among them the Earl of Shrewsbury and Sir William Cavendish. The name of the designer is not known, but it has been attributed to Smithson.

The features which first strike the viewers are the height of the house, and the enormous windows. The hall is a high room, with a fine fireplace and needlework by, possibly, Mary Queen of Scots, who was detained in the great house. The high Great Presence Chamber has a frieze in clear-coloured relief of the Court of Diana and the story of Orpheus running round the walls. The room is approached by a vast stone staircase which climbs through half the length of the building. The house is famous for its needlework. The long gallery, nearly 200 feet in length, is hung with tapestries from end to end which, until a few years ago, were so numerous that they were hung three and four deep. Many have now been moved to Chatsworth, and number among them some of the finest Gothic tapestries in existence.

Kirby Hall, near Kettering in Northamptonshire, was built about 1570 and, although in a ruined state, is a most impressive mixture of Gothic and Classic influences on a grand scale, the mason or architect being John Thorpe senior. There is an air of great restraint and calm in this fine building, in contrast with the more dramatic architecture of Bolsover Castle standing on a spur of land above a precipice.

Bolsover Castle was built by Sir Charles Cavendish, a son of Bess of Hardwick. The design of the keep is consciously mediaeval, and its construction is in the real Gothic tradition, but the splendid and elaborate decoration is of the Renaissance, and there are some remarkable painted rooms and unique sculptured chimney pieces of marble and alabaster. The Riding House has a gigantic Italian doorway, and gable after gable in the Dutch manner, but in date it hardly belongs to the early Renaissance period. Adjoining the keep is the immense and ruined range of rooms erected in 1634 by the Cavendish Duke of Newcastle for the entertainment, at vast expense, of Charles I.

Montacute, near Yeovil, with Levens Hall in Westmorland and Chastleton in Oxfordshire, and Burton Agnes Hall in Yorkshire, Losely in Surrey and Kelmscott in Oxfordshire, and above all Compton Wynyates in Warwickshire, form a group of houses in the traditional manner. Much of their charm derives from the fact that they were built by families of no particular importance, and the centuries have left them more or less as they have always been. In the more remote parts of the country, where building traditions were strong and died hard, the Tudor tradition flourished well into the seventeenth century in manor houses and cottages scattered about the countryside.

Compton Wynyates (1520) is one of the best examples of the houses built in the Gothic tradition. It was completed by Sir William Compton, a London merchant and a favourite of Henry VIII. The central courtyard, around which the house is planned, is entered under a low square battlemented tower having a four-centered archway

Little Moreton Hall, 1559: most picturesque of the black-and-white houses of Cheshire

93

surmounted by a three-light mullioned window. On the opposite side of the court is the hall with its oriel window, and on the south are the drawing room and chapel. The view of the house from above, with its charming mingling of stone, red brick and half-timber work is one of the most satisfying visual experiences in England.

Burton Agnes, built of brick with stone quoins (1600–10), is characteristic of homes erected at the turn of the sixteenth century with its great height and its front recessed between two projecting wings. It is one of

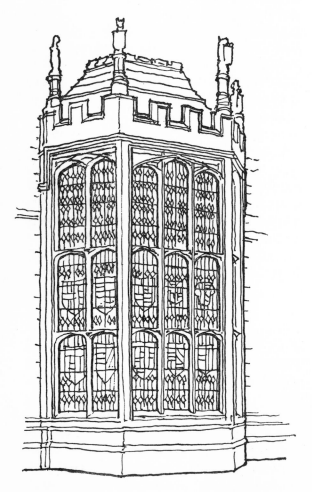

Hengrave Hall, Suffolk, 1525–8: typical oriel window

the most mature of the late Elizabethan designs and, inside, the decoration is luxuriant. The hall has a most elaborately carved screen surmounted by three tiers of allegorical plaster reliefs and the chimney-piece is also very richly ornamented. The unusual staircase has eight newels coupled into arches, the surfaces covered with carving, and other rooms retain their contemporary decoration.

Chastleton House (1603–14), near Moreton-in-Marsh in Gloucestershire, still retains its seventeenth-century furnishings, detailed in an inventory of 1633, and is one of the most perfectly preserved early seventeenth-century manor houses, owing to the fact that one family has lived there until almost the present day. The house closely resembles Burton Agnes in plan, although it is on a rather smaller scale. The long gallery at the top of the house has an unusual barrel vault patterned with roses.

Kelmscott Manor, near Lechdale in Oxfordshire, was built around 1550 in the traditional Cotswold style. It was once in the possession of William Morris, who bought it in 1871, and spent a great deal of money on the house. It had a very significant influence on his decorative ideas, which tended towards a revival of the traditional rather than the creation of a more modern idiom.

Fountains Hall, near Ripon in Yorkshire, is most romantically sited near the great ruined Abbey in the lovely little valley of the Kell. It was built with stones from the Abbey about 1600, and contains some richly carved fireplaces.

Knole, near Sevenoaks in Kent, was originally a palace of the mediaeval archbishops of Canterbury, and was added to continuously in the seventeenth and eighteenth centuries. Apart from some of the most interesting plasterwork in England, its furniture and contents are unrivalled of their

Compton
Wynyates,
Warwickshire,
1520

period. There are brocaded and cut velvet beds of James I, and one whole suite of bedroom furniture with a splendid bed hung with gold and silver tissue, made for the use of the monarch on the occasion of a royal visit.

Knole illustrates incomparably the first decade of the Jacobean period. It is not great architecture, but rather a rambling collection of buildings that look from a distance like an old and very picturesque village. Jacobean architecture is a continuation of Elizabethan although, after James ended the war with Spain, the release of wealth and energy resulted in an outburst of the arts and, in architecture, an emphasis on size and increasingly symmetrical planning, the ornament derived predominantly from Flemish patterns and the elevations continuing their picturesque variety of outline.

Hatfield House in Hertfordshire, the seat of the Salisbury branch of the Cecil family, was designed and built (1607–11) by Robert Lyminge and supervised by Simon Basil, who was a predecessor of Inigo Jones as Surveyor of the King's Works. The whole centre of the building includes the state rooms and the traditional great hall which suffered redecoration in 1878, the family living quarters being contained in the wings in comparatively modest scale. The house is E-shaped in plan, with the central hall and projecting wings set off by formal gardens, and the ornate south front is treated with Doric, Ionic and Corinthian columns superimposed to form a centre piece. There are the usual long gallery, chapel and grand staircase, the whole building displaying the wealth and grandeur befitting the country mansion of the most powerful nobleman in the kingdom.

Blickling Hall in Norfolk is of rose-red brick, built between 1616 and 1620 by Robert Lyminge, the designer of Hatfield. It is similar in plan to Bramshill and is H-shaped. The approach to the house lies between two lines of picturesquely gabled outhouses, in the Dutch manner characteristic of East Anglia. The grand staircase may have been carved by the same craftsman as that at Hatfield.

Bramshill, at Hartley Wintney in Hampshire, which was probably designed by John Thorpe, is an example of the use of classical ornament incompletely understood and applied. It was built between 1605 and 1612, so that the rose-pink brickwork of which it is built has weathered with the centuries to a most attractive texture, but the three-storeyed entrance doorway is plastered with somewhat coarse pilasters with a fretwork pattern in stone around the eaves. The long gallery, 130 feet in length, is imposing.

95

Audley End, 1603–16: the hall screen

Audley End, near Saffron Walden in Essex, is now only one-third of the size of the huge house built by Thomas Howard, 1st Earl of Suffolk, between 1603 and 1616, with a great outer court and tall angle pavilions stretching forward half-way to the river, and an inner court behind the existing hall range. At each end of the extremely ornate hall, which remains unaltered, is a pair of two-storeyed projecting porches in a Jacobean version of the classic style, but the pinnacled turrets, the mullioned windows and the importance of the hall continue the Tudor tradition.

Castle Ashby, near Northampton, is mainly Jacobean, and was built in 1642 (on the site of a castle crenellated in 1306) to a quadrangular plan. The fourth side was

96

completed in 1630 by Inigo Jones and is a two-storey building using superimposed Doric and Ionic columns. The great chamber is a fine room, with a large and ornate chimney-piece whose plasterwork typifies the transition in style from the Jacobean to the Palladian. The timber panelling and ceiling of the great hall show an early version of classic pilasters.

Few English architects of the period travelled abroad to improve their knowledge of continental taste. Combined with the innate English suspicion of new ideas they were slow to assimilate the true classical idea, and this explains the comparatively late entry of the mature classic manner to this country. There were, of course, some exceptions. John Thorpe appears to have travelled, for there are plans of several French châteaux among his many drawings. He studied Du Cerceau's *Les Plus Excellents Bastiments de France* and copied one of the plans which he modified to suit English conditions. He was a draughtsman of great competence who might, had he reached Italy, have been the means of introducing to England, with his fine drawings, the matured classical style. But it is not known whether he travelled thus far, and in the absence of any drawings of Italian buildings it may safely be assumed that he did not. He was a fascinating architect, and many more Elizabethan houses have been attributed to him than he could possibly have designed.

No buildings can be attributed to John Shute, who was sent by the Duke of Northumberland to Italy in 1550, and who made a collection of his drawings and notes for passing on to other designers.

Until the Earl of Pembroke sent Inigo Jones abroad to study architecture in Italy in the early 1600's there was nobody to end the pause in the development of the English Renaissance manner; yet before the end of the first quarter of the seventeenth century, Jones was producing designs in the manner of Palladio, whom he had assiduously studied, which were to divert English taste from the crude Elizabethan and Jacobean periods. Returning to England in 1603, at the age of thirty, he designed the background to Ben Jonson's *Masque of Blackness* and for many years designed stage scenery and costumes, the drawings of which may still be seen at Chatsworth.

Four years later Jones was appointed Surveyor to Henry, Prince of Wales, an intelligent youth of great taste whose lively, curious face may be seen in Cooper's drawing in the possession of the Duke of Buccleuch. The untimely death of the prince in 1612 left Jones without his patron, and again he went abroad. It was on his second visit to Italy in 1613 that he acquired knowledge of Andrea Palladio (1518–80), and his works in Vicenza and along the River Brenta, that were to have such a towering effect on the domestic architecture of England for the next century and a half.

He belongs, however, to the period of the full Renaissance in England, and his place is therefore in the next chapter, as the buildings he erected before 1625 are so many years in advance of the rest of English designers that they should be described with the buildings that followed directly after them in the mature Italian style.

Oxford University had grown from its early roots in the mediaeval monasteries when young monks and friars were sent there to benefit by the University teaching. Those from the Abbeys of St. Albans and Gloucestershire went to Gloucester College, now Worcester College; the Cistercian novices went to St. Bernard's College, founded by Archbishop Chichele, now St. John's College; the Augustinian Friars had their college where Wadham was later built; and the oldest foundation of all was the Priory of St. Frideswide.

It is impossible in a book of this size to study all the architectural treasures that abound in the University where architecture and history are inseparably linked. Christ Church has therefore been singled out as a typical example.

The cathedral had grown from the priory of St. Frideswide, Oxford's patron saint, the daughter of a king who founded the Saxon church in the eighth century. In the eleventh century, according to the chronicler William of Malmesbury, writing of the Danes, 'into the tower of St. Frideswide they were driven, and as men could not drive them thence, the tower was fired, and they perished in the burning'. Ethelred the Unready rebuilt the church and in the reign of Henry I it became a priory of Augustinian canons. Little but the foundations of the old Saxon church remain. The Norman part of the building with its massive pillars and round arches has withstood the onslaught of time, Wolsey, and the Civil War remarkably well. It is the only cathedral in England that can still boast of four Norman vaulted roofs.

Christ Church Cathedral presents, in its architecture, a particularly fitting shrine where students of today may worship inspired by the magnificent craftsmanship of their forefathers. Here the thirteenth-century builders crowned the Norman tower with a graceful octagonal spire soaring heavenward 144 feet; here they built the Lady Chapel with its clustered pillars and pointed arches; here the progress of vaulting may be studied, beginning with the unique early Norman barrel vault in the sacristy, the cross-vaults carried on the semi-circular arches of the choir aisles, the fourteenth-century ridge ribs of the Latin Chapel, the lierne ribs of the cloisters culminating in

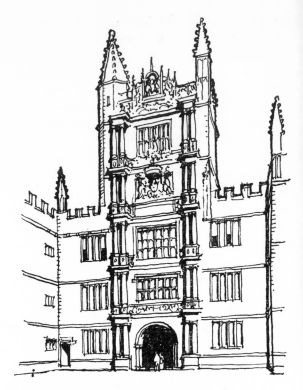

Bodleian Library, Oxford, 1613–36: the tower

the magnificent lacy fan-vault which the English masons built across the great Norman pillars of the choir. Here are stained-glass windows dating from the thirteenth century to Burne Jones. The martyrdom of St. Thomas à Becket is depicted in one of these windows with the head effaced by order of Henry VIII, who disapproved of all who obstructed the desires of kings, hence the fall of Wolsey four years after he had founded the great college which then bore the name 'Cardinal' in his honour.

In 1525 Wolsey obtained a Papal Bull enabling him to suppress the Priory of St. Frideswide or any monastery whose numbers were less than seven. Demolition of the old Augustinian Priory was begun and Cardinal Wolsey, himself a Fellow of Magdalen College, began the building of the largest and most generously endowed of all Oxford's colleges. The quadrangle, which is nearly 100 yards square, was laid out; it was his intention to enclose the vast area with a cloister whose buttress-footings and wall-ribs still remain, and a chapel, equal to King's College, Cambridge. The vast scale of Wolsey's project may be seen in the gigantic kitchen, built on the site of the Priory and part of the old city wall, virtually unchanged with the passing of the centuries.

Before his fall Wolsey saw the building of Christ Church Hall, the finest in Oxford with its wide hammer-beam roof and great Irish oak beams bridging the 40-feet span, a magnificent example of this period of Tudor architecture. The hall now houses a great collection of paintings, including works by Gainsborough, Lely, Kneller, Reynolds and Romney. The college gateway, however, was unfinished when the Cardinal fell from favour; building was stopped, and the college renamed Henry VIII College.

Before his death Henry reformed the diocese of Oxford, making the Abbot of Oseney the first Bishop of Oxford with what remained of St. Frideswide as his cathedral, and endowing the new Bishopric with the spoils of the Abbey of Oseney. In 1546 the former Cardinal College was put in charge of the Dean and renamed Christ Church.

Christ Church College, Oxford, c. 1529:
the great hall

99

Little building was done in Oxford during the Reformation. Chapels were pillaged and libraries destroyed, the city fell to the Roundheads and later became the headquarters of Charles I. The great stone stairway leading to Christ Church Hall winds around a single column on which rests a remarkable piece of fan-vaulting, built during this period of upheaval by a London stonemason named Smith. The Dean at the time was Samuel Fell, whose son, Dean John Fell, was later responsible for the building of the whole north side of the quadrangle as well as finishing the work of Wolsey on the east and west ranges. The quadrangle was given balustraded parapets and a terrace was built within the bases of Wolsey's cloister. These balustrades were replaced by fake battlements during restorations in the nineteenth century.

Work on Wolsey's gateway had stopped on a level with the adjoining balustrades, and the building was left open to the weather for some hundred and fifty years until, in 1681, Christopher Wren was called in to complete the work. He abandoned the idea of a Tudor oriel window, building up, instead, the well-known octagonal bell tower. This was finished in 1682 and the bell of the old Abbey of Oseney was first heard from 'Tom Tower' on the anniversary of the Restoration, ringing out its 101 peals, as it does to this day at 9.5 of an evening, in commemoration of the 101 students of Henry the Eighth's foundation.

The old Peckwater Inn, originally given to the college by Henry VIII, was replaced in 1706 by the Renaissance buildings, in Oxford stone, designed by Dean Aldridge, an amateur architect. The remaining side of the Peckwater Quadrangle designed by Dr. Clarke, also an amateur, was completed by the library in 1761. The ground floor of this building was originally intended to be an open piazza, designed on the classical formula, and built on columns, as at Trinity College, Cambridge, in order to keep the books raised above the damp.

To the south-east of the library lies Canterbury Quadrangle, on the site of Canterbury College, founded by Simon Islip, Bishop of Canterbury, in 1363. The present buildings were designed by James Wyatt and begun in 1773.

General restoration of the cathedral was begun by Sir Gilbert Scott in 1870. The west wall was removed, one bay was added to the nave and the present entrance was built. When the east window was removed, traces of a large Norman circular window were discovered. Scott restored the window most successfully on what was considered to have been the late twelfth-century design.

The layout of St. John's College, Cambridge, is on the Western European conception of the form any group of buildings should take. The mediaeval university consisted of a body of men who were qualified to teach by the possession of a degree. At first they only required a building for meeting and ceremonies, a library and schools for teaching. They did not undertake to provide for the students board and lodging any more than they do today. However, by the end of the fourteenth century, the Cambridge college plan consisted of ranges of buildings, including a gateway, a chapel, hall and buttery, a kitchen and sets of chambers, totally enclosing a roughly rectangular court.

St. John's comprises three such courts. Founded on the site of the ancient Hospital of St. John, established in 1135, it was converted into a college of the University by Lady Margaret Beaufort, Countess of Richmond. The foundress died in 1509 without living to see the building begun and the

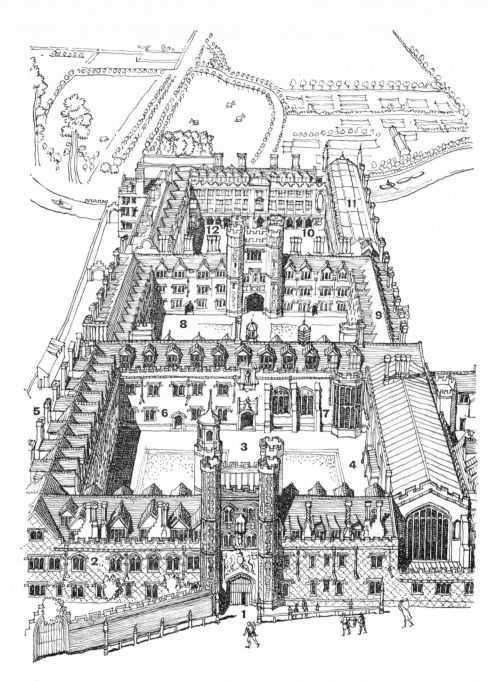

St. John's College, Cambridge, founded 1511 (from Loggan's view)

1 Entrance gateway	5 Chambers	9 Master's lodge
2 Library	6 Kitchen	10 Third court
3 First Court	7 Hall	11 Library
4 Chapel	8 Second court	12 Loggia

work was taken over by John Fisher, Bishop of Rochester.

The first court was begun in 1511 and opened in 1516. Cambridge has no good building stone and, from Roman times onwards, a local material, taken from the chalk bands in the south and eastern parts of the county, known as 'clunch', has been used in building. Clunch is suitable for infilling and internal work but weathers quickly, and the mediaeval builders found it expedient to face these walls outside with rendering, brickwork or imported stone. The gatehouse of the first court is of clunch and red brick and has an embattled parapet and octagonal angle turrets. The great oak doors are probably the original ones carved by Loveday. The hall with its original roof and loft screen is divided into bays by two-stage buttresses in one of which is an oriel three-sided window containing mediaeval and later glass. In the middle upper light a figure of St. John under a canopy can be seen, probably of the eighteenth century and formerly in the cathedral of Regensburg. The hexagonal timber louvre on the roof belongs to a later date and was doubtless erected to improve ventilation in the Hall.

The original library of the college is now divided into rooms, some showing the old roof trusses beneath the present ceiling, while most of the ground floor now forms the Junior Combination Room.

Building of the second court was begun in 1598 and the original drawings are preserved in the College archives. The walls are of red and yellow mottled brick with Northamptonshire stone dressings and the roofs are of green slates. The central feature is the gatehouse with its tower reminiscent of Hampton Court, now named the Shrewsbury Tower in memory of Mary, Countess of Shrewsbury, who provided a large sum of money for the building of the court. The tower is of three storeys with semi-octagonal angle-turrets carried above the embattled parapet. On the first floor a panel shows the arms of the Countess of Salisbury.

On the north side the Combination Room has a magnificent plaster ceiling, executed by John Cobbe in 1600, and wood-panelled walls of the same date. The gallery measures 93 feet by 19 feet. A staircase leads to the new library which occupies the entire north side of the third court. It is a fine example of Jacobean Gothic begun in 1623 and finished two years later, with the main library on the first floor. The construction is of mottled red and yellow brick with dressings of freestone and clunch on the inside. An interesting scheme for a library built on pillars extending west from the Shrewsbury Tower was rejected by Bishop Williams.

The west range of the third court rises up from the river in truly Venetian manner. Built in 1669–73 it is divided into five main bays by chimney projections and is joined to the library only by a lofty open arch, thus allowing the maximum light into the older building.

Two bridges cross the Cam from St. John's. Plans for the first were begun by Wren and Hawksmoor. Its three spans and balustraded parapet reflect peacefully in the quiet waters below. One panel carved in the Weldon stone of which the whole is built shows Father Cam, with the bridge and the College in the background. The high-covered 'Bridge of Sighs' dates from 1826 and is called after the famous bridge of that name in Venice.

On the west side of the river New Court was built in 1826–31 from the designs of Thomas Rickman and Henry Hutchinson, in the Gothic idiom. Unfortunately the original chapel, dating in part from the time of the old Hospital of St. John, was pulled down

102

in 1863 and replaced by the present Victorian 'Early Decorated' church by Scott.

The bed came into general use in England during the sixteenth century. It was probably the most elaborate piece of furniture in the household and its value lay chiefly in the rich draperies and the curtains of velvet, satin, silk or even cloth of gold which covered it. These hangings kept out the cold, and the frames were often richly carved. At the head and foot high panelling protected the sleeper from draughts.

With the wider distribution of wealth in the sixteenth century chairs became objects of daily use. English sixteenth-century chairs all had arms, and early in the seventeenth century began to be upholstered, the arms, backs and seats being covered with leather studded with brass-beaded nails or in needlework or velvet. Being made chiefly of oak they were heavy and solid, with upholstered rectangular backs raised above the seats on turned supports. Smaller and more movable chairs were made in France and Italy and later in England.

The chest was an extremely important piece of furniture, storing clothes, tools, armour and other possessions. Probably nearly every household had one, sometimes covered with metal, with large, rough iron keys to guard valuables, as there were no banks. There were special chests for travellers, with rounded lids and large square handles at each end. They were often elaborately carved and sometimes had rich Genoa velvet coverings embroidered with the initials or the coat-of-arms of the owner.

Practically the only remaining examples of the English mediaeval trestle table are the magnificent pair which still stand in the Barons' Hall at Penshurst, which date from the fifteenth century. Tables with the top fixed to the frame and legs did not come into general use until the sixteenth century. They were at first large and cumbersome, with oblong tops usually about 12 feet long and 2 to $2\frac{1}{2}$ feet wide and needed two or three people to lift them. The legs were thick, joined by wide stretchers and, towards the end of the sixteenth century, were elaborately decorated, being turned and carved in bulbous shapes, a fashion introduced by

103

Dutch immigrant craftsmen. Diners used a knife and spoon which they retained for personal use. It was the custom for the lord and his family to dine above the large standing salt, the most important object on the mediaeval table, a few examples of which are still extant in the possession of city companies and University colleges.

There was very little table glass until the sixteenth century, when it began to be manufactured by Protestant refugees from Lorraine. Queen Elizabeth, in 1575, granted a privilege to a Venetian, Jacop Verzelini, and later a company was established to make 'all manner of drinking glasses, broad glasses . . . and all other kinds of glasses, bugles, bottles, vials or vessels whatsoever'.

At table, manners of the sixteenth century were still crude by modern standards. Plates were wiped clean with bread, and the eater ate as much as possible in the shortest possible time, to the accompaniment of loud and appreciative belches. In his book on etiquette, *Galatea*, Giovanni della Casa writes in 1550 of those who 'thrust their snouts, like pigs, into their broth, and never raise their eyes or hands from the victuals, and gorge rather than eat with swollen cheeks, as if they were blowing at a trumpet or a fire'.

In the sixteenth century the English had the reputation of being the world's champion meat eaters; 'the Spaniard eats, the German drinks, and the English excel in both'. Parker, the Archbishop of Canterbury, bequeathed to his Cambridge college 'a tarte of marygoldes, primroses, or cowslips'. The sixteenth-century breakfast was a casual snack, with dinner at eleven a.m.

Both men and women servants were employed in the large town and country houses of the sixteenth century. The Earl of Derby had three officers—a steward, a controller and a receiver general—who supervised the household. Each had three servants at his disposal, the head of the household having a page and seven gentlemen-in-waiting. There were carefully defined tasks for each servant, such as looking after 'the seller that the wynnes be carefullie kepte and the plate belonge to the same well looked into' and making sure that 'in the scullerie . . . the vessell be well and cleanlie kepte'.

People in the Middle Ages were on the whole cleaner than those of the Renaissance or of the seventeenth and eighteenth centuries. There were many public bathing places, but as they gave too much opportunity for bawdy or even indecent behaviour they went gradually out of use. In the sixteenth century it was rare even for royal personages to take a bath. Queen Elizabeth having 'a bath every three months whether she needeth it or no', was considered most advanced in the matter of personal hygiene.

There was, however, no drainage system and the supply of water was unwholesome and insufficient. Although larger houses might have a courtyard into which all refuse was thrown, the general repository for filth of all sorts was the street, where a small stream running down a central gutter served as a sewer.

The Elizabethan farmhouse, one of the most natural and unpretentious of buildings, is also one of the most attractive. In Kent and the west country its chief ornament is the pattern of timber beams which constructed it, and in the eastern counties the sometimes very elaborate plaster work was one of its most pleasant features. Life in these surroundings changed but slowly, particularly when the main business was sheep rearing and the spinsters, or unmarried women, spent the long, quiet hours at their wheels, spinning the yarn which went to the weaving shops of the nearest town, or the lands beyond the seas.

At the village of Chiddingstone in Kent can still be seen a whole row of early Tudor cottages, side by side with others of Elizabeth's time. Buildings became more closely clustered where before they had grouped around a village green.

The communications of this period were slow and inconvenient. It was by no means infrequent for Henry VIII, in his journeyings to woo Anne Boleyn at Hever Castle, to be stuck fast in the mud of the Kentish clay and await the arrival of help to pull him out. Some of the great houses, such as Penshurst and Leeds Castle, became almost isolated in autumn and winter as no transport could reach them.

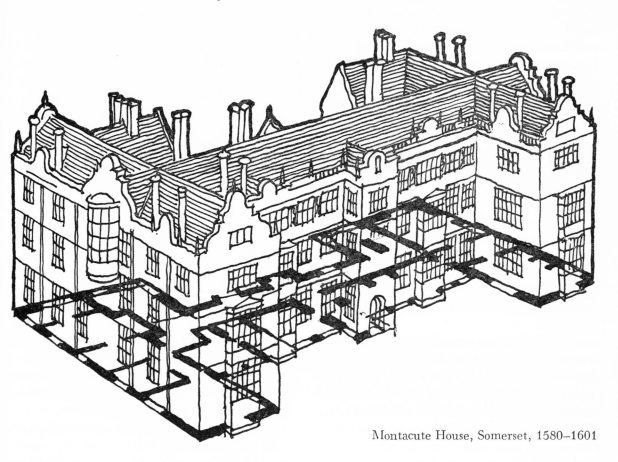

Montacute House, Somerset, 1580–1601

4

The Later Renaissance 1625–1830

England in the seventeenth century was still largely feudal, with a population that was predominantly rural. Traditional English manners and institutions remained strong, and new ideas from abroad were received with a native caution, for the long period of religious crisis caused a hesitancy between the various expressions of the Reformation, and while many solutions were tried, none commanded sufficient general support.

England was still, in spite of its ability to prevent a Spanish invasion, only a minor power, of extremely limited wealth, so that there was little incentive to foreign artists of any calibre to work in the fog-bound island, and certainly not to those from Catholic Italy. Leonardo da Vinci had visited the court of Francis I of France for three years and died at Amboise, and men of the fame and genius of Bernini could be attracted to the wealthy French Court of Louis XIV to prepare plans for a gigantic palace, the

Louvre; but not to England, as the country could not afford such luxuries. The only foreign artist of international repute to work here was Peter Paul Rubens, and he completed only one work, the ceiling of the Banqueting Hall at Whitehall. The Italian mural painters who followed him and worked in the great English houses were of much inferior quality and were often bettered by the native English painters.

This era is dominated by the classic influence of the Italian Renaissance. The work of Inigo Jones (1605–40) includes the Banqueting Hall in Whitehall, London (1619–1622), the Queen's House, Greenwich (1616–1635), St. Paul's, Covent Garden, London (1631–5), Stoke Bruerne Park, Northamptonshire (1629–35) and possibly Raynham Hall, Norfolk (1635–8), the additions to Kirby Hall, Northamptonshire (1638–40), Lindsay House in Lincolns Inn Fields (1640) and Barber-Surgeons Hall in London (1636), now destroyed by bombing. Mansions of this early period include Coleshill, Berkshire (1650–62), now destroyed by fire, Belton House near Grantham (1685–8) and Groombridge Place in Kent (late seventeenth century); Honington Hall, Warwickshire (1685) and Thorpe Hall, Northamptonshire (1653–6) are others.

The amount and quality of the work of Sir Christopher Wren (1631–1723) are phenomenal. It includes St. Paul's Cathedral, London (1675–1710) and the London City Churches of St. Stephen Walbrook (1672–1679), St. Mary-le-Bow (1671–80), St. Bride, Fleet Street (1675), St. Martin, Ludgate (1677–84), St. Clement Danes, Strand (1684), St. James', Piccadilly (1682–4), St. Mary, Abchurch (1681–6), St. Mildred, Bread Street (1677–83), St. Lawrence Jewry (1671–80), St. Benet Fink (1673–6), St. Mary-at-Hill (1672–7), St. Anne and St. Agnes (1677–80), St. Swithin, Cannon Street (1677–85), Christ Church, Newgate Street (1677–87), St. Magnus the Martyr, London Bridge (1676–1705), St. Alban, Wood Street (1682–5), St. Dunstan-in-the-East (1698), St. Mary, Aldermanbury (1711) and St. Michael, Cornhill (1670–2). At Oxford there is the Sheldonian Theatre (1664–9), the Library of Queen's College (1693–6), Tom Tower, Christ Church (1682), and the Garden Quadrangle of Trinity College (1668–1728). At Cambridge he designed Pembroke College Chapel (1663–5), Emmanuel College Chapel (1668–73) and Trinity College Library (1676–84).

His secular works include the Monument, London (1671–6), the Fountain Court and Garden façades at Hampton Court, Chelsea Hospital (1682–91), Marlborough House, Pall Mall (1709–11), additions to Kensington Palace (1690–1704) and the Greenwich Observatory (1675–6). He was mainly responsible for the great project at Greenwich Hospital (1696–1715) and the Cloisters in Pump Court (1680–1) in Middle Temple, London. Other secular works of the time are Abingdon Town Hall (1677–80), the Custom House at King's Lynn (1683) and Guildford Town Hall (1682).

The greater houses of the period include Castle Howard, Yorkshire (1699–1712), Blenheim Palace, Oxfordshire (1705–22), Seaton Delavel, Northumberland (1720–8), Holkham Hall, Norfolk (1734), Ditchley in Oxfordshire (1720–5), Moor Park, Hertfordshire (1720), Houghton Hall, Norfolk (1722-1726), Prior Park, Bath (1735–48), Wentworth Woodhouse, Yorkshire (1735), Harewood House, Yorkshire (1759–71), Kedleston, Derbyshire (1757–70), Wardour Castle, Wiltshire (1770–6), Heaton Hall, Lancashire (1772) and Stowe House in Buckinghamshire (1771–9). There are also Mereworth in Kent (1722–5), Syon House at Isleworth in Middlesex (1762–9), Osterley Park, Middlesex (1761–80), Luton Hoo in Bedfordshire (1768–75), Althorp in Northamptonshire (1787–9), Heveningham Hall, Suffolk (1778–99), Dodington Park, Gloucestershire (1798–1808), Downton Castle, Shropshire (1774–8), Lowther Castle, Westmorland (1806–11), Lee Priory, Kent (1783–90), Fonthill Abbey, Wiltshire (1796–1807), now destroyed, and in the Gothic Revival manner Ashridge Park, Hertfordshire (1803–1813) and Eaton Hall, Cheshire (1804–12). Sezincote House in Gloucestershire (1803–1815) preceded the Royal Pavilion, Brighton (1815–21) both in the domed 'Indian' style.

This era saw also the layout at Bath of the north side of Queen Square (1729), South Parade (1743), the Circus (1754) and the Royal Crescent (1767–75). After these came the Crescent at Buxton, Derbyshire (1779–1781). In London are the Mansion House (1739–52), Chesterfield House in South Audley Street (1766), demolished in 1937,

Ely House, Dover Street (1772), Lansdowne House, Berkeley Square (1762–8), now demolished, Apsley House, Piccadilly (1775), the old Courtauld Institute in Portman Square (1775–7) and the Adelphi development (1768–72), now demolished. Carlton House (1783–5) was pulled down in 1827, and the Quadrant in Regent Street (1818–1820) was destroyed in 1906–23.

Apart from the Wren churches others of the period are also remarkable for their pleasing proportions. In London we have St. Mary Woolnoth (1716–26), St. George's, Bloomsbury (1720–30), Christ Church, Spitalfields (1723–9), St. Anne Limehouse, and St. Alphege, Greenwich (both 1712–14), St. Paul, Deptford (1712–30), St. John, Smith Square, Westminster (1714–28), St. Mary-le-Strand (1714–17), St. George, Hanover Square, St. Martin-in-the-Fields (1722–6) and St. Giles in the Fields (1731–4). Towards the end of this period are St. Marylebone parish church (1813–18), St. Pancras, Bloomsbury (1819–22), All Saints', Camden Town (1822–4), All Souls', Langham Place (1822–5), St. George, Camberwell (1822–4), St. Mark, Kennington (1822–4), St. Mary, Wyndham Place (1822–4) and the Gothic St. Luke, Chelsea (1820–4).

The Bank of England (1788–1833) was one of the more important secular buildings. Some of London's older clubs were developed from coffee houses and number among them Boodle's in St. James Street (1765), Brooks's (1776–8), the Pantheon, Oxford Street (1770–2, destroyed 1792), the Athenaeum (1827) and the Travellers' (1829–31). London saw the building also of Somerset House (1776–86), the British Museum (1823–4), the Marble Arch (1825) and the screen at Hyde Park Corner (1825). At Oxford came the Radcliffe Library (1737–49), Queen's College, Oxford (1710–19), the Clarendon building (1712–15) and Worces-

ter College (1720), and Cambridge saw the building of Downing College (1807–20) and the Old University Library (1754–5). London University commenced with University College (1828).

Guildhalls were raised at Worcester (1721–3) and High Wycombe (1757) and bridges at Richmond, Surrey (1774–5) and Pulteney Bridge, Bath (1768–74). Bridges designed by engineers were built at Coalbrookdale (1779) and on the Stockton and Darlington railway.

This period of the Later Renaissance covered the transition of England from an agricultural to an industrial country. The speed of development increased over that of the preceding centuries, not because communications were any faster, but mainly because travel, particularly in the eighteenth century, became more popular. Nearly everyone travelled, the only exceptions being the small tradesmen and peasants or those who combined a well-assured position with lack of enterprise. It was rarely lack of money which prevented people from journeying to and fro and a good average was 20 miles a day. The charm of the eighteenth century lies in the fact that all the gains made by civilisation before the industrial age were at the disposal of mankind. The perfect balance between nature and man, between town and country, had been attained. In spite of the wars which ravaged it, Voltaire and Swift agreed that more estimable than the great military captains were those men who 'grew two blades of grass upon a spot of land where only one grew before' and who assisted mankind to 'cultivate its garden'. It was the century least troubled by doubts, heart-searchings and queries, coming as it did between the age of Cromwell, of Gustavus Adolphus, of Milton and Louis XIV, on the one hand, and on the other the nineteenth century, the age of scientific advances, of Bismarck, Darwin, of astounding material progress and swift transport.

Europe had maintained the tradition of classical learning and taste since the fall of the Roman Empire, and had brought the tradition to grand achievement in the Renaissance, and beyond it to the Baroque. The eighteenth century, graceful in manner, neat in thought and expression, a little sceptical, a little worldly, but in possessing the secret of life as far as men cared to inquire into it, was, in spite of grave shortcomings in its social and moral economy, an admirable and on the whole a serene and cultured age. As Talleyrand remarked to Guizot in a later and stormier time: 'He who has not lived in the years near to 1789 does not know how sweet life can be.'

The early years of the Tudor dynasty saw the entry into England of those influences which were to culminate later into the most tasteful period of English architecture. The seeds of culture and scholarship introduced from abroad in the sixteenth century by foreign artists into the courts of Henry VII and Henry VIII had, however, not fallen entirely upon stony ground, for curiosity about the new tastes and trends was first aroused in aristocratic circles, and it is to the interest of the Earl of Pembroke, a con-

noisseur of the arts, that we owe the career of Inigo Jones.

Jones was born in London in 1573, and is notable as the man who first introduced the mature Italian Renaissance style of architecture. When it is considered that his Banqueting Hall was completed in 1622, in the High Italian Renaissance manner, no less than seventy-two years before the completion of St. Paul's, we can place some measure upon his genius, for he stood alone, not only for his competence, but as the only English designer worthy of the name of architect who had travelled abroad. There was none other in England to compare with him.

He was a fanatical theatregoer, a very fine draughtsman, and the first and greatest English artist of the theatre, which may explain his attraction to Venice, where the puppet theatre was pre-eminent. A century later this same theatre was to attract the Asam brothers from Bavaria and inspire the fantastic altars at Rohr and Kloster Weltenberg, in Bavaria, where the Danube races between sheering cliffs above Regensburg.

To a man of Inigo Jones' theatrical temperament the Italy of the seventeenth century, and particularly Venice, must have seemed like a new and delightful world, for although the period of the high Baroque

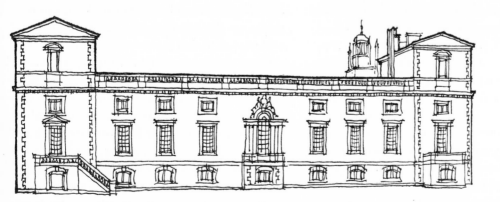

Wilton House, Wiltshire, 1647–9, by Inigo Jones

had not yet arrived (Bernini at this time was no more than a child), Italy was full of the finest works of art in Europe; the Library of St. Mark was not yet fifty years old, and Sansovino, Palladio and Vignola had been dead only a few years. Palladio's theatre at Vicenza was a mere twenty years old, and the villas and palaces at Vicenza and along the banks of the Brenta were new, alive and scintillating in the gay Italian sunlight.

Inigo Jones broke completely with the mediaeval tradition and introduced the pure straight lines and harmonious proportions of Palladio, whose native town of Vicenza was full of his works. The Queen's House at Greenwich (1617–35), which he built for Charles I's Queen Henrietta Maria, has the restrained elegance of a Palladian villa on the mainland near Venice, and the Banqueting Hall in Whitehall (1619–22) could stand on the Brenta or in Vicenza, for it is entirely Palladian in feeling.

The scheme for an enormous palace at Westminster was intended to include the Banqueting Hall and would have completed the grandest Renaissance conception in England, as the palace would have covered an area twice that of the great Spanish monastery-palace of the Escorial, near Madrid. A magnificent façade to the Thames was projected, and the main elevations would have been 100 feet high. It was a conception on a remarkably Baroque scale. The grand court (800 feet by 400 feet) would have been twice the size of the court of the Louvre, but the country did not possess the money to complete the scheme, and with the death of Charles I, an autocrat in the Baroque tradition, the English repudiated the whole concept of the style with its emphasis on, and support of, the power and prestige of the ruler, for which the palace was intended. Charles II did not dare continue it, or even build on a comparable scale, and his palace

at Hampton Court is, by comparison, a very restrained affair.

The Doric portico of St. Paul's, Covent Garden (1631), 'built likewise with the porticoes about the Piazza' with the royal chapels at Denmark House and St. James (the latter now destroyed) were all designed by Jones, but much doubt has been thrown on other works supposedly designed by him. Coleshill, in Berkshire (1650–62), now most unfortunately destroyed by fire, is attributed to him, but some authorities support as architect the claims of Sir Roger Pratt, for whose cousin, Sir Henry Pratt, the house was built. It was not too deeply Italian in feeling although somewhat in the style of the Venetian villa; the stucco ceilings were magnificent, and outstanding in an age of exuberant plasterwork.

A great deal of Jones' work at Wilton (1649), the great house of the Earls of Pembroke near Salisbury, has been destroyed, but the state rooms with their decorations on the first floor still remain, including the Banqueting Hall and the Double Cube Room (60 feet by 30 feet), hung with the Vandyck portraits of the Herbert family in frames designed by the architect. The doors with their broken pediments, the wall panelling divided by great gilded swags of fruit and flowers, the richly carved and painted ceiling and the gorgeous furniture by William Kent make up the most famous room in England, and one of the finest in Europe.

I have said that, with the death of Charles I in 1645, England repudiated the Baroque although, through the curiosity of her aristocracy, the Renaissance was introduced and accepted. The reasons for this are many and interesting.

Seventeenth-century England plunged into a civil war which resulted in the rising commercial class, ranged under the banner of Puritanism, destroying absolute monarchy in England and breaking down the barriers of mediaevalism to create a state responsive to the needs of the new commerce and the new industry. But Cromwell's autocracy could not last in face of the non-Puritan strength of the country, although when Charles II returned much had been changed and the kingly power had been greatly diminished for ever.

The Catholicism of James II caused the loss of his crown, although he and his descendants could have retained it had they been content to let England develop from absolute monarchy to aristocracy. After Cromwell's death and the decay of belief in the Divine Right of Kings, the one power strong enough to rule the country was the landed aristocracy, who found in Vanbrugh their architectural interpreter. The rising commercial classes were not yet ready to govern on secular grounds; the only possibly secular government was that of the great Whig families who ruled England for a period from 1688 onward. The Whigs used the Baroque to bolster their power and prestige, but only for a time. The influence of Palladio, introduced again by the powerful Earl of Burlington, became too strong, and more democratic theories gained the initiative. Moreover, the Faith of England, with the monarch in his diminished authority as its Defender, never attained the absolute ascendancy over the minds of its adherents as did the Faith of Rome, which

Seaton Delaval, 1720–8

found in the Baroque the perfect architectural expression of its aims and ambitions.

Earlier in the seventeenth century Francis Bacon set an example of sober practical thinking which the English mind has never since forgotten, and later, at the height of the Civil War, Thomas Hobbes elaborated, in sharp hostility to the doctrine of divine right, his famous theory of sovereignty based upon an all-embracing social contract. Hobbes preferred monarchy as being more efficient in the preservation of order, but recognised that his theories could be applied equally well to justify the absolutism of an aristocratic or democratic government.

The English architect of the seventeenth and eighteenth centuries was never called upon to give visual expression to the ideas of a vigorous and militant church, as on the Continent, or to advertise the glory and prestige of an absolute ruler. As found in England, the Baroque is essentially a compromise. In the great houses of Vanbrugh at Blenheim, Castle Howard and Seaton Delaval, in the steeples of Wren and Hawksmoor, and in the dome and the western towers of St. Paul's, there is a certain sense of display, but that complete unity of expression, that final control and integration of every part which marks the greatest Baroque designs, is lacking, and we never find in English Baroque the colour and combination of space compositions and unexpected vistas which characterise the great Baroque buildings of the Continent. One reason may lie in the lack of a classical training. Vanbrugh and Hawksmoor never studied abroad, and Wren journeyed no further than Paris.

Wren's reflections on the limitations of English designers are interesting: 'It was observed . . . that our English architects are dull enough at Inventions, but when once a foreigne patterne is sett, they imitate soe well that commonly they exceed the original. I confess the observation is generally true, but this shows that our natives want not a Genius, but education in that which is the foundation of all Mechanik Arts, to which everybody in Italy, France and the Low Countries pretends . . . .' (Letter dated 24th November 1694 to Mr. Treasurer Hawes of Christ's Hospital.)

Blenheim Palace, Woodstock, Oxfordshire, 1705–22

Another reason for the repudiation of the Baroque in England is that the appeal to the senses, on which Baroque depends entirely for its effect, is completely alien to the English temperament. The Puritan suspicion of visual pleasure had never been overcome, and when Vanbrugh was called upon, at Blenheim, to express the national sentiment in terms of architecture, he achieved a magnificence, a complexity of space composition and a theatrical grandeur that fulfils the Baroque demand more completely than any other English building but is still only an English version of the idiom of Bernini in Rome, of Fischer von Erlach in Vienna or of Jules Hardouin Mansart in Paris.

Then again there was the problem of money. The wealth of the Roman Catholic Church and the cheapness of marble in Italy made the work of the southern designers that much easier. Wren never had sufficient money to build as he would have wished, and was forced to erect his buildings as cheaply as possible. (Not so many years before the last war the main supports of the dome of St. Paul's, which had been filled with rubble inside their stone exterior, commenced to fail and were reinforced with concrete pumped in under great pressure.) It needed the experience of a Borromini, and the easy handling of classical forms resulting from long and familiar use, to achieve works of great sophistication with such inadequate means. For this reason the west front of St. Paul's, with its superimposed orders, is a weakness which could never have occurred in Rome.

Baroque is essentially a pictorial style in which architecture, sculpture and painting are concerned with problems of light and shade, the dissolution of the hard outlines of forms and the effects of movement and shadow which characterise the works of Rembrandt and Caravaggio, and was such an important development in seventeenth-century painting in Europe.

The Baroque influence is very noticeable in the interiors of Windsor Castle, which were carried out by Hugh May, the Controller of the Royal Works, in the 1670's. Little has survived beyond the decoration of a number of state rooms by Verrio and Grinling Gibbons; the Chapel and St. George's Hall are pictured in Pine's *Royal Residences* but the significance of the work lies in the collaboration of May, Verrio and Gibbons in their combination of architecture with painting and sculpture. It anticipated the union of Wren, Gibbons and Verrio at Hampton Court and of Wren and Thornhill in the Painted Hall at Greenwich. This union was most effective in the Chapel at Windsor, where Gibbons' decoration was very rich and elaborate in the stalls, the whole surmounted with a fresco by Verrio which included a painted order of twisted columns, and an altar piece, representing the Last Supper, painted as a *trompe l'œil*, in a truly Baroque spirit.

The staircases were further examples of the Baroque quality of May's work in their sense of movement, and anticipated the later work of Wyatt and Adam. The Queen's Stair, with a rail of wrought iron, ascended in a rectangular space, the walls of which were decorated by Verrio, who included painted niches containing statues in the manner of a *trompe l'œil*. Another staircase, named after the King, was also elaborately painted by the same artist. We can still see in the state dining room the quality of the planning and the combination of sculpture and painting which lays claim to our notice as a sincerely Baroque example.

Wren's own work is essentially English in its modesty of treatment in line and surface, but it is also essentially Baroque in its freedom of experiment and its frank adoption of devices which mask, for reasons of effect, the construction of the building (see the illustration on page 126). Moreover, he was free from the restricting influence of Palladio. His scientific background developed his interest in experiment, and the solution of a given problem in a number of different ways, which added flexibility to his mind and gave him that grasp and control of the complex constructional problems which faced him in the dome of St. Paul's.

Neither in the painting nor the sculpture of this Baroque period could England compete with the Continent. The best of the mural painters is the native Sir James Thornhill, in his work at Greenwich. He is on a superior level to the Italians who came here to work; the weakness of Verrio's figure composition, and his incompetence to carry out his grandiose schemes, place him in a position far behind the great seventeenth-century decorators in Italy and Germany. Laguerre was more capable, as his series of ceilings at Chatsworth testify, and Pellegrini's work at Kimbolton and Castle Howard show great capacity for this form of work. Antonio Verrio can be seen at Hampton Court and Windsor Castle. He came from Lecce in southern Italy, and covered vast spaces of wall at Chatsworth and Burghley, but he lacked greatness.

Thornhill's collaboration with Wren and Hawksmoor at Greenwich Hospital produced the greatest achievement of English Baroque, of which the most important feature is the Painted Hall, with its complex sequence of spaces in the domed vestibule and the rectangular space at the high table. The interior treatment of the large round-headed windows surmounted by smaller square windows is similar to that of the Chapel at Windsor, and may owe something to Hugh May. The painted pilasters behind the windows, and the external treatment of the windows, also resemble those by May at Windsor.

The splendid chapel, now destroyed, built by Wren in 1685 for James II, and decorated by Gibbons and Verrio, is a possible link between Windsor and Greenwich. Gibbons carved four figures in white marble of St. John, St. Peter, St. Paul and the Church, as well as the expensive columns. There was also an elaborate altar-piece by Verrio, crowded with figures, and richly carved thrones for the king and queen, just opposite the altar.

It is by no means easy, at Greenwich, to distinguish between the contributions of Vanbrugh, Wren and Hawksmoor. Even at St. Paul's the western towers, with their reminiscence of Borromini's St. Agnese in Rome, have been questioned, but there is little doubt that the Painted Hall, with its dome and colonnades, is Wren's. Vanbrugh and Hawksmoor collaborated so closely, and influenced each other so profoundly, that the task of distinguishing the work of one from the other is sometimes a matter of no small difficulty.

Several of Inigo Jones' contemporaries were still alive and active at the Restoration, among them John Webb (1611–72), Hugh May (1622–84) and Roger Pratt (1620–85). Pratt designed Clarendon House in Piccadilly (1664–7) for the unpopular Lord Chancellor Hyde, but it suffered demolition after his flight in 1683. Pepys, who admired the house, wrote that he was 'mightily pleased with the noblenesse of this house, and the rare furniture and pictures'.

Webb was unfortunate, and profited little from the Restoration. He had hoped for the Surveyorship, which was awarded to a talented young amateur, Mr. Christopher Wren (he was not knighted until 1673). He repaired the existing Whitehall Palace and had every reason to expect to be called upon to carry out the buildings projected by his

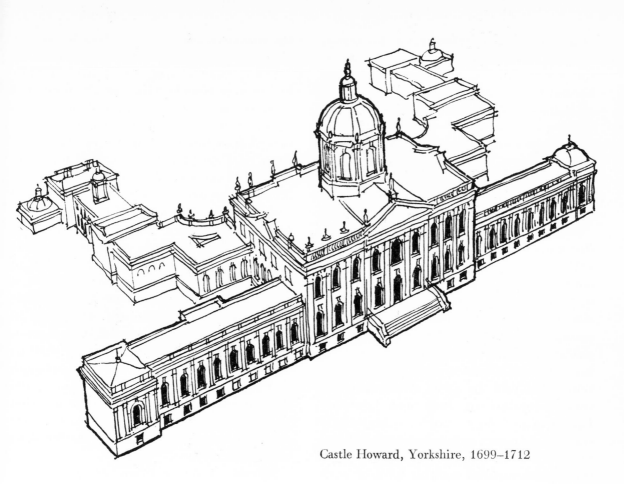

Castle Howard, Yorkshire, 1699–1712

master, Inigo Jones, nearly fifty years before. There is little doubt that Webb was the draughtsman, as well as the possible designer, of the Palace at Whitehall, and of the King Charles block at Greenwich. He went to Jones in 1628 at the age of seventeen and has been completely overshadowed by the genius of the older man, although he must have been an apt pupil and a highly competent character.

Thorpe Hall, near Peterborough, built about 1656 for Oliver St. John, Lord Chief Justice of Common Pleas, and a kinsman of Oliver Cromwell, is attributed to Webb, and is a handsome house with a fine cornice and massive chimney stacks. The ground floor is raised and contains the hall, library and dining room, with servants' quarters in the semi-basement beneath. Ceilings and panellings are charming, but the staircase is a magnificent example with a carved and pierced floral balustrade of a type which had a considerable vogue in late seventeenth-century England. There is an even more splendid example at Dunster Castle in Somerset (1681) and another at Ham House, Petersham, in Surrey. A small example is in the Guildford High Street, almost adjacent to the Town Hall, in a house that was until recently a tea shop.

Lamport Hall (1654–7), also in Northamptonshire, can more definitely be attributed to Webb, although the house has been much altered and little remains of his original work but the main entrance front. Ramsbury Manor in Wiltshire is another house

115

Thrumpton Hall, Nottingham,
1660–9: staircase

which may be by Webb, for it is simple in
design and admirable in proportion, but the
cornice is more restrained than that at
Thorpe. The ground floor is again raised,
with servants' quarters in the basement.

The staircase at Ashburnham House (1662)
part of Westminster School, is a masterpiece
built either at the end of the Civil War or
during the Commonwealth. It is considered
to be almost too good to have been designed
by Webb, but Inigo Jones was then nearly
eighty years old, and it is extremely doubtful whether it is his work. It is one of the
finest staircases in London, with its panelling and fluted columns and oval dome. The
only other staircase to compare with it is that
by William Kent in the interior of 44 Berkeley Square. The richly decorated staircases

116

at Ham House and at Thrumpton Hall, Nottingham, are of a more exuberant style.

A contemporary of Sir Christopher Wren, William Talman, 1650–1719, a Dutchman, was working on individual lines. He is best known for his great project at Chatsworth for the Duke of Devonshire (1687) and his work at Dyrham Park (1698–1700) a few years later. The fine Stuart suite of rooms at Chatsworth is unsurpassed in splendour in this country, and as the background to a great aristocrat is Baroque in conception.

Chatsworth is a superb example of a ducal residence. It stands on the slopes of the Derbyshire hills overlooking a spacious park, in a charming valley dotted with cattle and watered by a little stream. Built of local stone, it is simple and dignified in design. For some reason unknown, but probably at the request of his client, Talman placed the great reception suite on the second and top floors, the windows of which are therefore larger than those below, giving a somewhat heavy appearance to the façade.

Talman, about whom not very much is known, built Dyrham, in Gloucestershire, for William Blaythwayt, Secretary of State to William III. He designed also four of the Halls of the City Companies, the Fishmongers', Haberdashers', the Taylors' and the Drapers'.

The architect of Boughton, in Northamptonshire, which belongs to the Duke of Buccleugh, is unknown. It is French in influence, for the Duke's ancestor, the Duke of Montagu, had been Ambassador at Versailles, and it contains one of the finest collections of pictures and furniture still in private possession. Unknown, too, are the designers of Petworth in Sussex, and Badminton in Gloucestershire.

There is one other architect who maintains the Baroque tradition in this country. Thomas Archer (1668–1743) left Trinity College, Oxford, in 1689 and travelled abroad for four years. His subsequent career as an architect in England had been coloured by his studies of the Baroque in Rome, where Bernini, who had been dead only nineteen years, had transformed the city by his genius. Archer's designs show more Baroque influence than any other architect with the exception of Vanbrugh. His church of St. John, in Smith Square, Westminster, is as ponderous and dramatic as any work of the dramatist-architect. He designed also St. Philip, Birmingham, now the cathedral (1710–25), and worked on the north front of Chatsworth (1702–5).

Ham House, near Petersham in Surrey, has the most sumptuous interior of the Restoration period. If Hardwick Hall is famous for its needlework, Ham is outstanding for its use of timber, whether in floors, panelling or furniture. Originally built in 1610, the older rooms were redecorated in 1637–8 and the magnificent carved staircase was erected. Although the rooms are small in scale they retain most of the furniture listed in the inventory of 1679, but in spite of its comparatively late development and proximity to London the classic details are immature, although this in no way detracts from the charm of the old house overlooking the Thames.

Apart from Webb and Inigo Jones there was no outstanding English architect until the advent of Wren. The great age of English architecture commenced a little after the Restoration and the period of genius lasted over the Georgian era and a century of wealth and accomplishment. The age of Addison, Pope and Gray was the age also of the great craftsmen, of houses filled with walnut furniture and limewood carvings, with gorgeous stucco ceilings and a warmer and, in general, more original architecture than that of the cold Palladian style that was to follow. The paintings of Thornhill, Verrio and Laguerre too, were richer and more exuberant than the more precise Angelica Kauffmann, and Gabriel Cibber more human in his sculpture than the diluted Grecian forms of Flaxman.

There is a deep and fundamental difference between the Gothic and the Renaissance house. The former grew according to the whim of the owner and in comparatively haphazard manner, its merit or otherwise depending on the skill and experience of the mason in charge. To this we owe the picturesque quality of these houses, and their attraction is also due to the fact that they grew out of simple contemporary requirements and were built of materials that harmonised completely with their surroundings.

The Renaissance house was the product of one man and was designed in full before building operations were commenced, with plans and elevations drawn out to rigid rules of proportion, which were adhered to not always with the happiest results.

The change in the character of the plaster ornament, which developed into one of the finer English crafts, was almost entirely due to the influence of Inigo Jones. The ceiling of the saloon at Raynham Hall in Norfolk is a splendid example with the characteristic feature of his designs, the large central ellipse with its decoration of fruit and flowers encircled by a repetition of the great classic cornice. To obtain the effect he desired Jones imported foreign plasterers, for the English craftsman was accustomed to the more homely and fancy-free designs of the Elizabethan and Jacobean houses, and had had no experience of the far more luscious and sophisticated foreign style.

Coleshill, too, had incomparable ceilings of the same classical type, and the stucco work at Astley Hall, near Chorley in Lancashire (c. 1670), is the most extravagant display of Baroque virtuosity to be found in England. The compartments of the ceiling in the hall are decorated with plaster wreaths, cherubs and shields of extraordinary richness, the cherubs each modelled separately in the round and attached by wires, the wreaths built up of flowers and leaves each separately moulded. The ceiling of the drawing room is even more elaborate, the central feature composed of four large scallop shells with two pendant cherubs carrying festoons, all contained within a deep floral wreath. The remainder of the ceiling is filled with very large roses and other flowers and may have been made by a German or an Italian. Although the effect is somewhat heavy and overpowering due to the comparative lowness of the room which is surrounded by tapestries, it is of an extraordinary richness.

At Dunsland House, at Holsworthy in Devon (c. 1680), the north wing is decorated with plasterwork and carving of a very high order for so remote a district, and at Denham Place in Buckinghamshire, which was built in 1688 and is a four-square, red-brick, hip-roofed house, there is much fine woodwork and panelling of the period, and some particularly interesting plasterwork in the principal reception rooms. The ceiling of the drawing room is decorated with a panelled motif in which the sports of hunting, fishing and shooting are depicted in plasterwork with a trophy of musical instruments in the centre.

Christopher Wren (1632–1723), the outstanding architectural genius of the English Renaissance, was first a scientist and astronomer, a genius with an inquisitive, searching mind who became England's greatest architect almost by chance.

He went to school at Westminster, where his main studies were mathematics and the classics. Leaving Westminster at the age of thirteen he continued his studies under Sir Charles Scarborough, an eminent physician, who doubtless aroused his interest in anatomy, for, two years later, he was appointed assistant to the lecturer of anatomy at Surgeons' Hall.

As an Oxford undergraduate his interests were many and varied. He graduated in 1653, becoming a Fellow of All Souls' the same year and soon after being appointed Professor of Astronomy at Gresham College, London, a 'College for the promotion of Physico-Mathematical Experimental Learning', later to become the Royal Society.

For twenty years in Oxford and London, Wren lived and made his name by astronomy until the time when, as the King's Surveyor of Works and Architect to St. Paul's Cathedral, he became completely involved in architecture. In these twenty years he was interested in physics and made his own researches into Descartes' theories

St. Bride's, Fleet Street, 1670–8: steeple, 1701–3

119

of the influence of the moon on the tides. His drawings and studies inevitably came to the notice of Charles II himself, but he became widely known as a man of responsibility when he was commissioned 'to survey and direct the works of the mole, harbour and fortifications of the citadel and town of Tangier', which had come to Britain as part of the dowry of Catherine of Braganza, on her marriage to Charles II. It was Wren's reputation as a geometrician which prompted the offer, and it was further indicated to him that he would succeed to the Surveyorship on the death of the holder. The fact that he refused the offer on the grounds of health in no way appears to have prejudiced his chances. He may have been wise in his refusal, as the Tangier of the seventeenth century was a notorious centre of plague, and Wren had sufficient medical knowledge to appreciate the fact.

In 1661 Wren was appointed Savilian Professor of Astronomy at Oxford and in the same year became assistant to Sir John Denham, Surveyor-General of Works. His varied interests must have kept him extremely busy, and it is interesting to see, from a contemporary letter, that he was finding it difficult to keep pace with his varied commitments. Reproving Wren for not returning to the University on time, Dr. Spratt wrote:

'I must confess I have some little Peek against you; therefore am not much displeased that I have this occasion of telling you some ill news. The Vice-Chancellor did yesterday send for me, to enquire where the Astronomy Professor was, and the Reason of his Absence, so long after the Beginning of Term. I used all the Arguments I could for your Defence. I told him, that Charles II was King of England, Scotland, France and Ireland; that he was, by the last Act of Parliament, declared absolute Monarch in these his Dominions; and that it was this mighty Prince who had confined you to London. I endeavoured to persuade him that the Drawing of Lines in Sir Harry Savile's[1] School was not altogether of so great a Concernment for the Benefit of Christendom as the Rebuilding of St. Paul's, or the Fortifying of Tangier; for I understood those were the great Works in which that extraordinary Genius of yours was judged necessary to be employed. All this I urged; but, after some Discourse, he told me that he was not to consider you now as Dr. Bayley,[2] for so he owed you all kindness, but as Vice-Chancellor; and under that capacity he most terribly told me, that he took it very ill that you had not all this while given him any Account what hindered you from the Discharge of your Office. This he bid me tell you, and I do it not very unwillingly, because I see that our Friendships are so closely tied together, that the same Thing which was so great a Prejudice to me (my losing your Company all this while here) does also something redound to your Disadvantage. And so, my dear Sir, now my Spite and Spleen are satisfied, I must needs return to my old Temper again, and faithfully assure you, that I am, with the most violent Zeal and Passion, Your most affectionate and devoted Servant, Thomas Spratt.' (Spratt was historian of the Royal Society.)

Were all Wren's correspondence of an equally entertaining nature it is the more to be regretted that so little is now extant.

Wren's first essay in architecture was at Pembroke College, Cambridge, in 1663, which he designed for his uncle, the Bishop of Ely. It has a single order of Corinthian

[1] Founder of the Savilian professorship, then held by Wren.

[2] Dr. Richard Bayley, President of St. John's College and Dean of Salisbury.

pilasters, large pediments, a central window flanked by niches and a hexagonal cupola.

The date of Wren's first association with the Sheldonian Theatre at Oxford is not known. Gilbert Sheldon, the Warden of All Souls', wished to make a gift of some substance to the University on his departure to the Bishopric of London, and in 1663 Wren showed a model of the building based on the Theatre of Marcellus in Rome. Although architecturally immature, the building is of great interest from a structural point of view, for the covering of the roof posed problems of construction with which no architect had as yet contended, but with which Wren grappled with success.

It was through Sheldon, as Bishop of London, that Wren was first introduced to St. Paul's. The earliest church of St. Paul's was built in the seventh century by Ethelbert, King of Kent, and burnt down in the reign of William the Conqueror. A second church was built but this also was destroyed by fire in the reign of Stephen. The church which Wren was called in to repair was built about 1200 by Radulph de Diceto and completed about the middle of the thirteenth century. It was 586 feet long, the longest Christian church in the world, with a spire reaching the staggering height of 489 feet. When Wren began his preliminary survey in 1661, he found the ancient fabric in a dangerously ruinous condition, reporting that the pillars threatened to collapse and that the tower was leaning. The work of repair was begun but the Great Fire almost completely destroyed the whole building.

The reason why Wren never visited Italy is not known. The journey was certainly long and arduous and not without danger, but he could have gone by sea or across the Low Countries to the Brenner Pass, where communications were good and the speed of travel quite extraordinary, considering the state of the roads. The authorities at Oxford were most patient with the prolonged absences of their brilliant Professor of Astronomy; however, Wren may have decided that a visit to Italy for the purpose of study would tax their patience too highly. He did not go to Rome but he did the next best thing; he went to Paris, fortunately for himself and perhaps also for posterity, for he thereby escaped the Plague of London which was taking a toll of so many lives.

Wren could not have visited Paris at a more propitious time, for in 1665 building development in and around the city was commensurate with the dominant position of France in European affairs. The classical châteaux around Paris by François Mansart and Levau, the churches and mansions of Mansart in the capital city, the remodelling of Versailles by Levau, the great Collège Mazarin and the river-front of the Louvre, by the same architect, all proclaimed the strength and majesty of a vigorous and cultured nation. Wren met Bernini, who had been called to Paris to advise upon the rebuilding of the Louvre Palace, but the Italian genius granted him only the shortest inspection of his plans, evidently suspecting the probing, brilliant mind of the English architect.

A strong influence on Wren may have come from the church of the Val-de-Grâce (1645–50), by Mansart, with its altar by Bernini which is so reminiscent of the baldachino in St. Peter's and its twisted Salomonic columns. Bernini may also have suggested ideas to Perrault for the eastern façade of the Louvre, which is of a far more monumental character than the other façades of the great court, being comparable in many ways to the courtyard of the Ospedale Maggiore in Milan (1457) by Filarete, the architect and sculptor.

The church of the Sorbonne, with its fine

projecting portal, its saucer domes and its wide nave flanked by piers faced with Corinthian pilasters may have had a direct effect on St. Paul's. The influence of France on Charles II, also, was strong, for he had spent part of his exile at the French Court, and his favourite and deeply loved sister lived in France all her life. This may further explain the tenuous hold of the Baroque, through Wren, on English architecture, for the style never dominated the lively French as it did the more southern Latin countries.

Wren returned to England in March 1666, and found time in April to sketch designs for the repair of St. Paul's, for which he had been asked merely for his views. By September, the huge Gothic cathedral was a blackened ruin, and most of London had gone.

The Great Fire of London, in the early days of September 1666, destroyed nearly the whole of the City, with about thirteen thousand houses. The City, at that date, was entirely mediaeval in character and consisted of a maze of alleys, nooks, lanes and rookeries, without drainage or sanitation of any sort, foul and unwholesome, a sombre breeding ground for the plague which in the previous year had carried off one-seventh of the population. The frightful conditions had been noted before the fire by John Evelyn, the diarist, who had travelled in France and Italy and, as a friend of Wren, held very similar views on town-planning.

The plan Wren produced after the Great Fire of 1666 would, in itself, stand as a monument to his intellectual capacity. It was a completely new departure in the lay-out of a town and derived partly from plans by Domenico Fontana for the opening up of Rome for Sixtus V, and partly from what Wren had seen of the huge garden lay-outs by the French Court Gardener, Le Nôtre. Wren's achievement is all the more remarkable in view of the paucity of information concerning Renaissance planning on the Continent. Had this, his first plan, been adopted, St. Paul's would now have been viewed to the greatest advantage, and the appalling traffic problems of the City of London might never have occurred.

Even before the Great Fire the winding, ill-paved mediaeval streets of the City of London had proved quite inadequate for the rapidly increasing demands of both goods and people. The main route through the City was the river Thames itself, and contemporary painters and illustrations proclaim this fact in emphatic tones.

The way across the Thames at London Bridge and the roads leading up to and away from it had been, from the earliest times, the link between the important commercial routes of the Midlands with those of the south and the Continent. The principal line of communication, therefore, ran from north to south through the City, through Bishopsgate, and the other main line of communication from east to west, from Aldgate to Ludgate and Newgate. Another route from east to west linked the Royal Palace and the seat of government. These conditions were of paramount importance in any new plan, and Wren shows an outstanding appreciation of them.

The Fleet River was to have been straightened and deepened for shipping and a network of radiating and concentric streets, pivoting on a large octagonal open space, would have formed a kind of forecourt to the city. A great quay along the Thames was proposed, and from a square at the head of London Bridge four streets were to run to the city centre.

The plan is Baroque in providing for vistas and dominant architectural features, and when, in later years, Wren designed a setting worthy of St. Paul's he projected a huge and monumental area around the cathedral

122

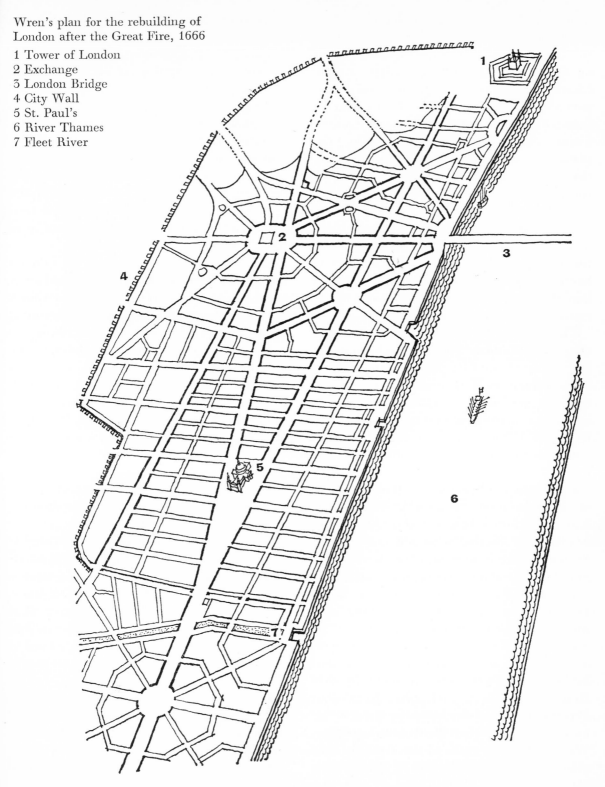

Wren's plan for the rebuilding of
London after the Great Fire, 1666

1 Tower of London
2 Exchange
3 London Bridge
4 City Wall
5 St. Paul's
6 River Thames
7 Fleet River

rather in the manner of the Place Royale, Paris. Before, however, Wren's plan could be put into effect the problem that arises in all great town planning schemes, that of deciding the ownership of the land, had first to be solved. Many ideas were put forward and surveys were made, but none was found to be practicable, with the result that, with the best intentions, the difficulties proved insurmountable and the fine plan was abandoned.

Wren was not entirely the loser, however, as he was appointed one of the six Commissioners for the rebuilding of the City and, with Roger Pratt and Hugh May, two men of wide architectural experience, he represented the Crown. With the three men appointed by the City, rapid progress was made in compiling new regulations for the rebuilding, and within three months these received the Royal Assent and became law. No half-timbered buildings were permitted. The new buildings were to be in brick and stone, and inspectors, appointed for the purpose, controlled the new building lines.

The rebuilding of fifty-three City churches by Wren occupied the next thirty-eight years of his life. They show an extraordinary imagination and a mastery of planning that is all the more amazing when the sites are considered. Most of them are small and awkwardly placed and called for extreme ingenuity in their planning, the more so as Wren broke completely with the mediaeval tradition and designed his new church spaces primarily as auditoriums. The decoration of these churches is mainly external, and the City of London is most fortunate in the richness and variety of their soaring towers and steeples. Wren was responsible for the design of these churches, although, with the vast amount of work entailed, it is doubtful whether the detail and supervision were his alone, which may explain the variation in quality.

The first churches to be rebuilt were

simple in plan, in the traditional idea. One such is St. Bride's, Fleet Street (1670–1), with its nave and aisles separated by rows of columns and a tower at the west end. It was gutted by incendiaries in the last war but has since been restored according to Wren's original plan. St. Stephen Walbrook (1672), at the back of the Mansion House, was also shattered but has also been skilfully restored. It is the first of the domed churches, the dome itself supported on a series of eight equal arches. Wren had at this time no idea of the final appearance of St. Paul's, and St. Stephen's is only a pointer to the direction of his thought.

St. James', Piccadilly, also gutted in the blitz, was most successful in plan, 'beautiful and convenient', and was consistently imitated for large new churches up to and after the Regency.

The quality of the decoration varied in all the City churches, but that of the steeples is consistently high. At St. Mary-le-Bow, Wren attempted a classical version of the old Gothic steeple, a fifteenth-century tower surmounted by four flying buttresses supporting a short spire. The result is one of the most satisfying and exciting steeples in the City, ranking with Christ Church, Newgate Street, St. Magnus the Martyr, and St. Vedast's. Wren's churches were planned always for lightness, and the decoration on the whole was restricted to wood-carving and stucco. There are no examples of exuberant ceiling paintings such as are found in the Baroque churches of Italy and Germany, no miracles of perspective and painting such as those by Gaulli in the Gesu or in S. Ignazio in Rome. But the woodcarving is often very rich, including pulpit, organ-case, pews, balustrades, reredos and reading desk, and ceilings are richly decorated in stucco with a wealth of garlands, heads of cherubs and shells.

By 1677 there were probably thirty churches in course of construction, and by 1685 the rebuilding of the City churches was almost complete. The Guildhall had been restored, the Halls of the City Companies and the Royal Exchange rebuilt in red and brown brick, with dressings of stone or wood.

The towers and steeples of Wren's city churches no longer dominate the skyline as they did in the eighteenth and nineteenth centuries, but their effect can be seen in Canaletto's 'View of the City with St. Paul's' at Windsor, and in other paintings of the time.

The Great Fire left the old cathedral of St. Paul's not entirely destroyed but in a most perilous condition. An attempt to repair it met with disaster and Wren was called in for consultation. Even before the destruction of the cathedral Wren had considered the possibility of a dome in place of the old Gothic spire which even then was in a dangerous condition. His knowledge of domes, however, was limited to a few illustrations. No such form of structure was known in the country and the obvious place for study was Italy, and above all Rome.

No drawings remain of the first design for St. Paul's, but Wren's 'Great model' of the design (1673), which he favoured, is still preserved, most beautifully made in wood, in the Trophy Room of the Cathedral. Its main feature is the dome, approached by a long and narrow nave, a feature which was to have been followed by Sir Edwin Lutyens in his design, never realised, for Liverpool Roman Catholic Cathedral. The contrast between the long narrow approach and the sudden burst and glory of a great space under the dome would have been magnificent, but 'the Chapter, and some others of the Clergy thought the model not enough of a Cathedral fashion'. So Wren was forced to compromise.

125

Left: section of a Gothic cathedral; right: flying buttress in St. Paul's concealed by screen wall. From *The True Principles of Pointed or Christian Architecture* by Pugin, 1841

In 1675 he produced the third or 'Warrant' design, so called because Charles II approved of it and issued the warrant for its commencement in 1674. The plan is similar to those of the mediaeval cathedrals, to Ely in particular, which Wren knew well through his uncle, the Bishop. It is interesting to remember that when the central tower of Ely had fallen in the fourteenth century it had been replaced by an octagonal construction (see the illustration on page 33) and the dome of St. Paul's also rests on eight piers and arches. The section of St. Paul's shows the nave supported by flying buttresses on the principle of the Gothic examples, but hidden by a screen wall which serves to lend consistency to the whole design and acts as a balancing weight to the thrust of the flying buttresses.

The Warrant design is distinguished by a high dome surmounted by a spire; the de-

sign of the dome went through various stages, one closely resembling that of St. Peter's in Rome, before it reached, in 1697, the form we know today. The design of the two western towers owes much to Rome, in particular to those of the church of St. Agnese in the Piazza Navona, by Carlo Rainaldi and Borromini.

Wren was fortunate in the craftsmen who worked on St. Paul's, many of whom were outstanding in an age of great craftsmen and, moreover, sprang mainly from the native genius in a manner that appears to be peculiar to that colourful age. England was, in character, the last European country to produce artists. The great age of English music had disappeared with the Elizabethan era: musicians of any calibre now came from abroad, from Italy and Germany; painters had come here from Germany, the Netherlands and Italy, and Tijou, the great artist in wrought iron, had come from France.

Among the names of famous English craftsmen who worked for Wren at St. Paul's are Grinling Gibbons, the masons Strong, father and son, Jasper Lathan and Edward Pearce, Samuel Fulkes and John Tompson. By 1697 they had built the cathedral up to the commencement of the dome itself, and a service was held there for the first time.

It is in the construction of the dome that Wren's quality as a mathematician stands forth. For interior effect, he designed a low, hemispherical dome. The lantern, weighing some 850 tons, is supported on a brick cone, 18 inches thick, springing from the same level. This cone is entirely closed by an external dome framed up in timber and covered in lead, which bears no weight and had no structural significance, but gives the impression of carrying the lantern surmounting it. This dome in turn surmounts a great drum. The reasons for the three domes are not only structural. The length of the nave necessitated the raising of the dome to a height where it could be seen. (At St. Peter's, in Rome, the nave is too long and the dome, from the front, sinks below the west front and cannot be seen fully except at a great distance.) Then again, the visual effect, in the interior, of a dome set on a drum would have been most unfortunate, the dome being too high, which gives the reason for the lower dome inside.

Wren was sixty-six when the dome was begun and seventy-seven at the completion of the structure. The last stone, on top of the lantern, was laid by his son Christopher, in the company of the masons Strong and their assistants. The great ball and cross were added, and the building was complete.

It is difficult to dissociate the form of St. Paul's from the favoured English Gothic shape. Unlike foreign examples, English cathedrals built up, in the main, to a central tower or spire instead of a great west front, as do most continental churches. Salisbury culminates in a central spire, and Canterbury, York, Lincoln, Hereford and others and, more grandly than all, Durham, build up to a dominating central tower just as St. Paul's culminates in its dome. The western towers are kept deliberately subservient to

St. Paul's, 1675–1710: cross section showing construction of dome

the overriding theme. Then, too, there is the similarity of the plan of St. Paul's to those of the Gothic cathedrals and to Ely in particular.

Wren's interior of Drury Lane Theatre, which was opened in 1674 after a fire had destroyed the old building, was completely altered by the Adam brothers in 1775. The perspective effects of the Bibienas, the Italian perspectivists, in the Teatro Olympico at Vicenza, may have influenced the transition of the auditorium to the stage by means of a tall Corinthian colonnade with a sharp foreshortening in perspective.

Work for the new Library at Trinity College, Cambridge, was begun in 1677. Wren had originally drawn up a scheme for a combined Senate House and Library, although the former building was never carried out to his design. The interior of the Library, with its fine proportions, noble simplicity and superb detail, is one of his most fortunate works, and in direct contrast with those of the same period in the Baroque monasteries of Austria and Bavaria, which are full of drama, movement and excitement.

The numerous wars of the seventeenth century resulted in hundreds of disabled soldiers being thrown on the streets to starve. Their plight aroused the sympathy even of that unfeeling age, and Louis XIV founded the Hotel des Invalides to house and care for his workless veterans. His example was followed in England by the foundation of the Royal Hospital at Chelsea, one of Wren's most felicitous designs, of which the King laid the foundation stone on 16th February 1681. The building was completed four years later, and additions were later made under James II and William and Mary. It is based on the university college plan with a range of buildings in the centre forming the focal point of the community life, with a chapel and refectory grouped around a vestibule. Dormitories and side wings attached to the main block form a court on the fourth side open to the Thames.

Wren's project for a palace at Winchester was commenced two years after building began at Chelsea. Commenced in 1683 the palace progressed rapidly and was nearly all roofed by 1685, when the death of Charles II stopped the work.

With the accession of William and Mary two further projects for palaces were started at Kensington and Hampton Court, the latter in July 1689, and schemes were drawn out which involved the destruction of nearly the whole of Wolsey's palace, but in the end shortage of money fortunately dictated a more economical scheme, combining a large number of rooms while harmonising with the existing Tudor work. The result cannot compare in any way with Versailles, either in scale or splendour. The national economy in any case would have forbidden any such idea, and the result is more in the nature of a large country house. But how charming is the mellow brickwork, with its background of Dutch domesticity, in such contrast to the grandiose and exuberant residence of the haughty French monarch. For Louis XIV was an autocrat in the full sense of the word, and represented a type that had here been repudiated in blood on a scaffold in Whitehall. By comparison, William and his *hausfrau* wife were comfortable and bourgeois, entirely suited to the quiet tones and lack of ostentation of the Thames-side palace.

The artists who collaborated with Wren in the decoration of Hampton Court Palace had few superiors in Europe. Jean Tijou, who worked also in St. Paul's, was probably the outstanding iron worker of his age, and Grinling Gibbons had no peer in the art of wood-carving. There was, however, no painter to compare with Tiepolo in Venice and Germany, although Verrio and Laguerre were competent enough. The sculptor was Caius Gabriel Cibber, capable but mediocre, and not of the calibre of the great continental sculptors. The whole project is, however, Baroque in conception, with its combination of architecture, painting and sculpture making up a single entity.

Wren made extensive alterations and additions to John Thorpe's old building lying in the midst of splendid gardens in Kensington. The new palace was built entirely of brick, which may have been due in part to the influence of Hawksmoor, who acted as Clerk of Works on the building, as he did also at Chelsea and Greenwich.

The French wars were responsible also for another great building project, the erection of a hospital for seamen at Greenwich, in which the Queen took a most lively interest. The site already contained Inigo Jones' Queen's House and the King Charles block, the only part actually built of John Webb's project for a Royal Palace. The Queen wished both buildings to be retained and the view from the Queen's House to the Thames had to remain unobstructed. With the accession of Queen Anne in 1702, changes were made in the organisation and Vanbrugh was introduced, although his influence was restricted mainly to the west front of King William's block. All the foundations of the scheme were, however, laid out before Wren finally withdrew, so that it can be considered as his own project and second only to St. Paul's in importance. It is certainly one of the greatest achievements of English architecture. In 1702 Wren was seventy years of age, and after that date he withdrew more and more from the scheme. The last two works carried out by the great architect were Marlborough House and the Chapter House of St. Paul's.

Wren, as an architect, stood alone until the appearance of Vanbrugh. He had little permanent influence on the Palladian movement which developed in the eighteenth century, and his fine London churches such as St. Mary-le-Bow, St. Stephen Walbrook and St. James, Piccadilly, had little effect on the tide of taste which continued to flow away from both these architects.

Nicholas Hawksmoor (1661–1736) became Clerk of Works to Wren at the age of eighteen. At this remarkably early age he was apparently the representative of the architect and thus had to bear a very considerable responsibility on projects of the size of Greenwich Hospital, St. Paul's, Westminster Abbey, Winchester, St. James and Kensington Palaces. He assisted Vanbrugh also at Blenheim and Castle Howard. Apart from his churches he designed Queen's College, Oxford (1709–30), part of All Souls, Oxford (1715–40), and the Clarendon Building, Oxford (1712–15). Vanbrugh, in fact, was most successful whenever he had Hawksmoor to help him, although the latter had not the playwright's extraordinary sense of drama or imagination. Hawksmoor's interior of Spitalfields Church, however, is rich and magnificent. His monument is the splendid Mausoleum at Castle Howard, whose stonework is decaying sadly and now awaits a possible grant from the government to prevent further disintegration.

The last forty years of the seventeenth century and the first forty years of the eighteenth century seemed to its contemporaries to be the period of supreme achievement of the arts in England. Goldsmith called it the Augustan Age, 'when language and learning arrived at its highest perfection'. It was an age which delighted in polish and elegance, in reason and control, distrusting all that was abnormal and freakish. It was the age of great English literature, beginning with the poetry of Dryden and Pope, and proceeding to Addison and

Steele. Apart from Kneller there was hardly a painter of any note, but in music the English tradition culminated in the operas and orchestral music of Purcell. Later Handel came to England and introduced the German oratorio to an enthusiastic public.

It was the age when the architect came, for the first time, firmly into his own, when architecture was no longer thought a part of the building trade but an art that was worthy of the study and attention of the best minds. A certain sympathy with the Baroque gave way, under the guidance of the Earl of Burlington, to the simplicity and grandeur of 'Roman' architecture, inspired by Palladio (1518–80) who had based his own buildings on those of ancient Rome. Great emphasis was laid on proportion and the balanced distribution of doors and windows, such as we see at Houghton Hall in Norfolk or at Stowe in Buckinghamshire.

The Georgian age which followed it lasted from 1714, when George I came to the throne, until the end of the century, when the Regency period saw the development of a more Grecian style of architecture. The Georgian period is notable mainly for the great number of large and small houses whose domestic character influenced even the churches and public buildings, and whose discreet solidity reflected the sober merchants and landowning democracy in contrast to the splendour and exuberance of contemporary foreign buildings in countries ruled by an autocrat. For the seventeenth and eighteenth centuries in most of Europe were the age of grandeur, when the Baroque style flourished as the background to the hundreds of grand dukes and princelings who ruled their little states and sought to emulate the glories of Versailles.

England owes her tradition of fine craftsmanship in brickwork to architects such as Wren, who were denied the use of marble and of stone on a big scale by the sheer need for economy. As the eighteenth century progressed detail became more delicate and window bars became increasingly slender. The houses themselves remained simple and symmetrical, rectangular in plan, built mainly in brick and with stone window sills and surrounds, doorways and quoins. In the earlier examples the sloping roofs projected over classical stone or wooden cornices, but later on the roof was partly concealed behind parapets.

Churches were symmetrical also in plan, with a tower at the west end over a pillared portico. More emphasis was placed on the word of the preacher than on the mysteries of ritual and the church became more of a meeting hall for listening to sermons.

The rise of the middle class in the eighteenth century saw the development of groups of domestic buildings as one architectural unit in squares, terraces and crescents that form the chief glory of towns like Bath, Bristol, and later at Buxton, Cheltenham, Brighton and Bloomsbury. In all these the individual house was subordinated to the general architectural conception, and reflected in fact the middle-class Englishman's ideas on 'good form'.

After what may be called the Baroque period of English architecture, there followed the inevitable reaction. As in Rome the architects of the sixteenth century had rebelled against the more classical tenets of the old Roman writer Vitruvius, then only recently rediscovered, and against Andrea Palladio and his more severe style of architecture, so in England a similar reaction followed at the beginning of the Hanoverian period. The Earl of Burlington, the leader of the new 'Palladian' movement, and his circle of architects may therefore have been responsible for preventing English Baroque from sinking into the decadence of its later

Stoneleigh Abbey, Kenilworth, Warwickshire, 1720

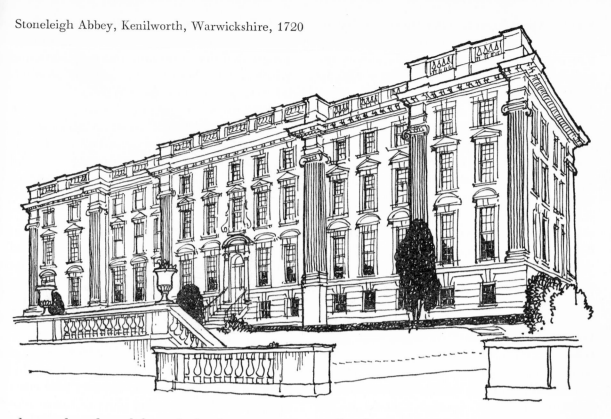

phases abroad, and for substituting a more balanced approach to architecture.

The first phase of Georgian art spanned the period of transition from Sir Christopher Wren and his school to the succeeding Palladian movement, and the second included the long reign of George II, the Regency and the reign of George IV. Both phases are fundamentally similar and based on the classical, but the latter phase became more refined, more scholarly and more economical.

The keynote of the Georgian style is proportion. It is typically English in its impressiveness and lack of ostentation, in contrast with the theatrical exuberance of the style of Vanbrugh. A good example is Stoneleigh Abbey.

Reaction against the school of Wren was followed by a revival of interest in the purer style of Palladio, introduced half a century earlier by Inigo Jones and encouraged by the Palladians of Lord Burlington's circle, beginning with Colin Campbell. A new interest in the Italian masterpieces influenced the work of James Gibbs, Isaac Ware and Sir Robert Taylor. The Senate House at Cambridge, by Gibbs, has more than a hint of Fontana, and in the work of Thomas Archer of Birmingham, at Wrest Park, there is a decided freedom in the manner of Borromini.

The first half of the eighteenth century saw the disciplined planning of Bath and a certain freedom in decorative details that is shown in the Baroque and Venetian characteristics of the work of William Kent, but later in the century the classical ideal can be seen at its best in Somerset House, by Sir William Chambers, the leader of the academic masters. A feature of this phase is the success of the provincial architects in

131

The Royal Crescent, Bath, 1789

towns such as York, Bath, Chester, Bristol and Plymouth.

The Adam brothers, sons of a well-known Edinburgh architect, travelled to Rome and Pompeii and discovered new forms of decoration which captured the popular fancy and formulated a style of decoration which became widespread for interiors, as well as for furniture.

After Archer there was to be no more Baroque architecture in England. The Rococo, or Baroque interior decoration, was to continue in various great houses for another century, but now the influence of Palladio, under the powerful and knowledgeable Lord Burlington, and with him, the architects who borrowed from Verona and Vicenza, swept the country, and the 'affected and licentious works of Bernini and Fontana' were to lose their appeal. Of this Anglo-Palladian phase, which continued until about the middle of the eighteenth century, when a revival of more Grecian characteristics

gradually superseded it, there were some very important figures.

William Kent (1685–1748) commenced his career as an apprentice to a coach-painter in Hull, journeying afterwards to Italy at the expense of three aristocratic patrons in order to study painting. For his patrons he bought pictures and antiques, and actually painted a fresco in a Roman church in 1717. In Rome he met Richard Boyle, 3rd Earl of Burlington (1685–1753) who, on the death of his father, had inherited large estates in Yorkshire and Ireland, as well as a house at Chiswick and Burlington House in Piccadilly. The times were favourable to those with rank and riches, and at twenty-one the Earl was not only a Privy Councillor, but Lord Lieutenant of the West Riding of Yorkshire and Lord High Treasurer of Ireland.

To men such as Burlington the country owes a great deal. They took the place of our present-day sources of travelling scholar-

132

ships, grants and moneys for research, in an age when, but for their generosity, it would have been quite impossible for the struggling artist or architect even to survive, much less travel to broaden and enrich his education. Burlington's taste was for architecture, which at this period enjoyed a very considerable vogue, and without a good working knowledge of which no gentleman was considered fully educated. He visited Italy for lengthy periods in 1714–15 and 1719 and acquired there a warm admiration for the works of Palladio, an edition of whose *Fabbriche Antiche* he published in 1730. From Italy he brought the young William Kent to Burlington House, whose exterior was being remodelled by James Gibbs and Colin Campbell.

The Earl was not only a patron of architecture, but a practitioner in no small degree, and must be given the credit for Chiswick House (1725), which although good in detail, fails on account of its meagre scale. It has recently been reconstructed in scholarly manner by the Ministry of Works. To Burlington must be given also the main credit for the dormitory of Westminster School (1722–30), the Assembly Rooms, York (1731–2), 29 Old Burlington Street and several other buildings. In these he probably enjoyed the help of Colin Campbell, Kent and others, with Henry Flitcroft (1697–1769), the architect of the immense Wentworth Woodhouse, as his personal assistant.

Kent was a man of varied and remarkable talents who, besides his competence as a painter, was a designer of the most superb doorways and mantelpieces. He designed the Royal Barge for George II in white and gold, with gilded dolphins writhing amongst the scallop shells and mermaids in the stern. The barge was in use until 1849 and is now in the Victoria and Albert Museum. As a painter, he carried out an altarpiece at St.

Clement Danes, painted a stair at Raynham for Lord Townshend, and at Kensington Palace he painted the walls to the King's staircase with a crowd of onlookers looking over a balustrade.

His Devonshire House in Piccadilly has now gone, but it suffered from the same meagre scale as Chiswick House, in spite of the splendid decoration. At 44 Berkeley Square, Kent designed a staircase of great ingenuity, considering the smallness of the space.

Kent's greatest work is Holkham Hall, in north Norfolk, in which Lord Burlington collaborated. There is a noticeable similarity between the exterior of the huge house and the Horse Guards, which he also designed, but Holkham, seen from outside, is depressing with its white brickwork, and the ground floor is rusticated in a dull and mechanical manner. On the south front is the inevitable Palladian portico, the angles of the main block emphasised by pavilions with 'Venetian' windows and an added storey.

But the interior of Holkham is superb, and the great hall, which is matched only by those at Kedleston and Syon, has a Roman magnificence, with its columns raised on a balustrade, its rich frieze copied from the Temple of Fortuna Virilis in Rome, and its gorgeous coffered ceiling, culminating in the great semicircle containing the staircase leading up to the saloon. Throughout the vast house, Kent's doorways, mantelpieces and ceilings proclaim the classical inventiveness of his mind. He had certainly repaid the early training of his patrons in Rome.

The Horse Guards (1750–8) is Kent's most successful building, far more imposing than Holkham, with the added advantage of Portland stone instead of white brick. The set of the cupola is perfect, the windows in proper proportion to walls, the side pavilions of the right size and projection. On each side of the cupola are raised storeys as at Holkham, but the Horse Guards is far more dignified, a fitting and most English background for the colourful military parades in front of it, and the brilliant uniforms of the Life Guards. It was unfinished at Kent's death and was completed by Vardy.

Kent was the designer of some of the most magnificent furniture in Europe. His finest mantelpieces, in marble, are in the stone hall and the dining room at Houghton, where Colin Campbell was the architect, and where he is rivalled as a designer of furniture only by Chippendale, whose craftsmanship lay with rare woods and marquetry. Kent's furniture is gilded and far more exuberant and Venetian in feeling and inclines more to the Rococo.

The Palladian school is distinguished by its interior stucco work and its decoration in the Rococo manner, carried out as often as not by Italian stuccadors with infinite invention and resource.

The other Palladians of Lord Burlington's circle included Colin Campbell (?–1729) whose early life is unknown but who emerged suddenly as the author of an immense book of architectural engravings, the *Vitruvius Britannicus*, of which the first volume appeared in 1715, the others in 1717 and 1725. This monumental work contains mainly illustrations of designs of great mansions, and was published under the patronage of Lord Burlington.

Campbell was the architect of Mereworth Castle, in Kent, whose design is based on that of Palladio's Villa Capra at Vicenza. On all four fronts the elevations are similar, the principal apartments arranged around the central circular hall, 35 feet in diameter, crowned by a dome. The subsidiary rooms are somewhat cramped, but the porticoes are splendid and Bagutti's plasterwork in the hall is delightful.

Houghton Hall is only partly Campbell. He certainly designed the great house, which was carried out by Thomas Ripley (1683–1758), while the interior decoration was left to Artari and Kent. The façade has great dignity, with its supporting colonnades on each side, joining the house to subsidiary blocks which contain kitchens and laundries, but the domes at each corner of the main block are uncomfortably low. The original raised attic storeys might here have been an improvement, but they were altered by Ripley.

Newby Hall, in Yorkshire, was designed originally by Campbell but altered so considerably by Robert Adam that it is in nearly all essentials an Adam house.

The Venetian, Giacomo Leoni (1686–1746), was another member of Lord Burlington's circle, and during the early years of his career was architect to the Elector Palatine, using his first book as an advertising medium in which he offered his professional services. The aristocratic commissions which came his way included Bramham Park, Yorkshire (1710), Clandon Park, Surrey (1732), Lathom House (1725), and Bold Hall (1730), both in Lancashire, and Moor Park, Hertfordshire (1720), which is now the headquarters of a famous golf club. This last great house has a splendid hall and marble doorways, superb stucco work and paintings by Thornhill and Amigoni.

Thomas Ripley, the least of the Burlington circle, designed the Admiralty (whose stone screen across the forecourt belongs to Robert Adam), as well as Wolterton Hall in Norfolk. Ripley furthered his career by his marriage to a maidservant of the all-powerful Sir Robert Walpole, but Isaac Ware and Flitcroft could rely on their more considerable talents.

Ware (?–1766) is said to have commenced as a chimney sweep, a thin, sickly little boy, who was seen by chance by Lord Burlington sketching in chalk on the face of a building. His talent was sufficient to arrest the attentions of the noble Lord, who gave him an excellent education and sent him to Italy. Ware held a succession of official posts from 1728 onwards and designed several notable buildings. He was employed at Houghton and refaced Chicksands Priory, in Bedfordshire, and Wrotham Park nearby. He was, however, at his best in London, where he designed Chesterfield House, with its elaborate Rococo decorations.

Henry Flitcroft (1697–1769) was apprenticed to a joiner when he attracted the attention of Lord Burlington, through whom he obtained employment under the Board of Works. He built two great English houses, Woburn Abbey, home of the Dukes of Bedford, and Wentworth Woodhouse, with its 600-feet façade, now threatened by surface coal mining. This huge house is no longer in private occupation and its fixtures and furniture have been dispersed, but it contains the 'Whistlejacket' Room with its

splendid paintings of horses by Stubbs, which in itself merits a visit to the mansion.

James Gibbs (1682–1754), the younger son of a well-to-do Aberdonian, visited Europe in his early twenties. His travels took him to Holland, France, Germany, Switzerland and finally Rome where he worked in the studio of Carlo Fontana. Here doubtless he was inspired by the great Renaissance palaces, and perhaps his round designs for the Radcliffe Camera at Oxford and his first plan for St. Martin-in-the-Fields, with its circular nave, were influenced by Bernini's San Andrea delle Valle or Borromini's San Carlo alle Quatro Fontane in Rome.

After his return from studying in Italy, Gibbs evolved a personal style in which respect for his patron Wren and knowledge of Italian Palladian and Baroque architecture combined to produce some of the masterpieces of the eighteenth century. St. Mary-le-Strand, begun in 1714, was his first London church. Here the Italian influence is very strong. It is interesting to note that the original design was for a church with a bell turret only. Gibbs converted the turret into

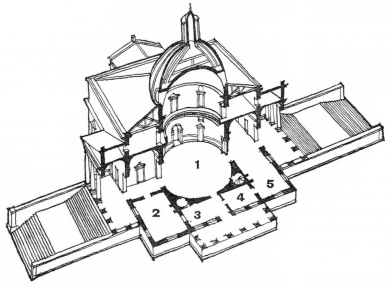

Mereworth Castle, Kent, 1722–5
1 Saloon
2 Reception room
3 Bedroom
4 Dressing room
5 Great gallery

135

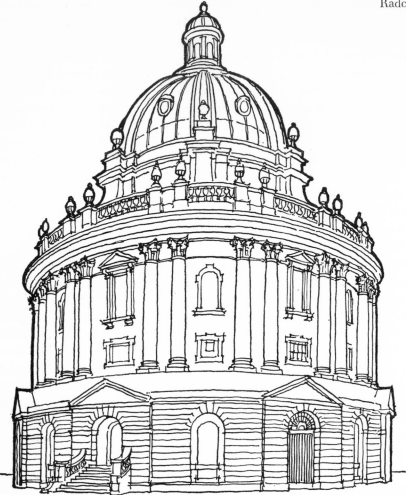

the commanding three-tiered spire, so familiar to Londoners, with great imaginative treatment. This he followed with the tower to Wren's church of St. Clement Danes, and finally his well-loved, intimate church of St. Martin-in-the-Fields. The first interesting circular design was turned down because of the expense involved but it did, nevertheless, inspire later architects to imitate the idea. Gibbs' second design is in the Wren tradition with its famous spire soaring gracefully above the seething traffic of Trafalgar Square.

Although the builder of the Senate House,

Cambridge, there is little to suggest his personal touch, and the design of the building is thought to have been by the amateur Sir James Burrough (1691–1764).

In the Fellows' Building, King's College, Cambridge, Gibbs' personal style may be seen to its best advantage, while the Radcliffe Camera Library at Oxford is probably his most famous work. His treatment of the circular building is full of imaginative invention. Here, in a last defiant gesture, Gibbs, with the assurance of the mature artist, gave free rein to the Italian influences of his youth. The building is now quite inadequate to hold the vast increase in the number of publications and it is interesting to note that half a million books are now housed beneath the adjoining lawns.

Gibbs' books were widely read, particularly his *Rules for Drawing, The Several Parts of Architecture* (1732) and *A Book of Architecture*. They had a far-reaching influence on the architecture of the eighteenth century in England and the New England States of America.

John Vardy (?–1765) was a humble bricklayer who rose, through the influence he acquired in several situations as Clerk of Works, to being a fashionable architect, a member of White's Club and the owner of a considerable fortune. He is best remembered for Spencer House in St. James's and as the architect who carried out Kent's design for the Horse Guards.

Matthew Brettingham of Norwich (1699–1769) was Clerk of Works under William Kent during the building of Holkham Hall. His own most important works were York House in Pall Mall and Norfolk House in St. James's Square, both of which have now been demolished.

One of the most satisfying buildings in England is the Palladian bridge at Wilton, designed by the 9th Earl of Pembroke whose grandfather had sent Inigo Jones to Italy. The noble amateur had the assistance of Robert Morris to advise on the construction, although, with the background of his studies in Italy, he was more than capable of designing in the Palladian manner and lacked only the technological experience of the practising architect.

With the production of *The Architecture of Andrea Palladio* by Leoni and *Designs of Inigo Jones* by William Kent, the Palladian movement was launched on its second and more triumphant phase. Whether this Italian style, which had grown naturally in Italy and was entirely suited to the less rigorous Italian climate, ever became successfully adapted to England's colder, less sunlit land is a matter of some doubt. We have become so accustomed to the long classic front and the central portico in so many country houses that the question has hardly arisen, and while it certainly provided a spacious background for the work of artists and craftsmen, in whom the eighteenth century was particularly rich, comfort and convenience were too often neglected, and Pope was inspired to write:

> . . . . '*Tis very fine,*
> *But where d'ye sleep, and where d'ye dine?*
> *I find by all you have been telling,*
> *That 'tis a house, but not a dwelling.*

In consequence the smaller Palladian house is a rarity, in spite of the fact that builders all over the country had never been more active in raising houses for the smaller squires and the rising professional classes. A constant stream of architectural pattern books gave all the necessary information on plans and elevations, down to the smallest details of staircases, doorways and chimney pieces. The result was a standard of taste in building that has never been surpassed. The horrors and the tragedies of the small speculative builder which we have to bear today were quite unknown, and the tradition established by Wren persisted in the quiet dignity of brick or stone.

One of the most prolific writers of pattern books was Batty Langley (1696–1751) whose books on the art and practice of building enjoyed immense sales. Other close rivals were William and John Halfpenny, writing similar manuals, while Robert Morris and T. Lightoler's *Modern Builders' Assistant* dealt exhaustively with details of building construction.

In the provinces there was no lack of

137

talent of a high order with Carr of York, the Woods of Bath and many others. Let us deal first with the London men before proceeding to the country. George Dance the Elder (1700–68) submitted in 1737 a design for the Mansion House, in competition with James Gibbs, Leoni and the Earl of Burlington, and was successful. He was responsible also for some of the City churches: St. Leonard, Shoreditch (1736–40), St. Matthew, Bethnal Green (1740–6), which was gutted in the blitz, St. Botolph, Aldgate (1741–4), together with the Fleet Market (1737), Surgeons' Hall (1745) and London Bridge (1756–60), since demolished.

A more conspicuous figure is Sir Robert Taylor (1714–88) who began his career as apprentice to a mason-sculptor, and was then sent by his father to Rome. He carved the sculpture of the pediment of the Mansion House and then turned architect, starting his day at 4 a.m. and working furiously. He was probably the most successful architect of his time until the advent of Robert Adam, and was responsible for the fine house at Heveningham, in Suffolk, with its lovely interior by James Wyatt. His great practice included the surveyorship of the Bank of England, of Greenwich Hospital, H.M. Customs, Lincoln's Inn, the Foundling Hospital, and the great Grafton and Pulteney Estates. He left his huge fortune of £180,000 (which could nowadays be multiplied at least ten times), to the 'Taylorian Institute' at Oxford.

Much of Taylor's interiors are on distinctly Adam lines; light, delicate and graceful, and a long way from the Palladians. He has more in common with Adam, Wyatt and Holland than with Kent and Flitcroft, and by reason of his enormous practice was one of Adam's chief professional rivals.

The end of the first quarter of the century saw the rise of Bath, with its squares, terraces and crescents in the fine Bath stone. The square was originally a French invention. The layout of Bath is associated with John Wood the Elder (1704–54) and his son John Wood the Younger (1728–81). The senior Wood was the son of a builder who worked for some years in London and Yorkshire before returning to Bath in 1727, where he laid out Queen Square, North and South Parades, and the Circus, which was completed by his son. The son designed the New Assembly Rooms (1769–71), the Old Royal Baths (1773–7) and Lansdowne Crescent. The well-known Pulteney Bridge (1769–1774), a favourite subject of Richard Sickert, is one of Robert Adam's most satisfactory projects.

Carr of York (1723–1807) is another provincial name of great merit. His Royal Crescent at Buxton derives from Bath, but his best known work is probably Harewood House, home of the Princess Royal, just outside Leeds. Carr was twice Lord Mayor of York, and enjoyed a very considerable practice that produced many fine country houses in Yorkshire, Westmorland and Notting-

Bridge at Shrewsbury, 1774

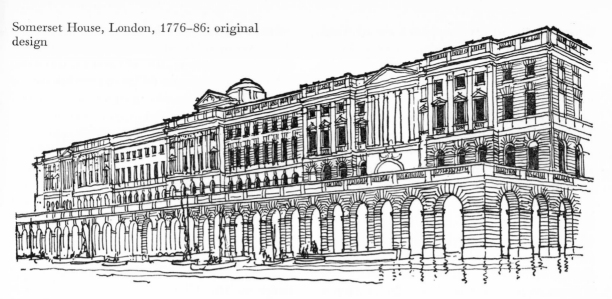

Somerset House, London, 1776–86: original design

hamshire, the stables at Wentworth Wood-house, the Assize Court at York, and Town Halls at Newark and Chesterfield. He designed many of the town houses of the northern towns in a period when county families would spend the winter in the local county town with its more sociable atmosphere, since the family residence on the remote Yorkshire moors might be cut off for weeks at a time by impassable roads or by snow. He left a fortune of £150,000.

James Paine is another provincial architect who designed with great fluency. Little is known of his early life, but at nineteen he was entrusted with the building of Nostell Priory, in the West Riding of Yorkshire. Paine rapidly became the rival of Sir Robert Taylor, both men conducting huge practices until they encountered Adam, Chambers and Wyatt. In an age of fine bridge building, he designed the bridges at Richmond, Chertsey, Walton and Kew, and the stables and bridge at Chatsworth (1758–62), the central block of Kedleston Hall, Derby (1757–61) and Brocket Hall in Hertfordshire (1760–70). Nostell was later added to by Adam but retains some of Paine's Baroque stucco frames.

Another typical bridge of this period, with reminiscences of Venice in its detail, is at Shrewsbury.

George Dance the Younger (1741–1825) left one masterpiece in London, Old Newgate Prison (1770–8), which was inspired by the Carceri, the fantastic series of prison drawings by Piranesi, the great Roman draughtsman. Dance had lived many years in Rome, and could well have known the sullen genius who sold his engravings in hundreds to the rich tourists who thronged the city.

The Palladian era in England ended with Sir William Chambers (1723–96), the son of a Scottish merchant in business at Gothenburg in Sweden. His considerable knowledge of the East was gained through entering the service of the Swedish East India Company, visiting Bengal and China, and studying architecture in Italy for five years, where he sketched with prolific ease, producing his first book, *Designs of Chinese Buildings, Furniture, Dresses, etc.* in 1757. His masterpiece is Somerset House, which originally, before the construction of the Thames Embankment, rose straight from the river and to which the barges tied up. We can now only imagine the original effect of the fine, long

139

façade with its three great water-gates lapped by the restless tide, as splendid, in its English way, as anything in Venice, and so courteous, in its restraint, towards the climacteric of St. Paul's.

In Canton he drew the gardens and pagodas of the mandarins, and in Paris he studied under Clérisseau, the great architectural draughtsman. His introduction to the Prince of Wales (afterwards George III) by Lord Bute led to the Pagoda and Orangery at Kew Gardens, which he laid out, together with sundry 'Classical' temples. His other masterpiece is the Casino at Marino, at Clontarf near Dublin, which is beyond the horizons of our survey, and he built the stables at Harewood for Lord Lascelles in 1755.

The sudden craze for landscape gardening in the later decades of the eighteenth century well illustrated the change in the tide of taste and feeling. The preference for the element of surprise over that of expectation was the reason for abandoning the formal garden, with its elaborate geometrical parterres, its lines of pleached elms and limes and its vistas of clipped yews in tubs.

The classic school of gardening, which had descended through Le Nôtre and Pliny, regarded the garden as the continuation and reflection of the architecture of the house. Le Nôtre with his superb designs provided a setting which enhanced the grandeur of the building. The elements of the whole composition were order, symmetry and balance in a geometrical pattern. Nothing was permitted which would destroy the feeling of disciplined repose.

The reaction was inevitable. John Evelyn, in 1679, saw with delight the designs at Cliveden carried out by William Wise for the Duke of Buckingham: grottoes and unexpected vistas made charming surprises; the whole layout formed an unexpected pleasure.

The fashion for the conventional spread to all classes with the result that the reaction against it became a matter of snobbery. Great landowners could no longer tolerate a garden layout that was shared by every London suburb. Moreover, the landscapes of Claude, Poussin, Salvator Rosa and the romantic painters were bought in Rome and found their way to the walls of many of the great English houses. The picturesque became fashionable and William Kent, the arbiter of architectural taste in the first half of the century, encouraged the tendency.

The finest example of English landscape gardening is at Stourhead in Wiltshire, the home of the Hoare banking family, who financed Oliver Cromwell. It was completed in 1772. Capability Brown and his son-in-law Henry Holland, together with Humphrey Repton, created the English park, probably the greatest English contribution to the arts. The cry was 'Back to nature', and the dislike of correctness extended from garden design and interior decoration to taste, to morals, and to behaviour. The reaction lead inevitably to the early stages of the romantic movement.

The latter half of the eighteenth century, known as the Adam Period, takes its name from the celebrated family of Scottish architects who, more than any others, cast their influence on the architecture and town planning of the period.

The father of the famous Adam brothers was an Edinburgh architect of means with an estate at Blair-Adam in Fifeshire, and a loyal supporter of the Hanoverian government. Most of the Scottish nobility were numbered among his clients, so that he was able to leave a flourishing architectural business to his four sons, who inherited also his shrewd business acumen.

Several bundles of letters, written by Robert and James Adam from Italy, recently discovered among Scottish family papers, throw an interesting light on the position of the architect in eighteenth-century England, and the methods of gaining patrons and commissions.

Robert Adam had two ambitions: to have a great career in architecture and to make a social and financial success of it.

The Grand Tour was the first necessity, to travel in Italy and study the great buildings of Rome and there to meet the young aristocrats who would provide him with commissions. He took a bold decision. From early work at Fort George, near Inverness, and from his father's estate he had amassed a fortune of £5,000, and with this extremely comfortable sum, worth at least ten times the amount today, he intended to keep himself for several years, living and travelling in affluent style. Only thus could he meet and mingle on equal terms with the young peers who were completing their education in Italy. He accordingly went abroad in 1750.

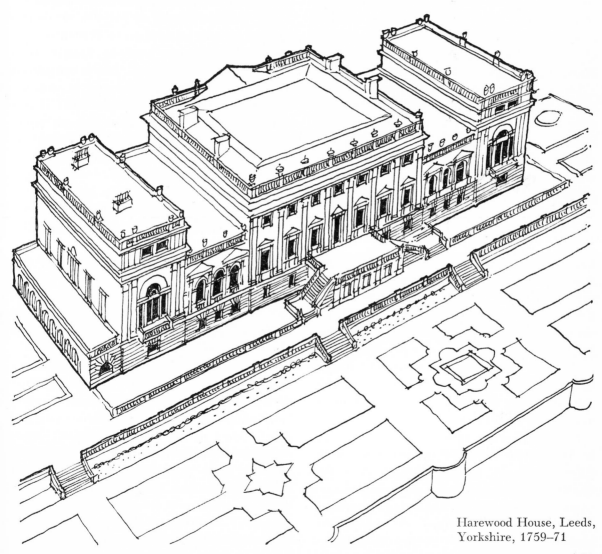

Harewood House, Leeds, Yorkshire, 1759–71

In Rome he shared expensive rooms with the Hon. Charles Hope, kept a carriage and valet and posed as an amateur of architecture, employing his own architects and draughtsmen. As a practising architect he would have been relegated to the level of the tradesmen and itinerant artists, which would in no way have suited his intentions. 'If I am known in Rome to be an architect, if I am seen drawing with a pencil in my hand, I cannot enter into genteel company.' [1]

Some writers maintain that Adam learnt his neo-Classicism from Clérisseau who, when Adam met him in Florence in February 1755, was without employment, having fallen out with the French Academy, where he had worked under a scholarship from 1749 to 1754. Adam retained his services for £100 a year, for which Clérisseau taught him perspective and drawing and acted as secretary to James Adam. Together they admired the 'antique incrustations' of Florence and Pisa, and visited the ruins of Herculaneum and the paintings on stucco of the seaside villas which had been overwhelmed and buried seventeen hundred years before in the cataclysmic eruption of Vesuvius.

Whilst in Rome in 1756, the Seven Years War with France broke out, which made Adam's return by land or sea a matter of some hazard, although it does not appear to have interfered with or caused any interruption of his studies, for, together with Giovanni Battista Piranesi, the famous engraver, he explored Rome, measuring and sketching the ancient monuments. It may have been Piranesi, too, who persuaded Adam to carry out his survey of the Palace of Diocletian at Spalato on the Dalmatian coast, in company with Clérisseau and two assistant draughtsmen.

The party sailed from Venice in July 1757 to Spalato, then under Venetian control, and

[1] *Robert Adam and his Circle* by John Fleming.

although at first they were suspected of spying out the fortifications under the pretence of sketching, their studies were allowed to proceed and the drawings of the great ruined Roman palace on the Yugoslav coast, which had such an effect on Adam's reputation, were completed.

On his return, already famous, to London, Robert Adam entered Parliament as member for Kinross-shire. His friendship with the Earl of Bute secured him the appointment, with William Chambers, as one of the Joint Architects of His Majesty's Works.

Adam was now well launched on his career with his brothers, and it was only a matter of time before they included among their clients the King and Queen, Augusta, Princess of Wales, William, Duke of Cumberland and many of the wealthier aristocrats. Their success was such that they even displaced architects who were actually at work on some of the larger mansions. At Croome Court, the Earl of Coventry dismissed Capability Brown in their favour, James Paine was suspended at Kedleston, and at Harewood House, which had been commenced by Carr of York, Lord Harewood persuaded the brothers to finish the great house.

The two masterpieces of Robert Adam, Kedleston and Syon, may be examined in detail, for these mansions are foremost in the architecture of the eighteenth century.

At Kedleston, Adam was called in after the building was begun, so that only the south front can be attributed to him with any certainty. The north portico can with confidence be placed to the credit of Paine, although it is as cold as his portico at Nostell. But the culmination at Kedleston is the great hall, which, with its twenty fluted columns of Derbyshire alabaster, is Roman in grandeur. The building, in common with many other great country houses of the eighteenth

Kedleston Hall, Derbyshire, 1757–70: south block

century in their adapted Palladian style, suffers by reason of its enormous scale and the difficulty of heating it adequately. The fireplaces of Derbyshire steel are, however, among the great technical achievements of the century.

Syon House at Brentford, still in the private possession of the Dukes of Northumberland, with its gardens running down to the Thames, is one of the most magnificent houses in Europe, although the exterior is plain and unassuming. The entrance hall in itself is superb and most elegant in a coldly classical way, but the anteroom leading out of it is in gorgeous contrast and beyond all praise. The twelve marble columns of *verde antique*, dredged from the Tiber by Sir Hugh Smithson, first Duke of Northumberland, with their gilded Ionic capitals and neckings, the entablature above of gold on blue, and the yellow and red and blue of the scagliola floor, form a picture that for sheer splendour is unsurpassed in England. The Dukes of Northumberland lived in tremendous style with their Swiss porters and their Northumbrian bagpipers, and even now, without the myriad servants and the panoply, the great house reflects the power and the prestige of this aristocratic family.

The dining room is in the usual Adam

manner, white and gold, but the red drawing room is a wealth of rich colour, the walls hung with a plum-red silk, woven at Spitalfields, and the carved ceiling, patterned in little diamonds and octagons, painted by Angelica Kauffmann. The doors in mahogany with gilded panels and the entablatures of gold on cream are as fine as anything in England. Syon House is open to the public at certain specified times, and forms in itself a world of enchantment, which judging from the comparatively small number of visitors, is still not sufficiently known or appreciated.

From Syon to Osterley, the residence of the Earls of Jersey, is a matter of only a few miles. Osterley cannot compare with Syon either in fantasy or imagination, but the furniture, and in particular the great state bed by Robert Adam, is very wonderful, showing, with the Doric orangery and the semi-circular conservatory, the inventiveness of his lively mind. Adam's weakness for over-decoration may be criticised here, for so covered are the walls with detail that it is impossible to hang a picture except in certain reserved places, and pictures were a very essential feature in the eighteenth-century interior.

Kenwood House, at Highgate in London, has now been presented to the nation by the Guinness family and is in the care of the London County Council. Its library, in pink and gold, with its curved and painted ceiling, is one of the finest rooms in England, and the mansion houses a small but splendid collection of paintings, among which is one of Rembrandt's most revealing self-portraits. The house, a less spectacular example of domestic architecture, gains in comfort by its lack of grandiose scale.

Robert Adam was the first architect to realise that the fittings and furniture of a house must bear a close relationship to the building which houses them, and that all should conform to a general scheme. He therefore set himself to design not only the furniture and carpets, but the upholstery, mirrors, fanlights, fireplaces, doors and doorways, and at Harewood House, near Leeds, he designed the window pelmets and valances, carved by Thomas Chippendale for the magnificent gallery, which were tinted blue to tone with the curtains. Some of the Reynolds' portraits too have Adam frames, and the ceiling was carried out to Adam's design.

In London the four brothers, with their driving sense of business, acquired the site of Durham House south of the Strand, bordering the Thames, which in those days was very inadequately banked in. It was an expensive enterprise, as the terraces they designed had to be supported by vaults and arches with all the necessary and costly foundation work, and from the start the brothers found themselves in financial trouble. The Government failed to use the vaults for storage, which would have helped to pay for their construction, and in order to raise money the brothers were forced to organise a State lottery, which barely paid their expenses. However, once completed, the Adelphi Terrace became one of the most fashionable residential quarters of London. The whole scheme was demolished many years before the war but the Society of Arts in John Adam Street still remains, with its fine doorways, fanlights and mantelpieces.

The houses in Portland Place and Mansfield Street, another speculative enterprise, were built for sale. Fitzroy Square, in which two blocks by the Adam brothers still remain, is reminiscent of their squares in the Scottish capital.

Two other country houses by Adam well worth examination are Nostell Priory, Wakefield, and Newby Hall, Ripon. At Nostell,

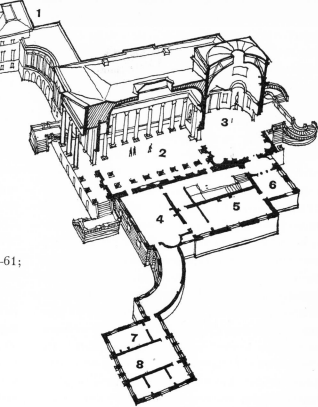

Kedleston Hall, Derbyshire: cross section.
Architects:
James Paine and Matthew Brettingham, 1757–61;
Robert and James Adam, 1765–70

1 Private wing
2 Hall
3 Saloon
4 Dining room
5 Bedroom
6 Anteroom
7 Laundry
8 Kitchen

James Paine had designed in 1735 a somewhat cold rectangular building ornamented by a heavy pediment on engaged columns. Robert Adam added a north wing some forty years later, a complete entity in itself with well-balanced projecting portico, Ionic pilasters and columns. Its tapestry room has a ceiling contrived out of an eight-pointed star. The saloon ceiling is decorated with pink, green and white.

Newby Hall has a sculpture gallery which houses a fine collection of Roman marbles and sculpture, but the most attractive room in the house is the drawing room, with its Boucher tapestries matched by the needlework sofas and chairs. The ceiling is lovely and unobtrusive, and the Adam carpet is in green, pink and brown on a cream ground.

In such an age of taste and elegance it is not surprising that Adam acquired a vogue without parallel. In his lively and inventive planning he was far superior to his predecessors, and his façades were so diverse and varied that no two are alike.

The Admiralty Screen (1760) is one of Adam's earliest works. Number 20 Portman Square (1775–7) and 20 St. James's Square are among his town houses. Lansdowne House in Berkeley Square was demolished many years before the last war, and other of his country mansions have been altered or demolished. Luton Hoo, home of the Wernhers, has been remodelled, and a wing of Bowood has been demolished. (Some of its ceilings by Kauffmann, and many of its elegant mahogany doors, have been incorporated into the Committee Room of the new Lloyds building in the City of London.)

At Stowe House, Buckinghamshire, the south front was remodelled from designs by Robert Adam, as was the estate where Capability Brown first developed his landscape art. The grounds of Stowe are rich in garden temples and other ornamental buildings by Vanbrugh, Gibbs, William Kent and Giacomo Leoni, and indeed features such as bridges, arches, grottoes and the like were normal embellishments in grounds of any size.

The brothers became associated in the 1770's and 80's with the development of Bath, and the Bathwick estate on the other side of the Avon from the main town. The owner of the estate, Sir William Johnstone-Pulteney, realised that its value would be greatly increased by the construction of a bridge between it and the town, and the project was carried out in 1770 to the designs of Robert Adam, who also prepared at least three plans for the estate, which it was proposed to develop on definite instead of haphazard lines.

The quiet and peace of Bath and the rest of England was not shared by the more volatile race on the other side of the Channel, for it was 1789, and on 14th July the Bastille was stormed by the Paris mob, while the Adam brothers in London were peacefully engaged on a scheme for the Haymarket Opera House. Their designs for Edinburgh University and mansions for the Scottish aristocracy are outside the scope of this book, and Robert Adam now had only three years of life before him. The obituary in the *Gentleman's Magazine* sums up his great contribution to English architecture. '. . . Mr. Adam produced a total change in the architecture of this country; and his fertile genius in elegant ornaments was not confined to the decoration of buildings, but has been diffused in almost every branch of manufacture.'

Robert Adam's contemporaries and rivals were no architectural nonentities, for in Wyatt and Holland were two of the most considerable of the eighteenth-century designers, and their work is preferred by some as more human and more dramatic than Adam's cold elegance.

Henry Holland (1745–1806) commenced as an apprentice in his father's building business, and eventually became a partner of Capability Brown, whose daughter he married. He was a consummate technician, a bold and intellectual designer; we have only to see the Subscription Room at Brooks's Club to assess his enormous competence.

Holland is, unfortunately, best known by his buildings which have now disappeared, of which by far the most important was Carlton House, which he designed for the Prince of Wales, later George IV, the most extravagant royal patron of the Arts since Charles I. It is possible to see it now only in the plates of Pyne's *Royal Residences*, for it was demolished in 1827–8. His East India House, too, has gone completely, with his Drury Lane Theatre, and his houses are not outstanding, although the porticoes of Broadlands, near Romsey, home of the Mountbattens, are admirable, and the interior is simple and elegant. Althorp, in Northamptonshire, is more successful in its interior, and the decorations show a strong French influence.

The Whitbread home, at Southill in Bedford, shows Holland at his most tasteful, and so also does Woburn, which he remodelled for the Duke of Bedford. Avenue House, Ampthill, which belongs to Sir Albert Richardson, is a successful example of his smaller houses, with its fine, late classic door and pillared porch.

Holland was the principal architect of Carlton House until his death in 1806, nearly a year after Trafalgar, when the building was carried on and completed by

Wyatt and Nash. Buckingham Palace was begun after its demolition.

Carlton House was the outstanding monument of the Regency period, for it represented all that was best in design and craftsmanship in this unique era. It was entered from Pall Mall under an Ionic screen, a long one-storey building with a great Corinthian portico, and a two-storey elevation facing St. James's Park. The entrance hall, which was entirely by Holland, had columns of yellow Siena marble with bronze capitals and bases, framing the four doorways, and the walls were stained green. Bronze busts and vases topped the heavy entablatures, the ceiling was coffered, and furniture was of mahogany and gilt to Holland's design.

From the entrance hall rose the grand staircase, opening on to an anteroom and then to the crimson drawing room, which was hung from top to bottom with crimson satin damask with gold fringes. This room, the heavy gilt furniture of which is now in Buckingham Palace, with its white and gold ceiling, its carpet of light blue velvet with the star and insignia of the Garter in the middle, its mantelpiece of black marble and the huge brass fender, may have been by Nash. Brilliant cut-glass chandeliers, comparable or superior even to those of the great palaces of Prague and Vienna, hung from the ceiling and completed the gorgeous scene.

Henry Holland's masterpiece, however, was the circular drawing room, with its great circle of porphyry painted columns matching the carpet, while the ceiling was painted to represent the sky, which must have given an illusion of unlimited space, in the Baroque tradition. Curtains and hangings were blue and silver, doors and cornice were lavender, with gilded ornament and arabesques, and a huge chandelier hung centrally from the 'sky' was reflected to infinity in the great mirrors.

The state apartments on the ground floor were not so successful, but they were improved by Nash and Wyatt. The golden drawing room, with fluted Corinthian columns, was entirely gilded, and the extraordinary dining room, with its columns and capitals of ostrich feathers, was designed in the Gothic manner and gave on to the conservatory, another Gothic fantasy with a cast-iron fan-vaulted ceiling.

James Wyatt (1746–1813) was one of Robert Adam's chief rivals, and started his training as a protégé of Lord Bagot, Ambassador to the Vatican, staying four years in Rome and two more in Venice, painting in the manner of Pannini. Returning to London at the age of twenty-five he started practice in spectacular manner by designing the Pantheon in Oxford Street, which immediately became the architectural sensation of London. It was opened in 1772 for concerts and masquerades and included a main hall under the cupola, a tea room below it of similar size and a suite of fourteen rooms. It remained a place of entertainment for another twenty years, when it was demolished by fire.

Heaton Hall, which he rebuilt for Lord Grey de Wilton, is one of his most important classic houses situated only four miles from the centre of Manchester. It contains superb mahogany doors, but incredibly, the Corporation of Manchester, when they bought the great house, sold off some of the specially designed furniture.

Heveningham Hall, in Suffolk, his most important classic house, has a superb hall with no less than eight magnificent mahogany doors and scagliola pillars in imitation yellow Siena marble. Walls and ceilings are painted in green with white details, and the floor is of stone with inlays of red marble and black marble lines. The staircase is less grand than that of Heaton Hall, the saloon

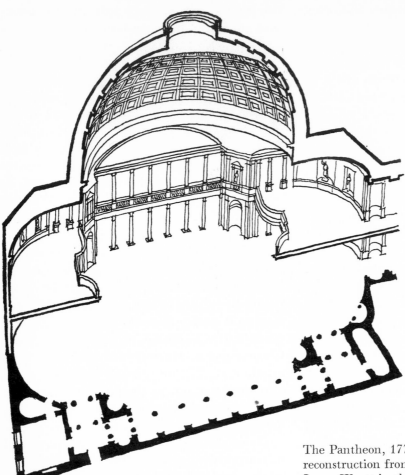

The Pantheon, 1772, burnt down 1792: reconstruction from the original drawings by James Wyatt in the Soane Museum

is painted entirely by Biagio Rebecca, the Italian decorator, and the dining room is one of the most enchanting rooms of the eighteenth century and worthy of more detailed description. The double mahogany doorway, with its painted lunette by Rebecca, is a most sumptuous piece of craftsmanship. The decoration of the room has been conceived as a whole. On either side of the door Wyatt's candelabrae stand delicately poised in oblong niches, which are surmounted by painted roundels in square frames. Over the mantelpiece is a great oval painting by Rebecca which leads the eye upward to the delicate stucco of the ceiling.

The fantastic Pavilion at Brighton, seaside pleasure dome of the Prince Regent, was designed by John Nash (1752–1835), who drew his inspiration from Sezincote, in Gloucestershire, built by Samuel Pepys Cockerell for his brother, who had done well in the East India Company. Humphrey Repton had designed the gardens at Sezincote and sent drawings and designs in this 'Hindu' style to the Prince Regent, all to no purpose, for Nash was appointed in 1815. Here again the great chandeliers catch the eye, in particular in the great Banqueting Room, lit by enormous candelabrae standing on the floor.

148

John Nash was a picturesque character who started as a speculative builder after a brief training under Sir Robert Taylor, and became the leading figure in the Regency period. After building in various parts of Wales he came to London to partner Humphrey Repton, the landscape architect. Together they built or altered a number of important houses, among them Sundridge Park in Kent (1799) and a mock-mediaeval house for his own use at East Cowes Castle, Isle of Wight (1789). But it was through his attractive wife, whom he married in the same year, that he came to the notice of the Prince of Wales and built for him the Royal Lodge in Windsor Park, remodelled Carlton House and built the Pavilion at Brighton.

Nash's stucco architecture of Carlton House Terrace and Regent's Park is peculiarly adapted to the London weather. In 1806, through his appointment to a minor post under the Commissioners of Woods and Forests, he laid out Marylebone Park, now Regent's Park, together with Regent Street, Carlton House Terrace and the adjoining streets. All Souls', Langham Place, is probably his best-known church, and his cottages could form a subject in themselves. We can but deplore the passing of his quadrant in Regent Street, for the buildings that have taken its place add little to our enjoyment.

All that we now have left of Nash in London are the houses of Carlton House Terrace and Regent's Park, among the latter some of the most interesting classical compositions of the period, where Cumberland Terrace, for instance, shows a picturesque variety of form and outline that is unsurpassed in the town planning schemes of this era. He was a brilliant if somewhat superficial designer, using a hard plaster stucco with impressive effect on a cheap brick at relatively low cost.

The development of trade with China in the eighteenth century saw the introduction of Chinese decoration, which gave a touch of the fantastic to designs for wallpapers, furniture and even buildings to which the French gave the term 'chinoiserie'. Chinese porcelain, lacquer and silks had reached this country as far back as the sixteenth century but it was not until later in the seventeenth century that Chinese influence made itself felt in the scenes and landscapes painted and lacquered in gold, scarlet, green and black on William and Mary furniture.

Sir William Chambers, Architect and Surveyor-General to George III, encouraged the style in his book *Designs of Chinese Buildings, Furniture, etc.* which he published in 1757. He had travelled to the Far East as a young man and had sketched and painted the buildings of Peking and other Chinese ports. He followed this book with another in 1772 on oriental gardening, and all over England, in the gardens and parks of prosperous citizens, appeared Chinese bridges and summer houses.

There is a Chinese room at Mawley Hall in Shropshire, and another at Badminton, whose bed, by Thomas Chippendale the famous furniture designer, is now in the Victoria and Albert Museum.

There is a complete Chinese dairy at Woburn, and more Chinese wallpaper, on a blue ground, at Moor Park, Cobham, Bowood and Nostell. At Claydon, in Buckinghamshire, there is a complete Chinese room, where the doorways are decorated with Chinese masks and faces, and the chimneypiece is another fantasy of Rococo and Chinoiserie. But the most remarkable feature is the alcove, which takes up almost one side of the room. The credit for Claydon's Chinoiserie must go to a certain Mr. Lightfoot, a carpenter contractor whose other work is unknown and whose workshops

149

produced the fascinating decoration inside the great house.

The Royal Pavilion at Brighton was decorated and furnished in the Chinese taste with Chinese wallpapers and lacquer cabinets and bamboo chairs, stools and sofas, made in China about 1800 for the European market. Later, when the Pavilion was enlarged in 1815, the interior was decorated with huge Chinese scenes in red, yellow and gold, with carved dragons and chandeliers in the form of lotus flowers.

Sir John Soane (1753–1837) is the last of the Neo-Classical architects, a title that might be ascribed to Sir Charles Barry later in the nineteenth century, were he not best known by his Gothic architecture in the Houses of Parliament. Soane was the son of a bricklayer who trained with George Dance the Younger, and after a period of travel in Italy set up practice in London and married the daughter of a wealthy builder. Through the influence of William Pitt he was appointed architect to the Bank of England, which he rebuilt between 1788 and 1833, was responsible to the Board of Works for the Palaces at Whitehall, Westminster and Hampton Court, built up a considerable private practice and was Professor of Architecture at the Royal Academy from 1806 to his death. With all this he was still a meticulous seeker after perfection, and his system of grooves and panels of incised and delicate moulding give the most charming results. His screen at the Bank was based on his version of the Roman Order of the Temple of Vesta at Tivoli, and his town house in Lincoln's Inn Fields, now the Soane Museum, contains a most interesting collection of pictures and *objets d'art* in a highly oriental setting. One of his best and most typical buildings was the Mausoleum and Picture Gallery at Dulwich (destroyed by German action in the Second World War),

built to house a collection of pictures and the remains of Sir Francis Bourgeois. Soane's country house, Pitzhanger Manor, at Ealing, now the public library, recalls Adam's garden front at Kedleston.

Meanwhile the Romantic tradition still persisted strongly in England. In J. and J. C. Buckler's *Views of Eaton Hall* can be seen the great sham Gothic pile that was built by William Porden for the first Marquess Grosvenor, one of the richest men in England. In its original state it must have been a most impressive place, with its huge fan-vaulted drawing room and its romantic silhouette, but later in the nineteenth century it was rebuilt by Alfred Waterhouse in a most lavish Gothic manner that bore no comparison in delicacy or interest with the earlier version, whose destruction deprived us of one of the most fascinating examples of Gothic revival in this country.

The first third of the nineteenth century was one of our most flourishing periods in the arts: in painting there were Sir Thomas Lawrence, J. M. W. Turner and Constable; in poetry Byron, Keats and Shelley. There were, however, no architects of the first order, although some of the most interesting developments in English towns belong to this era. At Cheltenham John Buonarroti Papworth laid out the Montpellier estate, with its charming caryatids in white stucco between the shops in Montpellier Walk. This same white stucco decoration is typical of many of our seaside towns, Weymouth, Scarborough, Bridport, Hove and Hastings among them, which express the domestic requirements of the time better, perhaps, than any other element of the architectural scene. Papworth also helped in the interior decoration of Boodle's Club, in the publisher Ackermann's premises in the Strand, and at Brockwell Park at Dulwich.

Two great and enlightened builders dominated the house-building programme at this time. James Burton worked with his son Decimus, who, apparently, never studied classical architecture at first hand in Italy or Greece until late in life. They built an estate in Bloomsbury (where their name is still commemorated by Burton Street), together with Cornwall Terrace in Regent's Park and the fine screen (1825) at Hyde Park Corner, as well as the various lodges in the Park, of which the villa illustrated is typical. The two best known buildings in London by Decimus Burton are Charing Cross Hospital and the Athenaeum Club.

Thomas Cubitt's fame is perpetuated by the layout of Pimlico and Belgravia, with George Basevi's scheme for Belgrave Square as the architectural climacteric. With its stucco Corinthian orders and fine proportions it is now the centre of the social and diplomatic life of the capital and amply does it fulfil its function. Apart from the Fitzwilliam Museum at Cambridge, he collaborated with Sydney Smirke at the Conservative Club in St. James's Street, whose fine staircase has now, unfortunately, been demolished in order to extend the Club.

Many of the imposing squares and terraces of Brighton were laid out at this time by the architects Wilds and Busby; at Hove, Decimus Burton designed Adelaide Crescent and the impressive Brunswick Terrace and Square. Kemp Town is a most picturesque quarter of the town, with its delicate cast iron and its copper hoods.

In London the older clubs, Brooks's, Boodle's and White's, grew out of coffee houses, while the Italian Renaissance palace was the model for the Travellers', founded by Castlereagh, the Reform, and other later clubs. Crockford's and the Oriental were built (1826–77) by Benjamin Dean Wyatt, eldest son of James Wyatt, and the Senior United Services Club was built by Nash in

Villa in Regent's Park, 1820

1827 in Waterloo Place on a site that had been cleared by the demolition of Carlton House. Burton, when he designed the Athenaeum Club opposite, was only in his twenties, but its fine Grecian design shows no sign of immaturity, and it remains to this day as the most successful and dignified club building in the country.

The Pandolfini Palace in Florence, by Raphael, is probably the model for Barry's Travellers' Club, and Sangallo's Farnese Palace in Rome, now the French Embassy, gave the same architect the inspiration for the Reform Club next door.

William Wilkins (1778–1839) is one of the last of the 'Grecian' architects, very versatile but sometimes variable, although a Sixth Wrangler and a Fellow of Caius, who commenced by designing Grange Park in Hampshire in 1810 in the Greek Doric manner. His least successful work is the National Gallery in Trafalgar Square with its poor, coarse Corinthian columns that had come from Carlton House and had to be incorporated in the building. The result in no way dominates the square, and since the emphasis is rather with St. Martin-in-the-Fields, there is a somewhat unbalanced feeling where the effect should be the epitome of classical planning.

Wilkins could not design a dome. That on

151

the National Gallery is meagre and weak, and although at University College in Gower Street he designed one of the finest porticoes in the country, the effect is spoiled by the low drum of the dome. The quadrangle in front of it, although unfinished, is most impressive with its fine trees, although so obviously unappreciated by the University authorities that they have done nothing to prevent the spoliation of its fine lawns by the erection of some hideous and quite inexcusable prefabricated concrete buildings.

Temperamental in character and unpredictable in outlook, Wilkins' work at Downing College is praiseworthy if on a somewhat small scale. His St. George's Hospital at Hyde Park Corner is, however, one of the dullest buildings in London.

Castle Howard, 1702–14. The culmination of the Baroque in England

5

The Age of Revivals 1830—1939

The introduction of iron into the framework of buildings was an event of tremendous importance not at first fully appreciated. Architecture as a whole developed into a battle between a revival of the Gothic and the Classic, and building became mainly a matter of copying traditional styles. A century of great wealth saw the building of many large mansions in town and country. In London there were Bridgewater House, St. James's (1847–57), Alford House (1872) and Dorchester House (1851). In the country Harlaxton Hall, Lincolnshire (1834–55) and Scotney Castle, Kent (1837–40), High-clere Castle, Hampshire (1842–4), Cliveden in Buckinghamshire (1849–51) and Scarisbrick in Lancashire (1837–52) were typical.

Many churches were built mainly in the revived Gothic manner in London, All Saints, Margaret Street (1849–59), St. Giles, Camberwell Church Street (1842–4), an exception being Westminster Roman Catholic Cathedral (1895–1903) in the Byzantine style. The Gothic Liverpool Cathedral was commenced in 1903 and Truro Cathedral in 1880. Public buildings include the Travellers' Club, Pall Mall (1829–31), the Reform Club next to it (1838–40), the Fitz-William Museum, Cambridge (1837–47), the Houses of Parliament (1840–60), the Ashmolean Museum, Oxford (1841–5), St. George's Hall, Liverpool (1842–54), the University Museum, Oxford (1855–9), the Foreign Office (1860–75), the Albert Memorial (1863–72), the Natural History Museum, London (1879–80), the Law Courts (1874–82), New Scotland Yard (1887–1888), County Hall, London (1912–22), and the Town Hall (1868–77) and Rylands Library (1890–9) in Manchester. Many of the greater town halls are of this period, such as Colchester (1898–1902), Norwich (1938), Cardiff Civic Centre (1897–1927) and Swansea (1930–4).

The invention of the steam engine and the development of the railways saw the building of the great railway termini at Euston (1846–9), St. Pancras (1866–71), King's Cross (1851–2) and Paddington (1852–4) and the introduction of iron built the Crystal Palace (1850–1) and the Conservatory at Chatsworth (1836–40), the Coal Exchange in Lower Thames Street, London (1846–9) and the Reading Room of the British Museum (1854–7), also, hotels such as the Ritz (1905–6) and the Piccadilly (1905–8) in London, and many of the great bank headquarters. But reaction is almost inevitable after a period in which development of a particular style has been carried to a point beyond which no advance is possible. This applies equally to social as well as to architectural history, and although the classical school never lost its influence throughout the nineteenth century the time had come for a change.

This change was fostered by an increasing inclination towards the romantic and the picturesque, inspired partly by the histori-cal novels of Scott, and occurred not only in England but in the other great English speaking nation across the Atlantic. In the United States, with its small population and unspoiled countryside, the creations of Andrew Jackson Downing and other architects arose along the Delaware valley, taking the form of castles and houses in the Gothic manner that harmonised naturally with the wild and often savage countryside.

What was the reason for this revival of the styles? The nineteenth century was an age of great discoveries, many of which were applied to the needs of everyday life. Science and increased knowledge were pressed into the service of humanity, and photography brought an awareness of art and architecture for the masses, while transport was revolutionised by steam. Coal in unlimited quantity provided the power to a country whose industry served the world and whose predominance in trade was not seriously challenged until the end of the century.

All this remarkable advance in knowledge,

Peckforton Castle, Cheshire, 1846–50: example of the mediaeval romantic revival by Anthony Salvin

however, was applied in no instance to the arts. In painting, revival again was the order of the day, and young painters went back to the earlier classical schools in Italy for their inspiration. The reason would appear to lie in the Victorian temperament, on which the writings of Ruskin had a tremendous impact. It was an essentially moral age, somewhat dull, in direct contrast to the Georgian era, which was essentially latitudinarian and irreligious. Ruskin, a great moralist, believed profoundly that ugliness was sin, although he was certainly responsible for much that is ugly in art, and he saw in Gothic architecture the expression of Christianity at its noblest, in direct opposition to the Classical, the outcome of a pagan civilisation; moreover, he believed the classical Renaissance to be an expression of Popery in its worst possible form.

He had a passionate disgust of the horrors of rampant industrialism, and the evils of poor housing and overcrowding associated with it. His inherited wealth provided the means for the travels which brought him probably his greatest happiness, but he was no narrow archaeologist. Realising that honesty and integrity were the basis of all good architecture he appreciated that a modern building could never be an honest creation and at the same time a mere copy of something that had gone before, however meritorious. He realised that a new world demanded a new style, and here he differed from A. W. N. Pugin with his more limited horizons and his preoccupation with the mediaeval.

This new style, in his imagination, must be as honest in its construction as the Gothic, its ornament based on natural forms, its shape arising naturally from its function. His theories were sound enough and are in line with the best contemporary thought, but his outlook was limited by his ignor-

Plate glass Louis Quatorze built in Regent Street in the 1830's:
from Whittock's *Shopfronts of London*

ance of the possibilities of engineering and the new horizons to be opened up by new materials and new methods of using them.

Gilbert Scott designed the St. Pancras Hotel and station in the picturesque garb of the Victorian Gothic, and the Law Courts, by George Edmund Street, provided a most interesting contrast in silhouette in the London sky-line, but the search for the picturesque in both these buildings led to confusions in plan and a variety of conflicting interests in the elevations. The work by which Scott is unfortunately remembered best is his Albert Memorial, lavish in its decoration and overpowering in its sculpture, a monument to Victorian fashion and the futile search for Romantic exuberance.

There was a further danger in reviving the past. Once the principle was accepted there were no limits to the imitation of past glories. Marrett's *Descriptions de l'Egypte*

155

appeared after Napoleon's campaign in Egypt. Italian villa designs joined the Greek and Gothic forms as accepted models for country houses and may be seen to this day with their flat low-pitched roofs, projecting eaves, square campaniles and arcaded or colonnaded piazzas, looking completely alien to their surroundings.

The *New York Mirror* in its review of a periodical publication of home designs in America in the new romantic style (1846) could equally be applied to England:

'. . . These cottages have nothing to commend them but a picturesque profile . . . They are the most costly and least convenient houses that can be built . . . They are the imitations of the natural expression of an age of semi-civilisation and gross ignorance . . . It was quite pardonable in Horace Walpole and Sir Walter Scott to build gingerbread houses in imitation of robber barons and Bluebeard chieftains; they were poets and had written Gothic romances: they would fill their houses with rusty old armour, lances, drinking horns and mouldy tapestry, and they were surrounded by the memorials of the times they were idly trying to revive. But there can be nothing more grotesque, more absurd, or more affected, than for a quiet gentleman, who has made his fortune in the peaceful occupation of selling calicos, and who knows no more of the middle ages than they do of him, to erect for his family residence a gimcrack of a Gothic Castle . . . as though he anticipated an attack upon his roost from some *Front de Bœuf* in the neighbourhood.'

The crying of the critics of this period, that we were the heirs to all the ages, excused the further use of traditional styles. They pointed out that in the past Mesopotamia had borrowed from Egypt, Greece from both and Rome from Greece, but they failed to appreciate that great architecture arose from the successful solution of the problems of the times, using the best available methods of construction and the most suitable materials. The sudden access of wealth created a new class, restless, half-educated, eager to express their riches in the most expensive styles; eager also to learn, whether stumbling through the Roman forum or gliding softly through the silent canals of Venice, whether gazing awestruck at St. Mark's and the Library of Sansovino, or, in Ravenna, whispering beneath the mosaics of St. Vitale, or sending the echoes flying in the Baptistry of Pisa.

The wave of Romantic feeling leading to the revival of Gothic architecture had commenced much earlier. The old tradition of Gothic building had never completely disappeared and still continued in more remote parts of the country, but the new trend away from the Classical tradition was encouraged by the landscape architects—Capability Brown and later Humphrey Repton, whose designs for the immediate surroundings of great country houses were marked by their complete lack of formality. Wren had built his Tom Tower at Christ Church, Oxford, in the Gothic manner, and Hawksmoor in 1735 had added the Gothic towers to the West Front of Westminster Abbey. His other exercise in Gothic is, of course, the towers of All Souls' College, Oxford. In 1750 Horace Walpole embellished his cottage at Strawberry Hill with Gothic detail on the exterior, a Holbein chamber within, and a gallery with fan-vaulting. Beckford described it as a sort of Gothic mousetrap.

In the 1750's Henry Keene designed the Gothic church at Hartwell in Buckinghamshire, with its fan-vaulting, and Sanderson Miller may have been the designer of Shobdon Church in Herefordshire, of about the same date, but such churches were few.

Penrhyn Castle, 1827–40: the great hall, based on the style of Durham
Cathedral. Designed by Thomas Hopper, the castle was one of the first to apply
the Norman style to domestic architecture

The first practical exponent of the Gothic
revival was James Wyatt (1746–1813)
whose alterations and renovations at Salisbury Cathedral earned him an unenviable
reputation as 'The Destroyer'. His huge
houses at Ashridge and Fonthill Abbey
were built on a vast scale for two of the
richest men in England. We are told that at
Fonthill the coal was perfumed and carried
in gilded baskets, which may well be believed, as Beckford, the heir to the greatest
fortune in England, for whom the house
was built, was charming but capricious. His
first intention had been merely to erect a

folly in the form of a Gothic ruin, and from this developed the fantastic palace which, with its surrounding 12-foot wall, became a place of mystery and curiosity for miles around. The house measured no less than 312 feet by 250 feet, the tower at the crossing rising to 278 feet. The hall was 78 feet in height, higher than the nave of Salisbury Cathedral, with a vast flight of steps rising through a soaring Gothic arch to the saloon. The glass was covered with the armorial bearings of the noble families connected by marriage with the Beckfords. The other rooms, cloisters and corridors were detailed with the most lavish Gothic decorations, and housed a magnificent collection of pictures, furniture and *objets d'art*. The construction of the great tower, however, was in line with that of many of the early Gothic towers. The impatience of the owner forced the employment of some hundreds of workmen who operated day and night until the completion of the job, but supervision must have been faulty, and an essential part of the structure was omitted, with the result that the tower, which had already fallen once, crashed in a gale, bearing down with it a large part of the Abbey beneath. It was never repaired. It had been the wonder of Wiltshire and had cost in the region of £273,000.

Wyatt's other grand house, Ashridge, remained uncompleted at his death in 1813 in a carriage accident and was finished by his nephew, Jeffrey Wyatt, who carried on the Gothic tradition in his very extensive alterations to Windsor Castle, improving it immensely and with imagination in his heightening of the Norman Round Tower. The multiplicity of small and inconvenient rooms in the Castle gave way under his direction to an impressive and grand interior. It is to him, in addition to its magnificent position, that

Fonthill Abbey,
Wiltshire, 1796–9

the Castle owes its present stately, and on the whole most attractive appearance. It was the success of this great commission, and the pleasure it gave the sovereign, which brought him his knighthood and the change of name from Wyatt to the more romantic and historic name of Wyattville, which he assumed with the permission of the grateful monarch. In this amusing form of snobbery he was by no means alone. Wealthy merchants and rich coal-owners, in attaining knighthood or peerage, or even without a title of any sort, changed their names by licence to others of a mediaeval character, with no more pretensions to ancient lineage and feudal ancestry than Wyatt himself.

Both Wyatt and Wyattville were the more considerable figures of the Gothic revival, although the classic tradition showed through the Gothic veneer of their exteriors in the formality of their planning. The man who more than any other influenced the course of the battle between the Gothic and Classic styles was Charles Barry, whose early experiment in the Gothic manner at Todding-

ton Manor (1830) in Gloucestershire may be compared with his later achievement at Westminster.

On the 16th October 1834 a devastating fire destroyed the old Houses of Parliament and the following year saw the competition for the new buildings. The conditions laid down that the style was to be either Gothic or Elizabethan, so firm was the mediaeval tradition in the popular imagination. It was a courageous choice, for no secular building had yet been erected in the Gothic style. The main reason for the choice, however, was the fact that two most important parts of the building still remained. Westminster Hall and its magnificent timber roof had by some miracle escaped, and although in ruins, popular sentiment demanded the restoration of St. Stephen's Chapel. Obviously neither of these could have been incorporated in a classical design.

The competition was won by Sir Charles Barry (1795–1860) with the assistance of the younger Pugin (Augustus Welby Northmore, 1812–52), son of that Charles Augustus

159

Pugin (1762–1832) who had so stimulated the revived Gothic style with his publications on Gothic details. A. W. N. Pugin was a convert to Roman Catholicism. As with most converts, his zeal was deeply sincere almost to the point of fanaticism, and with Ruskin he saw in Gothic the true expression of Christianity, in whose great buildings he took a personal and particular interest. The younger Pugin, too, was one of many extremely brilliant and articulate writers who were able not only to interest the specialist but to move the population in general. He produced numerous books in which he upheld the ideals of Christian architecture and derided the Classic. There is, in fact, sufficient evidence to support the contention that the design of the new Houses of Parliament owed more to Pugin than to Barry, to whom the former had, however, sold his services and collaboration.

The new Houses of Parliament were certainly more classical than mediaeval in plan. On one occasion, when passing the buildings by river, Pugin had exclaimed to a friend: 'All Grecian, Sir; Tudor details on a classic body.' Barry could, of course, design with equal facility in the classical manner or in the mediaeval. The result of the competition set him firmly on his career, and he produced a brilliant design in the perpendicular Gothic manner. It has tremendous vitality. With its long low frontage to the Thames it has all the repose of a great work of art, and the contrast between the long river front and the height of the Victoria Tower and the tower of Big Ben is extraordinarily satisfying. The style was followed widely.

Barry's sons carried on his huge practice. Charles designed Burlington House, which contains the Royal Academy as well as many learned societies, and Edward designed Covent Garden Theatre and the additions to Wilkins' National Gallery. Another son, who became Sir John Wolfe Barry, was the engineer who designed Tower Bridge.

A. W. N. Pugin was barely twenty-five when he received the commission in 1832 to build Scarisbrick for the richest commoner in Lancashire, Charles Scarisbrick. The result was one of the most interesting buildings of the Gothic Revival in England, with its fantastic clock-tower based on that of Westminster. For John Talbot, 16th Earl of Shrewsbury and Waterford, he built 'the princely towers and enchanted gardens of Alton' in Staffordshire. The house is on an immense scale, the dining room copied from the Sainte Chapelle in Paris, and the entrance hall based on the nave of a cathedral. One huge room was built in the form of an octagonal chapter house with central clustered shafts from which sprang the stuccoed tracery of the roof.

Pugin's grateful client was an extremely wealthy Catholic who spent £20,000 a year on the building of churches, the total expenditure on charity and ecclesiastical building during his lifetime probably exceeding half a million pounds. He employed Pugin on the bulk of them. In all, this energetic architect erected over sixty-five churches in the United Kingdom, including Roman Catholic churches at Birmingham, Nottingham, Derby and Ramsgate, culminating in the fine Roman Catholic Cathedral of St. George in Southwark, which was burnt out in the last war and has now been rebuilt.

Pugin was the most brilliant and picturesque figure of the Gothic revival, with an unrivalled knowledge of mediaeval decorative detail, but his highly strung temperament and his intensely nervous energy drove him to insanity and death. In his writings he criticised the buildings of his day, contrasting them unfavourably with those of the Middle Ages, and through his

Harlaxton Hall, 1834–55: example of the Tudor Gothic revival by Anthony Salvin

books he influenced the popular taste for Gothic and attempted to revive the spirit of self-sacrifice and sincerity which produced the great Gothic cathedrals. Until fairly recently it has been fashionable to decry the Victorian era, but none can deny the integrity of the Victorian architectural conscience.

With Pugin there began the second phase of the Gothic revival, the period of Scott, Street, Waterhouse and Salvin. This is the period of calamity for many of our great cathedrals, whose 'restoration' at the hands of some of the less sensitive Gothic architects reached a point of despoliation that was achieved only by Oliver Cromwell and his iconoclasts.

And now, throughout the country, there arose a mass of secular buildings in the fashionable manner, designed by a host of ingenious, courageous and vigorous architects who lacked the one essential virtue of taste. Their powers of design were obscured nearly always by the most abominable materials in a terrifying range of colour, but William Butterfield (1814–1900), with his craze for black and yellow brickwork against a feverish red, surpassed them all in horror. His brickwork at Oxford clashes aggressively with the lovely old colleges although, mercifully, it is sited away from the centre of the city. He designed Keble College with assurance and aplomb, together with the unpleasant chapel at Balliol, and churches and cathedrals in England, Scotland, Australia, South Africa and India.

Fortunately not all the architects of this period followed the Butterfield tradition. One of the finest Gothic buildings in the country, St. Philip Neri, crowns the hilltop at Arundel, near the great castle. It is French in character, built with impressive height and a mass of flying buttresses. It was designed by Joseph Aloysius Hansom (1792–1870), a Catholic architect whose name is immortalised by his invention of 'the gondola of the London streets'—the hansom cab. He was the architect of the warehouses at St. Katherine's Docks (1850–1858), the Euston Station hotel (1836–9), the classical stone buildings in Lincoln's Inn (1835–42), and the Birmingham Town

Hall in the form of a Corinthian Roman temple.

William Burgess (1828–81) was a complete mediaevalist who designed in the early nineteenth-century French manner. In spite of his many large works he is best known as the architect of his own house in Melbury Road, Kensington, but he designed cathedrals at Cork, Brisbane and Lille, and was employed on the rebuilding of Cardiff Castle and at Worcester College, Oxford, as well as churches at Stoke Newington in London, Skelton and Studley Royal.

G. F. Bodley (1827–1907) is another whose churches are, on the whole, sensitive and free from the heaviness which marred much contemporary building. The chapel at Queens' College, Cambridge, the gateway at Magdalen and the tower over the Hall staircase at Christ Church, Oxford, are typically successful works. His competence was shared by J. L. Pearson (1817–97) the designer of Truro Cathedral.

Bodley was employed also on the restoration of Westminster Abbey and designed many London churches, including St. John in Red Lion Square with its chancel modelled on the cathedral of Gerona in Spain.

A typical town hall of the period is at Northampton, designed by E. W. Godwin, whose main claim to fame was his elopement with Ellen Terry after her child-marriage to G. F. Watts. John Raphael Brandon built the Catholic Apostolic Church in Gordon Square for a group of virtuous business men who expected the imminent ending of the world. It is one of the more successful large churches of this period, and has weathered to a pleasant texture that in no way detracts from the Early English style in which it is designed (1854).

R. C. Carpenter (1812–55) was the designer of two of the better known public schools, Lancing (1848) and Hurstpierpoint (1849), and cathedrals at Inverness, Jamaica and Ceylon. His restorations at Chichester Cathedral and Sherborne Abbey have mellowed with time, and are now almost indistinguishable from the original building.

The outstanding figure of the later Gothic Revival was Sir Gilbert Scott (1810–77), assured, successful, completely representative of the Victorian character in his business acumen and his somewhat smug morality. He was the first of the famous architectural dynasty and, as the son of a village clergyman, owed no artistic pretensions to his forebears. He commenced his career by winning the competition for the Martyrs' Memorial at Oxford in 1840, and followed it in sensational manner by winning the great international competition for St. Nicholas Church in Hamburg, which launched him upon his enormous practice, and a continuing flow of bad and indifferent architecture. Scott was always very proud of the design of this church, although it was never built.

It was the winning of this competition which directed his attention to continental Gothic architecture, and in particular the French cathedrals. In Venice he met Ruskin, and for the first time came into contact with Italian Gothic, which at first repelled and then attracted him.

His work at Oxford and Cambridge is generally condemned, together with most of his work at the cathedrals of Salisbury, Ripon, Lichfield, Hereford and Ely, but his Victorian clients were certainly not in accord with the critics of today. His practice grew to vast proportions and included practically every kind of secular building. An enormous amount of research, by freehand and measured drawing, gained him a very wide knowledge of his subject, although it is a pity that it is in such disturbing contrast to the inadequacy of its application. An instance of this is his rebuilding of the seventeenth-century chapel at Exeter College, a solidly constructed building which had literally to be blown up by the architect to replace it by the present peculiar edifice, which is supposedly modelled on the Sainte Chapelle, although its silhouette has some Romantic merit. He added to and altered the chapels at All Souls', New College and University College, but his worst buildings are probably the block in Broad Street. At Exeter College, too, he replaced the Georgian Library with his own in the 'Methodist Decorated' style, although his work at St. John's is more restrained.

At Peterhouse, Cambridge, his work has been less criticised. The great chapel at St. John's is not popular, but his hall at Peterhouse is among his better University works. One of his more successful churches is St. Mary Abbotts, Kensington (1869), which has a noble spire and is altogether a most digni-

fied work, but the monument which has probably received more execration than any other in the country is the flamboyant Albert Memorial, opposite the Albert Hall, which combines all that is worst in Victorian Gothic Decoration. His St. Pancras Hotel has also received more criticism than most, mainly owing to its completely inappropriate style.

Scott's long quarrel with Palmerston arose out of the competitions for the Foreign Office and the War Office in 1856. The story is not without interest. Scott's design for the Foreign Office was placed third to Coe's winning entry, and he was beaten too for second place by Barry and Banks. Garling won the War Office.

Palmerston, however, in typical high-handed manner, quashed the awards and appointed Sir James Pennethorne (1801–71) who followed Renaissance rather than strict classic lines and who had been an assistant to Nash. Scott, however, was not the man to take this sort of treatment lying down. At a meeting with Barry, Beresford Hope and Digby Wyatt, they agreed to place the matter in the hands of the Royal Institute of British Architects, but in the meantime there had been a change of government and Lord John Manners had taken over the Office of Works. On the advice of the R.I.B.A., a select committee was convened,

Manchester Town Hall, 1877

163

who recommended a choice between Scott and Barry, and Scott was appointed in 1858. The decision not to proceed with the building of the War Office further complicated the situation. Scott contacted Digby Wyatt, architect to the India Office, which at the time was looking for a site in Whitehall. Wyatt and Scott agreed to collaborate, and drawings and designs were in hand when Sir William Tite (1789–1873), the architect of the Royal Exchange and Member of Parliament for Bath, opposed the whole idea of a Gothic Foreign Office, and was naturally supported by Palmerston.

Scott might have won the day had there not been a crisis on the Continent. Napoleon III had invaded Italy and Palmerston was once more at the head of the Foreign Office. He sent for Scott and told him bluntly that he would have no Gothic Foreign Office. After a great deal of hedging and delay Scott finally produced the building we see today, a compromise if ever there was one, but still possessing a certain dignity.

The limited competition for the Law Courts resulted at first in favour of E. M. Barry, son of Sir Charles Barry and architect of Charing Cross and Cannon Street Hotels. Scott was placed second although the heads of the law offices preferred his design to Barry's. In the end, George Edmund Street (1824–81) was appointed. He had spent five years in Scott's office before setting up his own practice in 1849, and had a highly successful career in the building of churches both at home and abroad. He restored five cathedrals and wrote two books, *Brick and Marble in North Italy* (1855) and *Gothic Architecture in Spain* (1865), but the work by which he will be best remembered is the Royal Courts of Justice (1874–1882). The site was an awkward one, and this was the last attempt in London to apply the revived Gothic style to a secular building for which it was quite unsuitable. There were later attempts in the provinces, but the style was in decline and architects born in the 1830's foresook it in their later careers. One such was Alfred Waterhouse.

Alfred Waterhouse (1830–1905) can be compared with Scott as the founder of an architectural dynasty. He built up his enor-

Knebworth House, Hertfordshire, 1843: built by Edward Bulwer Lytton, 1st Lord Lytton, the famous Victorian novelist

164

mous practice, as many other successful architects have done, by winning one of the larger competitions, in his case the Manchester Assize Courts (1859) which were so badly damaged in the last war that they were demolished exactly a century after their completion. It was a typical Victorian Gothic arrangement with high pitched and pavilioned roofs, somewhat similar to his Town Hall, Manchester (1868–77), which still remains. His Prudential Assurance Building in Holborn has some merit in silhouette but cannot be compared with his St. Paul's School at Hammersmith, which from the playing fields has great dignity, although the hard red brick with which both buildings are faced jars unpleasantly, even with their covering of London soot.

The Natural History Museum in Cromwell Road, Kensington, would again be more acceptable were it not for the unpleasant texture of its materials, and University College Hospital, again in his favourite hard red brick, is an astonishing building altogether, in its inappropriate style and materials. The plan, however, on such a restricted site is not without much ingenuity, and this we find with most of the great Victorian architects. They were good planners, but of taste they possessed extremely little.

The Duke of Westminster was probably the richest man in England, and Waterhouse expressed this wealth in exuberant form at Eaton Hall, Cheshire, where he surrounded William Porden's 'Cathedral Gothic' with a dazzling display of flamboyant and expensive ornament, double rows of ornate Gothic arches and vaulted ceilings.

One of the most romantic houses of this period in the country is Knebworth House, Hertfordshire, the home of the Lytton family. It was built by Edward Bulwer Lytton, the successful Victorian novelist, and is today the home of a former Governor of the Bank of England.

The peak of the Greek revival period was reached and passed in the 1820's and by 1840 was completely at an end in England, although it lingered in Scotland until after the middle of the century.

Of the Classical school of architects the most distinguished was Decimus Burton (1800–81) whose father, a builder in a very large way, laid out estates at Tunbridge Wells, Brighton and St. Leonards with the help of his son.

Although he lived to 1881 Decimus Burton, on the strength of his father's fortune, retired at an early age, to the great loss of English architecture. In the comparatively short time in which he produced buildings he was responsible for some outstanding architecture, designing the Entrance Screen at Hyde Park Corner and the Triumphal Arch at Constitution Hill, which now forms the centre piece of the new roundabout at Hyde Park Corner, and the United Services and Athenaeum Clubs in Waterloo Place. In the 1840's he worked with the engineer Richard Turner on the Winter Garden in Regent's Park and the Palm Houses at Chatsworth and Kew Gardens.

Sir Robert Smirke (1780–1867) had one of the biggest practices in London, and, although never an exciting architect, combined scholarship with industry and reliability. Smirke travelled widely on the continent and particularly in Italy, after a period of apprenticeship with Sir John Soane, with whom he was temporarily completely out of sympathy. He had a certain flair, and his portico of the Royal College of Physicians, opposite the National Gallery, is as impressive as anything of this period.

Above all his other works, his plan of the British Museum is monumental, and the tremendous frontispiece of giant Ionic columns

is magnificent in scale and most meticulous in execution. One has an uncomfortable feeling, however, that the architectural character is emphasised at the expense of a more workable plan, although the fine building lends a superb air of grandeur to this part of Bloomsbury, and is in attractive contrast to the sheer and naked functionalism which is rampant today. It is infinitely to be preferred to the dull mass of the London University Senate House skyscraper behind it, or to the heavy and uninspired School of Tropical Medicine not far away. He had, too, a great capacity for speed, and his King's College, which joins on to Somerset House and with which it had to match, was designed and completed to the allotted time schedule.

He was the architect, also, of the Customs House, which had originally been designed by a pupil of Sir John Soane. The building was completed in 1817, but owing to faulty construction the riverside elevation had to be demolished. Smirke rebuilt it with his favourite Ionic order, but during the last war the building was badly damaged, and

has been reconstructed by Professor Sir Albert Richardson in a manner that in no way detracts from the dignity of Smirke's building and contributes an added liveliness to Smirke's somewhat dull design.

There follow some lesser architects in Louis Vulliamy (1790–1871) and Benjamin Dean Wyatt (1775–1850). Wyatt had no natural flair for architecture whatsoever, but he inherited a huge practice from his father, and he was the nephew of Samuel Wyatt and cousin of Jeffery. His connections, therefore, in such a conservative age, were invaluable, and he could hardly fail to profit thereby. As a young man he was sent to India as Wellesley's secretary and consequently, on his return, received the commission for Apsley House at Hyde Park Corner, the town mansion of the Dukes of Wellington. Wyatt altered and enlarged the house, which is satisfying and solid with its Bath stone and Corinthian columns. He was the architect also of the Duke of York's Column at the bottom of Regent Street in London. He succeeded his father as Surveyor to Westminster Abbey and the Oriental Club in Hanover Square (1826–7), and of York House, now Lancaster House, overlooking the Mall.

Louis Vulliamy was one of the more distinguished of Smirke's pupils. His Corinthian façade of the London Institution in Albemarle Street has great dignity, but his masterpiece was Dorchester House (1848–1857) in Park Lane, which was modelled on Raphael's Farnesina Palace in Rome. The great town mansion, once the home of Sir George Holford, the South African millionaire, has now been destroyed to give place to the Dorchester Hotel. It had a magnificent monumental staircase and a surrounding gallery on the first floor, from where the crowds of celebrities climbing the marble stairs could be surveyed and criticised. Doors and fireplaces were designed by Alfred Stevens, here seen at his best, and the great reception rooms housed one of the finest art collections in London. Vain efforts were made to save the mansion for opera, for which it was, of course, quite unsuitable.

Philip Hardwick (1792–1870), second of three generations of Hardwicks, was architect of the great Doric Arch, which has now been demolished, at Euston Station. With his son, P. C. Hardwick, he designed the monumental booking-offices and hall (soon to follow a like fate if the proposed rebuilding of Euston is carried out) which owe their detail to the Massimi Palace in Rome. Philip was the architect also of the imposing Goldsmiths' Hall, which survived the London blitz, of Seaford House in Belgrave Square, and, with his son, of the station hotel at Paddington and the Great Hall, Euston Station. He designed also the Hall and Library in Lincoln's Inn (1843).

One of the best known churches in London, St. Pancras Church, with its row of Greek caryatids based on the Erechtheum on the Acropolis at Athens, is the work of William Inwood (1794–1843) and his two sons, both of whom died in their forties. It is unusual and scholarly, and their St. Peter's, in Regent Square, with its fine Greek detail, green scagliola columns and coffered ceiling, is one of the most splendid churches in London.

One of the most monumental and exuberant public buildings of the nineteenth century is the Fitzwilliam Museum at Cambridge. It has an imposing portico of eight Corinthian columns with a sculptured group in high relief in the pediment above, the whole supported by two wings with Corinthian pilasters. The architect was George Basevi (1795–1845), a cousin of Disraeli, who evidently shared some of his famous relative's flair for flamboyance. He

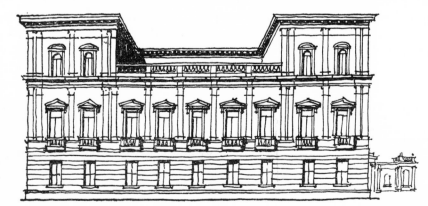

Dorchester House, Park Lane, London, 1848–57: the design by Louis Vulliamy was based on the Farnesina Palace, Rome

167

Fitzwilliam Museum, Cambridge, 1845

was a draughtsman of some competence who designed Thurloe Square, Belgrave Square and Pelham Crescent as well as the Conservative Club in St. James's Street.

Sir Charles Barry (1795–1860) is best known by his biggest building, the Houses of Parliament, but his buildings in the Classic manner are no less worthy. As a young man he travelled widely in Europe, and in Egypt, Syria and Palestine. The Manchester Art Gallery (1824) is his first building in the Classic manner, and his Travellers' and Reform Clubs (the latter based on the Farnese Palace in Rome, with its great cornice designed by Michelangelo) are among his best known works. His Treasury buildings in Whitehall (1848) are straightforward and in telling contrast to Scott's somewhat simple, unbalanced design in the Foreign Office, and his enormous classical houses at Cliveden, and Bridgewater House in London for the Earl of Ellesmere, are out-

standing in a century that is renowned for scholarship in its best buildings. Cliveden, built in a magnificent position above the Thames at Taplow, Buckinghamshire, was designed on the lines of an Italian Palazzo for the Duke of Sutherland. His Halifax Town Hall is an interesting mixture of Gothic form and classic detail.

C. R. Cockerell (1788–1863) was one of the more enthusiastic classical architects who commenced by touring the Near East and, with some archaeologists, discovered the Temple of Apollo at Bassae, with its unusual Ionic order, and the marbles of Aegina. He drew and measured extensively in Florence and Rome, and later entered unsuccessfully but indomitably many of the great open competitions for the Houses of Parliament, the Royal Exchange, the Carlton Club and University College. His reward came in 1839 when he won the competition for the Ashmolean-Taylorian

168

Museum at Oxford, which was completed in 1845. The four huge Ionic columns on the east front, surmounted by statues, appear to be stuck on to the building, with its rather heavy storey above the cornice. He completed the Fitzwilliam Museum at Cambridge after the death of Basevi, and St. George's Hall at Liverpool after Elmes' decease. The Sun Fire Office in Threadneedle Street, now altered, and buildings for the Bank of England at Manchester, Bristol and London, all follow in his competent manner.

Harvey Lonsdale Elmes (1815–47) is known by one supreme work, his St. George's Hall at Liverpool, one of the most monumental buildings of any country or any age. It contains a vast circular concert hall which is based on the tepidarium of the Baths of Caracalla in Rome. Elmes died of

Town Hall, Halifax, 1860–2: Gothic form clothed with Classic detail consumption, a fairly common disease at the time, in Jamaica at the early age of thirty-two. He was an architect of great promise who, after winning the St. George's Hall competition, followed in the next year by winning the first premium for the Liverpool Assize Courts, for which he chose the Greek Doric Order, but which it was decided to incorporate with his other winning design in one imposing building.

Sir James Pennethorne (1801–71) is a considerable name in this period of the Greek classical revival. An assistant of Nash who was influenced by Barry, he was more inclined to follow Renaissance rather than the strict Classical manner, and was renowned for the refinement of his detail. His Civil Service Commission buildings (1866) in Burlington Gardens, at the rear of the Royal Academy, are distinguished if not sparkling. He added the western wing of Somerset House in 1852.

One of the best known buildings in London, and the least appreciated, the Albert Hall (1868), was designed by Captain Fowke (1823–65) and General Scott (1822–83). Fowke was a captain in the Royal Engineers who built parts of the Victoria and Albert Museum in 1865 and the Imperial Institute block in 1861, afterwards merged on to the new buildings designed by Aston Webb and Colcutt respectively. The latter block is now to be destroyed and replaced by a huge development for London University by Norman and Dawbarn. The Colcutt tower has been the centre of a fierce controversy, but it is likely to be allowed to remain.

With these great Greek classical buildings we reach the end of an epoch. There was no lack of architects to carry out works which added distinction to many provincial towns, and they are certainly worthy of note. There was John Foulston of Plymouth, whose Theatre Royal and Royal Hotel were destroyed in the blitz on the town in the Second World War. There was Thomas Harrison, who designed the Liverpool and Manchester Athenaeums, and John Dobson of Newcastle who designed the monumental Central Station (1849) and improved the city with his street-planning developments. There were Edward Walters who designed the flamboyant and now destroyed Free Trade Hall at Manchester, and Cuthbert Brodrick who built the Leeds Town Hall, with its unpleasant dome spoiling the effect of a most impressive, if heavy, Corinthian façade. All these men were distinguished for their scholarship, based in most cases on wide research and travel in their youth. Their example has been followed in this century by Le Corbusier, the acknowledged architectural prophet of the age, whose early years were spent in travel and who is a most powerful exponent of draughtsmanship and advocate of the pencil.

Richard Norman Shaw (1831–1912) started his career in promising fashion by winning the Silver Medal, and the next year the Gold Medal and Travelling Studentship of the Royal Academy Schools, where Cockerell, in old age, was still Professor of Architecture. Shaw travelled widely in Europe in 1853–4, sketching mainly the larger French cathedrals (which he published in a book of drawings entitled *Architectural sketches from the Continent*) and other continental buildings with whose designs he intended to influence those of his own country.

On his return to England he entered the office of G. E. Street and remained with him until 1865, when he left to take up private practice in partnership with W. Eden Nesfield. Shaw was a High Churchman with a great admiration for Butterfield, which may have been coloured by that highly ques-

Cliveden, 1850: the formal gardens are adorned with sculptures from the Villa Borghese in Rome

tionable architect's undoubtedly virtuous character, although this same admiration had apparently, and fortunately, little effect on Shaw's actual work, for he became disillusioned with the Gothic revival at an early age and never worked in that style.

It is doubtful whether Shaw was ever fected directly by William Morris, but at least he shared his sympathy with the mediaeval. He rapidly achieved what must have been the largest practice in domestic architecture in the country. It was a day of great house building, and Shaw worked with fluency and rapidity. He was said to have designed the huge house of Cragside in Northumberland (for Lord Armstrong of Vickers-Armstrong fame) in the few hours his host was out shooting. His best known mansion is probably Bryanston, in Dorset, which was modelled on Coleshill, and was built for Lord Portman. It was converted to the well-known public school in 1928.

The experiment at Bedford Park, at Chiswick, is of interest. The client, Jonathan T. Carr, proposed a middle-class type of garden suburb with church and shops and public house, all of which Shaw carried out.

'The Ballad of Bedford Park', published in 1881 in the *St. James Gazette*, explains the idea.

In London town there lived a man,
   a gentleman was he,
Whose name was Jonathan T. Carr,
   (*as has been told to me*).

'*This London is a foggy town*',
   (*thus to himself said he*),
'*Where bricks are black and trees are brown,*
   and faces are dirtee.

'*I will seek out a brighter spot,*'
   continued Mr. Carr,
'*Not too near London, and yet not,*
   what might be called too far.

'*Tis there a village I'll erect*
   with Norman Shaw's assistance,
Where men may lead a chaste, correct,
   aesthetical existence.'

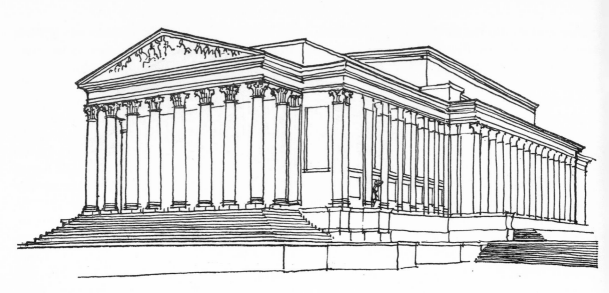

St. George's Hall, Liverpool, 1839

With red and blue and sagest green
were walls and dado dyed,
Friezes of Morris there were seen,
and oaken wainscot wide.

There was a village builded
for all who are aesthete,
Whose precious souls it fill did
with utter joy complete.

And Jonathan and Norman
found so much work to do,
They sold out to a Company
to put the business through.

Thus art and business acumen were mingled in true Victorian manner. The experiment created a sensation and Shaw progressed successfully to the daring design for New Scotland Yard (1891) and the Piccadilly Hotel (1905). This last work formed part of the rebuilding of Nash's Regent Street, but the massive ground-floor arches restricted the display desired by the shops and the remainder of the Quadrant was rebuilt by Sir Reginald Blomfield in a style that strongly suggests cardboard and in no way compared in character with Shaw's more vigorous design.

With the exception of Bryanston, Shaw's experiments in the classical tradition were never very successful. He was far better in his very romanticised Tudor manner. He built the first big block of flats in London, the Albert Hall Mansions (1879), and improved greatly on the antiquated system of Victorian sanitation which nearly killed the Prince of Wales of typhoid in 1871. His experimental, Renaissance style London houses at 180 and 196 Queen's Gate, Kensington, are not convincing, and his half-timber work in his country houses is inclined to be fussy, but his houses, on the whole, are far superior to those of other architects of the period, typical of which are William Burgess' own house, Gothic and turreted, in Melbury Road, Kensington, Manor Farm, built by Basil Champneys for his own use, the house and studio for Sir Frederick Leighton, by George Aitchison, with its extraordinary Arab Hall, the house for Val Prinsep by Philip Webb and the house and studio for G. F. Watts by Aitchison and Frederick Pepys Cockerell, son of C. R. Cockerell, but far below his distinguished father in quality.

Among Shaw's office buildings his New Zealand chambers (1872), in Leadenhall Street, are a remarkable and original experiment in a sort of romantic Jacobean style, while his Alliance Assurance building in St. James's Street is in a form of Flemish which recalls streaky bacon, a criticism aimed at more than one building of this period. New Scotland Yard is generally accepted as Shaw's masterpiece but the general effect, though solid and imposing, is restless with its combination of granite, Portland stone and brick. It is far more successful in silhouette, particularly in a London mist or at dusk, when the detail is obscured. Shaw can hardly be rated a great architect, but he certainly improved on most of the deplorable architecture which followed the decline of the Classical revival.

The other architect who influenced the general taste away from the Gothic revival was Ernest George (1839–1922), who was some eight years younger than Shaw. He also was a draughtsman and water colourist of competence, whose work, like Shaw's, consisted mainly of large country houses, streets of houses in Kensington and Mayfair, such as Collingham Gardens and Mount Street, and the Guildhall School of Music off the Embankment (1910–11). He adopted the Jacobean tradition for his country houses, and his London street frontages display a fondness for fussy Flemish detail which is anything but unpleasant to look upon, and forms an effective contrast to the more severe contemporary building of modern London. He exercised an influence on English architecture which was multiplied many times through his famous pupils, Sir Guy Dawber, Sir Herbert Baker and

Sir Edwin Lutyens, all of whom made their mark in emphatic manner on the architecture of England, Africa and India.

Sir Thomas Graham Jackson (1835–1924) also built confidently in the Jacobean manner but is best known by his Examination Schools in The High at Oxford. He entered the office of Sir George Gilbert Scott in 1858 after a brilliant career at Oxford and began practice in London in 1862, building mainly scholastic and ecclesiastical buildings. At Oxford he built exteriors to Brasenose, Balliol, Corpus Christi and Lincoln Colleges, and added various school buildings to Eton, Harrow, Rugby and Winchester. His restorations at Winchester Cathedral, Bath Abbey, Christchurch and the Hospital of St. Cross at Winchester are harmless, if undistinguished.

Two of Norman Shaw's pupils who achieved fame were Ernest Newton (1856–1922) and W. R. Lethaby (1857–1931) who became better known as a teacher and particularly as a writer. Newton's country houses, through which he exercised considerable influence on English country house design, maintained a high and consistent standard. They are mainly Tudor in style, or in a manner closely allied, and he used weather-tiling and boarding with much success and pleasant effect. The interiors are always in good taste.

Lethaby was a mediaevalist who, with Walter Crane, William Morris and Burne-Jones, became involved in the Arts and Crafts movement which was initiated in 1887. He was a revolutionary in architectural thinking, anticipating Le Corbusier's dictum that 'a house is a machine for living in' by his own, that 'we must have houses as efficient as a bicycle'. He went further, in 1922, when he expressed the thought that a cathedral could be constructed in concrete as adequately as an industrial building. But his very forward thinking was supported by a sound traditional training which he expressed in another famous theory, that 'No art that is only one man deep is worth much.' His Eagle Insurance building in Birmingham, which he designed with J. L. Ball, reflects his balanced thinking, although the huge window to the ground floor appears incongruous and on an altogether different scale from the rest of the building.

Although a mediaevalist, Lethaby was no bigot, and surprisingly, in an essay entitled 'Beautiful Cities', which he wrote for the Arts and Crafts movement, he criticised the contemporary London scene in vigorous language and proclaimed that Waterloo Bridge (the Rennie design) was 'second in importance only to St. Paul's and must be preserved at any cost and sacrifice'.

The phase of Victorian architecture which followed the era of scholarship may be termed the Romantic, and was to a large extent influenced by the thought and writing of one man, William Morris, not, perhaps, to the same direct extent as Pugin or Ruskin, but with possibly as much general effect. His theories sprang from a healthy mind in a particularly healthy body, in contrast to poor Ruskin's physical impotence, and the misery of a ruined married life which could not but affect his work.

Morris was a man of singular charm of manner. He spent one year (1856) in the office of Street, and in the following year, with Burne-Jones, began the decorations of the Oxford Union. He was not only a poet, but a creative artist, sincere and genuine in his search for the best possible in everything, whether in design, materials or execution. A man of considerable private means, he graduated at Oxford with the intention of taking holy orders, but abandoned the whole idea for painting and poetry. It is quite evident that the more practical and mundane side of architecture, which is essential in the erection of buildings, made no appeal to him although he spent a lot of time superintending the building of a house to his own idea, the actual architect of which was Philip Webb. This was the famous Red House near Bexley Heath in Kent, which was finished in 1860, and his dissatisfaction with the type of furniture, fabrics and materials then being produced led to the formation of the firm of Morris & Co., whose partners included Webb, and the pre-Raphaelites Rossetti, Ford Madox Brown and Burne-Jones. Morris himself designed much of the furniture, wall-paper and fabrics produced by the firm. His constant plea for simplicity and honesty in design and craftsmanship had great influence on the architecture of this period.

The invention of steam traction brought phenomenal changes to the country. Between 1830 and 1860 about 25,000 bridges, large and small, were constructed, many in iron, like the tubular Britannia Bridge across the Menai Straits, many in stone, like the viaducts at Chapel-en-le-Frith in Derbyshire, and others in brick, like the Digswell or Welwyn viaduct in Hertfordshire, which carries the main line railway from King's Cross to the North. This viaduct is typical of many brick viaducts which march across the countryside with all the power and vigour of the Roman aqueducts. They were built to fulfil a function; their long horizontal lines are extraordinarily satisfying and they share the grace and repose of all great architecture. The building of the Digswell viaduct is a demonstration of the pioneering spirit of the Victorian builders and sheer determination to achieve against great difficulties.

The Mimram valley extends from Welwyn in the west to Hertingfordbury in the east. Twenty-four miles north of London,

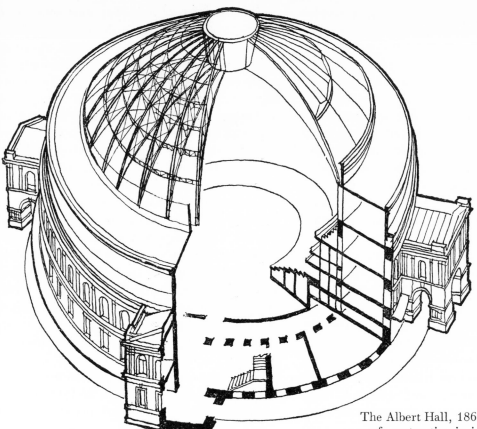

The Albert Hall, 1868: section showing roof construction in iron

and nearly a mile wide, it had to be spanned if the Great Northern Railway, first projected in the 1840's, was ever to become a reality. There was plenty of opposition. It was pointed out that the waterlogged and swampy bed of the valley could never support the foundations of a railway bridge carrying heavy traffic, and that it would be better to make a detour, however long and costly.

The energy and organising genius of one man overcame all difficulties. Thomas Brassey was the son of a Cheshire farmer, a man of the people, who rose on the crest of the great Victorian railway boom to be a highly successful railway contractor. He was given a four-year contract by the railway company.

Sheer man-power was the only source of energy. It was fortunately cheap. Five or six thousand of the toughest and roughest were set to work with pick and shovel to dig an enormous trench 2,000 feet long, 300 feet wide and 100 feet deep. Thousands of tons of earth and saturated clay were dug out by the sweating labourers. Masses of burnt clay and mortar were packed into the huge trench to form a firm and indestructable base for the bridge foundations, and the colossal task of building began.

Five million bricks were made on the spot. The winter of 1849–50 was bitterly cold and the cursing, frozen workers had only a shanty town in which to live. Conditions became appalling but Brassey scourged them on. Little more than two years after the

175

start, the 40 arches of the bridge, each spanning 40 feet, were complete; 100 feet high, and 2,000 feet long, the viaduct was opened on 8th August 1850. It still carries the main line expresses from King's Cross to the North.

The use of steel in building is regarded by most people as a comparatively recent innovation, and the modern steel and glass development as something that has occurred only over the last few years. In actual fact its use goes back for nearly two centuries, and it is to this country that the credit must be given for the early experiments, not only in engineering but, later, in buildings such as the Crystal Palace. The development of the railways in this country gave us a lead over other countries which we were quick to exploit industrially, but in architecture, in which in the nineteenth century we failed to carry on any form of experiment, we lagged well behind the more advanced technology of France and Germany.

Buildings in England were constructed in brick, stone and timber up to the end of the eighteenth century, but with the Industrial Revolution iron began to be used, at first sparingly but later, after its conversion to steel, in ever-increasing quantity. Before the eighteenth century, iron had been used in the chains encircling the domes of St. Peter's in Rome, and St. Paul's in London, to counteract the outward thrust of the great arched forms, and in Florence tie-bars of iron were extensively used to prevent the spread of the delicate arches resting so lightly on columns. Wren, too, had used bands of wrought iron at the base of the spire of Salisbury, but its use, apart from decorative purposes, was naturally extremely limited as no structural problems had as yet arisen that could not be dealt with adequately either by a timber beam or a brick or stone arch.

The use of coal and the blast furnace in smelting made possible the casting of iron in larger dimensions and in increasing quantities. The iron bridge over the Severn at Coalbrookdale, in Shropshire (1779), has a span of 100 feet and consists of five semi-circular iron ribs, each cast in two pieces. The architect is generally accepted as T. F. Pritchard.

The second cast-iron bridge to be built was far more ambitious, and is still in existence. It crosses the Wear, at Sunderland, and spans 240 feet, a very great advance in so short a time, for it was erected in 1793, only fourteen years after Coalbrookdale. It is an interesting example of a new form of construction imitating the old in appearance. Between the six ribs are perforated blocks of iron imitating radiating stone *voussoirs*, held together with wrought-iron arcs, fitting in grooves and secured by bolts.

The design for the new London Bridge, by Telford, showed a yet further advance, the arches attaining a span of 600 feet at a height of 65 feet above high-water level. It was never built, and the drama and beauty of the great sweeping arch are lost to us. Other bridges followed: Telford's Menai suspension bridge, with a span of 579 feet, was built in 1818, and the younger Brunel's suspension bridge, over the Avon gorge at Clifton, has a span of 702 feet.

John Rennie (1761–1821), probably the most distinguished architect-engineer of the nineteenth century, built his first cast-iron bridge in 1803, spanning the Witham at Boston in Lincolnshire. It gave no indication of his later fine bridges at Southwark and Waterloo, which have been replaced. This last bridge is particularly to be regretted; with its two massive granite Doric columns to each pier and its rusticated masonry, it harmonised magnificently with Somerset House. Rennie's Naval Victualling Yard, at Stonehouse, Devonport, uses a sombre classic style with impressive effect.

The vital stimulus to building in iron was the advent of the railways, although James Walker's Vauxhall Bridge (1816) and Rennie's Southwark Bridge (1819) had been built before the railway era. The first railway bridge to be built mainly in wrought iron spanned the river Gaunless at West Auckland and carried the Stockton and Darlington railway.

Robert Stephenson's best known work is the Britannia Bridge over the Menai Straits, built in 1852, in the form of a box girder. The two centre tubes span 460 feet and each weighs some 1,600 tons; the two outer spans are 230 feet and are supported on masonry piers. The bridge still safely carries the main railway line to Holyhead.

Brunel's Royal Albert Bridge at Saltash, near Devonport, crosses the Tamar with two main spans each of 455 feet. It is most original in conception and a tribute to his engineering genius. The two main spans consist each of a large wrought-iron tube, half an inch only in thickness and elliptical in section, 16 feet 9 inches wide and 12 feet 3 inches high. This form of tubular iron, while comparatively light, is immensely strong, and the bridge still carries the main Western Region line to Penzance. The Forth Bridge was later built on a similar principle.

Cast-iron columns were used by John Nash in 1816 in the Royal Pavilion at Brighton. They were used also in Lancashire cotton mills, and cast-iron beams made their appearance in 1801 in Manchester. Brick or concrete arches were used between the beams, and the modern method of steel frame construction was born. Wrought-iron beams were used in 1845, flanges were added at top and bottom, and the modern H-sectioned beam was evolved.

The Saltaire Mills in Yorkshire, built by Sir Titus Salt, were completed in 1853 by a similar method. The four-storey building is 550 feet long by 50 feet wide, the floors supported by iron beams resting on iron columns, with flat segmental brick arches between the beams. The outside walls are of stone. Meanwhile, another and lighter form of building was taking place. Joseph Paxton, head gardener to the Duke of Devonshire at Chatsworth, who was building greenhouses there with timber frames, visited Paris in 1834 and may have seen Rouhaults's conservatory of iron and glass which had been built in 1833 in the Jardin des Plantes, for in 1837–40 Paxton built the great conservatory at Chatsworth with iron ribs. He designed also a machine for making metal window bars and thus anticipated prefabrication and mass production. Decimus Burton's Palm House at Kew, begun in 1842 and completed in 1866, is similar in design.

The great dome of the reading room at the British Museum, 140 feet in diameter and 106 feet high, was constructed by Sidney Smirke with iron radiating ribs in 1857. It is still 2 feet less in diameter than the dome of the Pantheon in Rome which was built in A.D. 120–4 by the Emperor Hadrian, and has a diameter of 142 feet 6 inches.

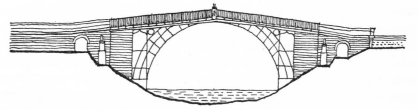

The first cast-iron bridge built at Coalbrookdale, 1775–9

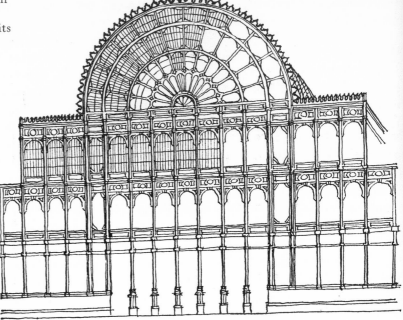

The Crystal Palace, 1850–1: main
entrance and barrel vault,
construction by prefabricated units

The most significant constructional event of the nineteenth century was the building of the Crystal Palace, for the Hyde Park Exhibition, commenced on 26th September 1850 and by 14th January 1851 almost complete. It was the world's first demountable structure. The utmost use was made of units of a standard size, which were prefabricated and assembled rapidly on the site. Paxton, the designer and architect, could thus thank the experience he had gained at Chatsworth, for the principles employed there were used to supreme effect on the Crystal Palace, which was in fact a huge greenhouse. The building covered an area of 772,784 square feet, and took about sixteen weeks to erect. St. Paul's, by comparison, occupying 55,000 square feet, took thirty-five years. With his engineers, Fox and Henderson, Paxton pioneered the modern method of prefabrication in building. Curiously enough, after the removal of the Crystal Palace to Sydenham in 1853, the lesson was completely ignored and building continued on the old

traditional lines for over half a century longer. The great Palace which went up at Sydenham was not the building which came down in Hyde Park, as it was considerably enlarged and was given a semi-cylindrical glass vault, but it was undoubtedly a creation of considerable beauty. Since its re-erection it lay neglected in a London suburb, used only occasionally for a dog show or a brass band contest, until its destruction by fire in 1936.

The story of its origin is not without interest. The success of the French Industrial Exposition of 1844 was pointed out to the British Government, together with the probable advantages to British commerce, but the government remained unco-operative. In 1848 a proposal for a self-supporting exhibition of the products of British industry to be directed by a Royal Commission, was submitted by Prince Albert, whose interest had been keenly aroused, but met with no better success with an obdurate government. 'Meanwhile,' a contemporary writer tell us, 'the popular feeling in favour of such an experiment was rapidly strengthening, and the success which has attended the experiment may, in large measure, be referred to the freedom of action which this dissociation from the timed councils of the government secured for its projectors'—which rings a familiar bell. A report by Digby Wyatt, the architect, on the French exposition further supported the idea.

Prince Albert thereupon took over the whole project. 'But, indeed,' continues our writer (*Art Journal, 1851*), 'for his indefatigable perseverance, his courageous defiance of all risks of failure, his remarkable sagacity in matters of business, and the influence which attached to his support, the whole project, notwithstanding the great exertions which had been made to secure its realisation, must have fallen to the ground.' Subscriptions poured in, commemorative medals were struck, and support and enthusiasm rose to a high pitch.

But when the time came for making definite arrangements for the erection of the building the Commissioners found they had only £35,000 in hand. Nothing daunted, an international architectural competition was opened for a building not exceeding a coverage of 900,000 square feet. The time allowed for the preparation of the drawings was limited to the fantastically short time of one month, but in spite of this, 233 designs were submitted, many of a highly elaborate character. Of these, 38 came from abroad,

128 from London and vicinity, and 51 from provincial competitors. The rejection of the whole of the plans of the competing architects by the Building Committee under Digby Wyatt created, we are told, no ordinary dissatisfaction, and astonishment rose further when it was learnt that the Committee had meanwhile prepared a plan of their own, with working drawings. It was ugly, cumbrous and costly, and public opinion forced its prompt rejection.

Among the contractors who had accepted the invitation to tender for the building were the firm of Fox and Henderson, who sent in a price for a building of an entirely different character. This was Joseph Paxton's. At the time he was erecting a greenhouse for the Victoria Regia lily in the grounds of Chatsworth for the Duke of Devonshire, and at a meeting of the directors of the Midland Railway he sketched, on a piece of blotting paper, the idea for the building. The tender was accepted.

No time was lost. Fox worked eighteen hours a day for seven weeks on the working drawings, which he drew himself, while his partner Henderson directed the prefabrication of the cast-iron parts.

The site was a rectangular piece of land in Hyde Park between Rotten Row and Queen's Drive of about 26 acres. The transept, with semi-circular roof enclosing some tall trees, which were allowed to remain, was 108 feet high and 72 feet wide. Other trees were retained and enclosed by open courts. The plan of the whole building formed a parallelogram 1,848 feet long and 408 feet wide, the nave, 72 feet wide and 64 feet high, running the entire length of the building.

The secret of its amazingly rapid construction was prefabrication. On the experience gained at Chatsworth, Paxton designed a building based on the manufacture of

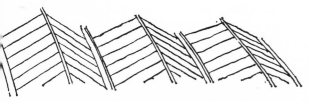

The Crystal Palace: detail of cast-iron roofing to the barrel vault

thousands of similar cast-iron parts which could be rapidly assembled, while roof and walls were infilled with 896,000 square feet of glass. Hollow cast-iron columns, 24 feet apart, supported open work girders, the roof covered by Paxton's favourite ridge-and-furrow glazing.

The building was unique, an enterprise of astonishing courage when it is remembered that, in the eyes of the Victorians, the function of the architect was to camouflage the structure as far as possible. All, however, was sacrificed for speed. The business methods employed were no less unique. No contract had been signed between the Commissioners and Messrs. Fox and Henderson, who relied with complete confidence on the good faith of the Royal Commission, backed by the Prince Consort. No order was received by them for the building, no payment on account for work done was received, and they had incurred the risk of expending upwards of £55,000 without being in a legal position to call upon the Commissioners for the repayment of any part of it.

With the further development of the railway in England, iron came into ever-increasing use. Some of the most impressive results are shown in the great termini built around and since the middle of the nineteenth century. The roof of Euston Station (1848), a series of iron and glass sheds supported by iron columns, is undistinguished, but Paddington, by the younger Brunel, has three elliptical iron and glass roofs resting on columns crossed by two impressive transepts. Probably the finest of these early roofs is at St. Pancras Station, built in 1868 by P. W. Barlow, and shaped, possibly in sympathy with Gilbert Scott's hotel and offices, like a late Gothic arch, which is particularly suited to the wide span of 243 feet. Cannon Street and Liverpool Street were built between 1865 and 1890 and are far happier in

appearance than the later roofs of Victoria and Waterloo, which are entirely undistinguished. Of the larger London stations of any architectural merit, Lewis Cubitt designed King's Cross (1851–2), with its two huge brick arches expressing the structure of the station behind them.

The Coal Exchange (1846–9) in Lower Thames Street, London, was demolished recently in spite of distinguished opposition. It was notable for its iron-framed glass dome over the internal court, which was some 60 feet in diameter and 74 feet high, and the cantilevered access balconies.

One of the most satisfying iron structures of the period is the Boatstore in the Royal Naval Dockyard at Sheerness (1858–60) by G. T. Greene, the Director of Engineering and Architectural Works to the Admiralty from 1850–64. Its construction is particularly advanced, the stanchions having the 'H' section which came into general use only some years later. It is 210 feet long and 135 feet wide, lit from the top and sides, and four storeys in height.

The use of cast iron encouraged the development of the architect-engineer and inaugurated an era unique in the history of English architecture.

Thomas Telford's design for the Buildwas Bridge over the Severn was influenced by the bridge at Coalbrookdale, but it is more economical in its use of iron and thereby shows an advance in the theory of iron bridge building. His bridge over the Birmingham Canal, built in 1829, was still sturdy enough to carry the heavy tanks of the last war, and his warehouses at St. Katherine's Docks (1824–8) and his canal schemes for the Earl of Ellesmere, connecting the Dee, Mersey and Severn, all stand as monuments to his industry. Telford was a unique character in that he was actually more architect than engineer. His architectural structures have

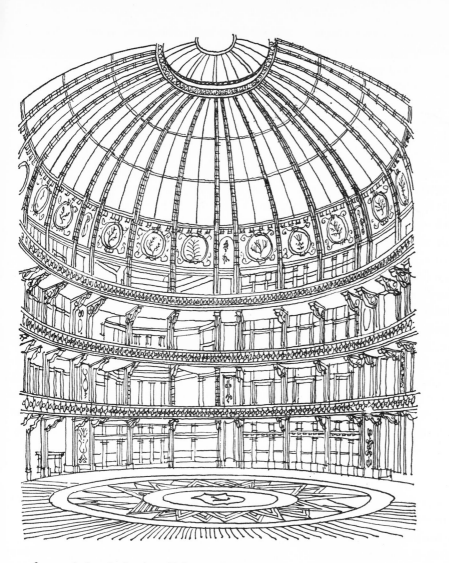

Coal Exchange, Lower
Thames Street, London,
1846–9:
architect, J. B. Bunning

much merit in their simplicity and complete lack of all ostentation and unnecessary ornament.

The Bessemer process for converting iron to steel was invented in 1856 on a large and economical scale. In this process a little carbon is introduced to produce steel, and a smaller quantity to produce mild steel, used mainly for the structure or skeleton of the building. The sections most commonly used in building are the 'I', or 'double tee', and are made in standard sizes.

The most remarkable development in the modern use of steel construction is in bridges, which must be regarded as a branch of architecture in the light of modern thought. These developments should be studied as they will increasingly influence modern buildings as the architect and engineer collaborate even more closely.

Suspension bridges were first built in England during the first half of the nineteenth century and set the standard with Telford's Menai Straits bridge, built in 1818 and spanning 579 feet. The younger Brunel's Clifton bridge, spanning 702 feet, was

181

designed in 1832 but not completed until 1864. The Americans have gone further than the rest of the world in this graceful form of construction, culminating with the huge Golden Gate bridge at San Francisco with a main span of nearly a mile.

The largest suspension bridge in England, by Mott, Hay and Anderson, is now under construction and is due for completion in 1963. It crosses the Severn at a narrow junction of the river between Beachley and Aust, just above the point where the river Wye joins the Severn and about 25 miles below the nearest existing road bridge over the Severn at Gloucester. The main span will be 3,240 feet with side spans each of 1,000 feet, and two carriageways each 24 feet wide will carry the traffic. Constant experiments have been carried out, including tests for wind pressure, and a revolutionary design has been adopted which consists of a continuous box section constructed of welded steel plates, the road deck forming the upper side of the box. The footpath and cycle track will be cantilevered at each side to streamline the section against wind forces. The result of these modifications and experiments is confidently expected to reduce the cost of the great structure by about a million pounds, which demonstrates the advantage of continuous research in building, such as some of the University Schools of Architecture are carrying out today.

With the closing years of the nineteenth century a new method of construction had gradually come to the fore. This is known as reinforced concrete. The principle is demonstrated by the illustration. Concrete is made up of a mixture of water with cement, sand and ballast in certain proportions, as a rule 1 : 2 : 4. This mixture, when set, is enormously strong in compression but extremely weak in tension, so weak, in fact, that in calculating the strength of a rein-

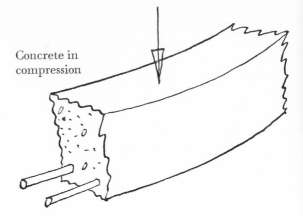

Weight on reinforced concrete beam tends to bend beam

Concrete in compression

Steel rods in tension

forced concrete beam its tensile strength is ignored, the whole of the tension being taken by the steel, which again can withstand enormous pull. The effect of a weight on a reinforced concrete beam is to bend it down, so that the concrete in the upper part of the beam resists the resulting compression, which it is well able to do, while the steel reinforcement near the bottom of the beam, which tends to crack apart and is therefore in tension, resists the pull. The advantage of this method of construction lies in the economic use of steel, which is expensive, and, again, is practically everlasting, as no weathering can effect the concrete, and the steel, by reason of its covering, cannot rust. Another advantage is that, in case of fire, the steel, which would otherwise warp and bend in the heat, is protected by the concrete. An instance of this occurred in a recent fire at the *Daily Mirror* building while in course of construction. The fire attacked one of the main supports carrying a weight of some 3,000 tons and reinforced almost solidly with steel bars, but while the concrete covering was badly calcined the steel was not affected, and a new covering of concrete repaired the damage.

The theory of reinforced concrete was discovered by the Romans. The dome of the Pantheon in Rome is generally supposed to be of concrete, and bronze reinforcing rods have been found in the remains of the Baths of Caracalla. Roman concrete was formed of stone or brick rubble and a mortar of which the important ingredient was pozzolana, a volcanic earth found in thick strata in and around Rome and the neighbourhood of Naples. It is a much superior substitute for sand, and when mixed with lime and wetted it produces mortar of very great strength and tenacity. It will even set under water. The dome of the Pantheon, constructed probably of solid concrete, could therefore be monolithic and would rest vertically on the supporting wall without any outward thrust, which may be the reason for its still perfect structural condition over an enormous lapse of time.

The secret was lost until the eighteenth century, when John Smeaton, carrying out building research for his Eddystone Lighthouse (1774), produced the necessary building material in cement. Smeaton had discovered that quicklime mixed with clay hardens under water, and for the foundations of the lighthouse he used a concrete composed of quicklime, clay, sand and crushed iron slag.

With the discovery of Portland cement a hydraulic cement, superior to any previous kind, was produced. Experiments with the new material, using anything from flat iron rods to iron meshing, were made until, by the end of the century, reinforced concrete engineering became an exact science. Over this period the French were well to the fore in their experience of the material, with the Germans a close second.

England, however, lagged behind the rest of Europe in the use of the new materials. The age of revivals, the period which covered nearly the whole of the nineteenth century, had almost come to an end. Architecturally, it had been a barren period, for it is impossible to revive a style of architecture without reviving the civilisation and the kind of life which produced such a style. The growing awareness of the approaching scientific age and the incongruous attempts to revive the architecture of a long dead past produced a ludicrous situation, but so conservative is this country that, even today, the average house-buyer yearns nostalgically for the Tudor or half-timbered style, with its reminiscence of Merrie England, and the sea-girt island safe from all foreign affray. The advent of reinforced concrete in this country was delayed by restrictive building regulations, although it appeared in the extensions to the General Post Office, London (1907), by Sir Henry Tanner.

At the end of the nineteenth century and in the early years of the twentieth there began a striving for originality, and a freer treatment of Classical and Gothic architecture. The Paris Exhibition of 1900 had a marked effect on English architecture, in particular on the work of two great firms of architects, Mewes and Davis, and Lanchester, Stewart and Rickards.

Mewes and Davis are best known by their Ritz Hotel (1906), in Piccadilly (with its arcade, based on the Rue de Rivoli), by the Royal Automobile Club in Pall Mall and the old *Morning Post* building at the corner of Aldwych. Davis had been trained at the Beaux Arts in Paris, and Mewes had carried out considerable work in Germany as well as in France. There is therefore a very strong Third Empire feeling in their work. The Ritz Hotel was the first steel-framed structure in London, a most outstanding building that adds an air of distinction to this part of Piccadilly. The *Morning Post* building, too, has an atmosphere of old world culture entirely lacking in the new General Electric building which occupies the site of the Gaiety Theatre on the opposite corner. The Royal Automobile Club in Pall Mall is large and impressive with its oval entrance hall and its Egyptian swimming pool.

Lanchester, Stewart and Rickards laid out the University quarter of Cardiff, with the Town Hall and Law Courts. Rickards was a fine draughtsman in pen and ink and a competent designer. Their Central Hall (1906–12) at Westminster and their Neo-Baroque Bermondsey Town Hall still stand as monuments of their versatility.

Many of the larger Whitehall buildings appeared about this time. The heavy, stolid War Office (1906), by William Young, and the Home Office all lack the distinction even of Gilbert Scott's Foreign Office, but the County Hall, won in competition by Ralph Knott, is impressive, in a rather ponderous way, on the southern bank of the river.

The revival of the early Renaissance manner is seen in Sir Aston Webb's Victoria and Albert Museum, completed in 1908, with its symmetrical plan and late Gothic detail, its red brick with stone dressing and Dutch influence.

Westminster Cathedral stands on what was once Burlinga Fen, a marshy district reclaimed and made productive by the monks of the Benedictine Abbey of Westminster, to whose Thames-side monastery it belonged for six hundred years before the Reformation. After the eviction of the monks in 1540 these lands were used for a variety of purposes, and finally, in 1826, a prison was built on the site which Cardinal Vaughan bought in 1892. John Francis Bentley subsequently made good use of the solid foundations of the old prison when planning the Cathedral, which became the largest Byzantine monument in England. This style was chosen in

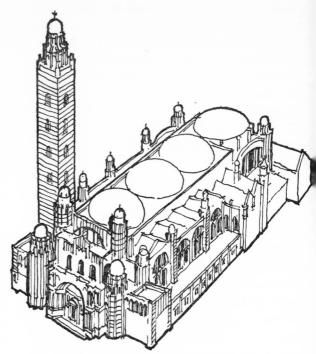

Westminster Cathedral, 1895–1903

preference to the revived Gothic or Classic style for several reasons, of which the most important were speed of construction, relatively lower cost and the need to build for a large congregation for great ceremonial occasions.

The cathedral is Byzantine in spirit and decoration but it is not built to the typical oriental square plan culminating in a massive dome, as in St. Sophia's in Constantinople and St. Mark's, Venice. Bentley covered his 360 by 156 foot nave with four saucer domes.

Building was begun in 1895 and completed in the remarkably short period of eight years. The exterior walls are of dark red brick with ornamental courses of yellow brick banding. Twelve and a half million hand-made bricks were used in the construction of the cathedral, the interior decoration being purposely left to the future when funds and time would be adequate to do justice to the rich Byzantine mosaics designed to clothe its rough brick walls. During the past fifty years the mosaics of many of the side chapels and some of the nave have been finished with varying degrees of success.

The massive dark green monolithic columns which support the galleries come from the same Greek quarry as those of the basilica of St. Sophia. The quarry, forgotten for centuries, was rediscovered in the nineteenth century, and the Westminster columns were among the first to be hand hewn from the re-opened pits. At the time of their transportation to the port the Greeks and Turks were at war with one another, and for a period the columns were confiscated by the Turks and held as spoils of war. All the columns in the cathedral have intricately carved, individually designed capitals in white Carrara marble. Other marbles came from France, Norway, Switzerland and Ireland.

St. Edward's bell tower, for half a century a dominating landmark but now sharing the London sky with several skyscraper blocks, rises 273 feet to a copper dome.

Most churches of the Victorian era were built in the derived Gothic manner, but the vast cathedral at Liverpool by Giles Gilbert Scott shows a certain originality. In 1900 a disused quarry on high ground overlooking the city was chosen as the site for a new cathedral. In an open competition, in which Norman Shaw and G. F. Bodley were assessors, young Giles Gilbert Scott, then only twenty-three, was placed first, although Bodley, with his wide experience, was appointed joint architect in view of Scott's youth.

Scott later altered his original plan, so that the whole composition culminated in the massive tower which dominates the city.

The cathedral is built of red sandstone from the Woolton quarries a few miles away and will, when completed, be one of the largest Gothic churches in Christendom. The plan is symmetrical about the central tower, and is designed with a breadth of feeling, a power and a dignity that are most impressive. The interior, too, is on an enormous scale. It is a prodigious design for so young a man, supremely confident and competent, thrilling in its contrasts between tremendous size and the puny human scale.

It is this sense of daring contrast that makes the best of Scott's works so memorable. The height of the Charterhouse Chapel outside Godalming, emphasised by the tall, narrow windows and the dramatic lighting, is not easily forgotten. The elegance and simplicity of his Waterloo Bridge make it a worthy successor to Rennie's nineteenth-century masterpiece, and his designs for the Battersea Power Station some ten years before created a style for brick power stations that has been followed to this day.

English domestic architecture had great influence on that of Europe in the latter third of the nineteenth century and the early years of the twentieth. Philip Webb (1831–1915), commissioned by William Morris to design the famous Red House at Bexley Heath in Kent, tried to carry on the mediaeval tradition of honest and efficient building from the point where its development had been interrupted by the intrusion of the Renaissance, and his total output, although comparatively small, was of much significance, although his real importance lies in his connection with Morris, and the movements they led for the improvement of design and craftsmanship.

C. F. A. Voysey (1857–1941), a leader of the movement towards simplicity in domestic architecture, left his mark on continental trends at the beginning of this century, and designed also in stained glass, wall-papers, textile fabrics and furniture.

Webb, Norman Shaw and Voysey were followed by a group of rather less competent architects, among whom Baillie Scott's designs appear almost deliberately mediaeval, and in consequence are somewhat artificial. Ernest Newton (1856–1918) and Sir Edwin Lutyens (1869–1944) inclined on the whole towards the symmetrical in their planning, and found it difficult at times to adjust their elevations to the internal arrangements in a satisfactory manner.

The movement towards greater simplicity in architecture, which originated in the late nineteenth-century domestic architecture of England, was much encouraged by an outstanding building in Glasgow which, although outside the scope of this book, cannot be ignored by reason of its significance. This was the Glasgow School of Art, designed and won in competition by C. R. Mackintosh (1868–1928), a building which made him a pioneer of the modern movement. The fashion spread. Buildings by the firm of Adams, Holden and Pearson were characterised by an almost severe lack of unnecessary ornament, and an appreciation of the value of unadorned surfaces that anticipated the later style. The Kodak building in Kingsway, by Sir John Burnet (1857–1938), built in 1910, expresses the steel frame with which it is constructed with a refreshing lack of unnecessary ornament, and the Stationery Office of Sir Richard Allison, built two years later, had a reinforced concrete structure that was honestly reflected in the severity of its façades.

Although England was, all unconsciously, the first to realise the potentialities of steel and glass construction, it was the continental architects who developed the style and built on the foundations laid in this country, creating a type of structure which can be used for any form of building, the purpose of the building dictating the design, and resulting in a living architecture which has arisen directly from the needs of the time and owes nothing to traditional forms.

In the years following the First World War traditional designs still dominated the architecture of England. Although the larger buildings were steel framed they were still covered with brick and stone and the mantlings of the eighteenth-century Renaissance. At this time the Quadrant in Regent Street was built by Sir Reginald Blomfield (1856–1942), in a Renaissance manner, as well as Brocklesby Park and several other large country houses in a similar style. The United University Club and the Carlton Club followed, with the Menin Gate.

Sir Edwin Luytens built in a neo-Georgian style in every way superior to that of Blomfield. He had far more imagination, and his huge practice embraced almost every form of structure. In the City he built Britannic House (1926) in Finsbury Circus, and the headquarters of the Midland Bank in Poultry, using a green and most expensive African marble in the main hall, so hard that, the story goes, it ruined every instrument used to cut it. For many of his earlier professional years he built country houses of varying size but unvarying expense up and down the country. He had an unerring sense of fine proportion and his Cenotaph in Whitehall is a masterpiece of subtle architectural design.

The later secular buildings of Sir Giles Gilbert Scott show an increasing awareness of structure and are influenced but mildly by the reigning Renaissance fashion. His Whitelands College at West Hill, London, and his additions to Clare College, Cambridge, are fine pieces of design in brickwork, but his University Library at Cambridge is somewhat heavy.

Heal's, in Tottenham Court Road, is one of the best buildings of this inter-war period, showing a simplicity and an awareness of the structure underneath. Devonshire House in Piccadilly, by Sir Charles Reilly, is retrograde and less expressive of its steel structure, but Adelaide House at London Bridge, by Sir John Burnet and Partners, is a most impressive industrial building, reflecting the massive construction beneath and, in its extremely restrained decoration, acknowledging only in the mildest form the architecture of the past.

With the Royal Horticultural Hall by Easton and Robertson, built in 1923–6, architecture takes a great step forward. It is a curious thing, and worthy of note, that English architecture is usually seen at its best in the form of a greenhouse, whether at Chatsworth or Islington. Tall, semi-elliptical concrete arches span the hall and support a series of bays which step inwards, diminishing in height towards the top. The appearance of the hall derives directly from its structure, and it is one of the happiest works of this distinguished firm of architects.

Another outstanding building of this time was the Shakespeare Memorial Theatre (1928–34), won in an international exhibition by Elizabeth Scott. The plan is efficient and is designed admirably for its purpose, but the appearance of the building, in one of the loveliest sites in England, is bleak and harsh, entirely out of sympathy or harmony with its setting on the river.

A finer building in every way is the London Passenger Transport Building (1929) at Westminster, by Adams, Holden and Pearson. The planning, to permit the maximum use of natural light, is extremely ingenious, and its façades, based on classical precepts, are plain and dignified. Epstein's sculpture, which raised a storm at the time, is rugged and strong, and contrasts admirably with the simplicity of its background.

Sir Giles Gilbert Scott dominated the ecclesiastical building of this time in a strongly individual style. The War Memorial Chapel at Lancing is typical, and while it is Gothic in feeling the detail is treated with great restraint and much emphasis is laid on large and unadorned wall spaces with impressive effect.

The complete breakaway from the traditional forms which still influenced this country was made in 1930–2 by an engineer, Sir Owen Williams, who was later to design the M.1 motorway. At the Boots chemical factory at Beeston, Nottingham, he anticipated the new architecture in England by twenty years. The appearance of the factory derives directly from its construction, which is based on the mushroom type of reinforced concrete structure first used on the Continent by Robert Maillart in 1908.

The factory covers an area of about 14 acres. The mushroom construction, which is possible only in reinforced concrete, gives wide column spacing, more unimpeded space on the floor, and obviates the necessity of beams in the ceilings. The floors are cantilevered beyond their supports so that it is possible for the outside wall of the building to be entirely of glass, a practice that is now general, and ensures adequate daylight throughout the entire building.

One of the most important considerations from the aesthetic point of view is the way in which the concrete has been allowed to remain visible in its structural form. It was not until some years after the war that the idea was followed by Le Corbusier in his Unité d'Habitation at Marseilles, whereupon shrill acclaim broke from a section of the English *avant garde* who, it seems, must ever look outside this country for all they consider meritorious.

Boots Factory, Beeston, Nottingham, 1930–2: part section showing mushroom reinforced concrete construction and glass walls

The *Daily Express* building at Manchester, also by Sir Owen Williams, again anticipates the post-war use of glass covering the maximum area of external wall, its appearance being dictated by its reinforced concrete construction, a flat slab type carried by supports with caps of cruciform type. Here, as in the Fleet Street building, black glass was used as a covering between the large areas of window, as the material is easily cleaned in the soot-laden Manchester atmosphere. Cantilevered projecting beams around the top of the building support a rail from which a movable platform can be suspended for cleaning the big expanse of glass, a practice which has been followed in most modern buildings. The *Daily Express* building in Fleet Street, again by Sir Owen Williams, with Ellis and Clarke as architects, is again framed in reinforced concrete. The cantilever construction permits the formation of long strips of glass windows, while the building is faced with polished black glass, a form of wall covering which anticipated all or most of the post-war office development, and gives, with its highly polished surface and vertical metal strips, a very brilliant effect. One of the most successful buildings in the country, considering its function, it aroused widespread interest at home and abroad.

In the 1930's, as a result of the persecutions by the Nazis under Hitler in Germany, many Jewish refugees fled the country. Albert Einstein, for whom Erich Mendelsohn had built the Einstein Tower at Potsdam in concrete used in plastic form, went to Princeton University, and Mendelsohn himself, with a vast experience of industrial and architectural design behind him, came to England. Almost immediately he won the competition for the De La Warr Pavilion at Bexhill, a distinguished and scholarly design for a concert hall and restaurant. He did not remain in England for long, and went on to Israel, where he still lives.

Mendelsohn is an artist and an extremely imaginative draughtsman who can express his architectural thought in line with the greatest of ease and fluency, as do most of the leading architects. Le Corbusier, the French architect who has dominated European architectural thought for the last forty years, is similarly gifted, and is a supreme and outstanding draughtsman. The early training of the two men was based on the Classical tradition, Le Corbusier in particular spending many of his youthful years sketching and measuring in Italy and Greece. Both men, however, realised early on that the architecture of today is that of an industrial and scientific civilisation: that machines or buildings must be designed for the purpose they are to fulfil. In his *Towards a New Architecture* Le Corbusier points out that the same principles of design apply equally to the building of a Parthenon or to an aeroplane, and that the one, by reason of the perfection of its design, can be as beautiful in its way as the other. It therefore follows that the possibilities of beauty in the new architecture, using new materials and new techniques, are as great as those of any building of classical Greece.

Another architect who came to England by way of Moscow, Vienna and Paris, where he worked under Perret, was Berthold Lubetkin, who moved to London about 1930 and, with five young English architects, founded the firm of Tecton. Their Penguin Pool in Regent's Park Zoo (1933–1935) is a spatial adventure in reinforced concrete, and their two blocks of flats at Highgate, known as Highpoint I (1934) and II (1937), and their Finsbury Health Centre are well to the fore in contemporary English architecture.

In the Spring of 1919 Walter Gropius became head of the Weimar High School for design, the famous Bauhaus, which was dedicated to the training of artists for the production of beautiful objects of use by the machine. The new Bauhaus buildings at Dessau were erected in 1925–6 and had an enormous influence on the architecture which followed on. In appearance they are of the utmost simplicity, the whole of the exterior walls being of glass, giving a very light and graceful air to the building.

In 1835 the idea of the circular library was put forward by the French architect Benjamin Delessert, for the Bibliothèque Nationale. Before this the Radcliffe Library had been built in 1738 at Oxford. The idea of the circular library influenced the Librarian of the British Museum, Sir Anthony Panizzi, who collaborated with Sydney Smirke, the architect of the Museum, in the construction of the great dome over the Reading Room.

The Manchester Reference Library, the largest municipal library in Great Britain, was designed by E. Vincent Harris in 1929 and completed in 1934. The plan is based on that of the Pantheon in Rome, the only complete Roman building still in use, whose huge concrete dome is some 15 feet larger in diameter. The reading room at Manchester is placed on the first floor, a most dignified space 127 feet in diameter, encircled by a colonnade of 28 columns, the reading tables arranged radially. The service is one of the most efficient, the circular service counter in the centre connecting with the book stack beneath enabling books to be delivered in the shortest possible time.

Although the building is based on a steel frame, there is no indication of this in its appearance, which is of a large classical monument. There have been criticisms of the circular form of its rooms, whose shape increases the problem of supervision.

The other notable library building of this time is the University Library at Cambridge (1931–4) which is sited beyond the Backs on the same axis as the Clare College Memorial buildings by the same architect, Sir Giles Gilbert Scott. The central tower, 160 feet high, dominates the University town; the structure is steel, which is expressed in the elevations, but here, again, the efficient functioning of the building has been sacrificed to some extent for the sake of a symmetrical plan. The appearance of the building, in brick of a pale fawn colour, gives no cause for objection, and the decoration of the interior is most pleasant and restful, with its blue chairs and silver-grey tables.

There was a considerable amount of church building in England between the two World Wars, the main reason being the rise of population and the spread of new residential areas, with a tendency to plan the churches as social as well as religious centres, many also providing for meeting rooms and school rooms. The style in general use was traditional in feeling, although the need for economy dictated a simpler and unadorned design.

The two English architects who at the time were well to the fore in church building were Sir Giles Gilbert Scott, whose huge cathedral at Liverpool placed him in the forefront of ecclesiastical designers, and Sir Edward Maufe, whose prize-winning design for Guildford Cathedral made him Scott's chief rival in this sphere. Maufe favours brick as the exterior material for his churches and even for Guildford Cathedral, and he uses the material in masterly fashion. His church of St. Thomas at Hanwell anticipates Guildford Cathedral, and although his buildings are dominated by traditional feeling the Gothic forms are simplified, and his fine sense of design, although conservative, has built up an enviable reputation in a country which is inclined to be suspicious of innovations where its deeper feelings are concerned. None of the English churches of the inter-war period matched the advanced stage of contemporary design of the continental churches, some of which, notably the German, broke right away from the traditional and used the most up-to-date materials in their construction, with novel and sometimes sensational effect.

The open architectural competition has often been the means of establishing the reputation of an architect, sometimes early in his career, and this practice is often pursued wherever a large and important building is projected. Many English town halls had been built in the nineteenth century and by this time were either too small or, by reason of their design, could no longer fulfil their function in a satisfactory way.

In the case of a large town it is a matter of great importance to erect a building that, in the dignity of its appearance and the efficiency of its planning, will conform in every way to the number and variety of the demands made upon it. It is the seat of local government and may house some hundreds of officials as well as the dignitaries that perform the civic duties of the town, so that its design calls for vast architectural experience and imagination.

The solution, in most cases, is to throw the design open to competition. A panel of assessors, appointed for their varied experience and their outstanding reputation, is appointed. In consultation with the civic officials they draw up a set of conditions, enumerating the needs of the building under discussion. A definite time is stated for the submission of designs, and architects are invited to submit their ideas.

In the nineteenth century the main feature of a town hall was its main hall, designed for concerts, balls and meetings of all kinds. Great stress was laid on the importance of the suites of rooms around the Mayor's Parlour, and heavy emphasis was given to the dignity of the more ceremonial side of civic life. All this has tended to diminish in the interests of economy and the lessening of civic pride, which has inevitably followed the greater ease of communication by road and air. There is now less money for lavish civic entertainments, and the expenses of mayor or councillors are carefully scrutinised and paid out. The endless and varied demands of modern life have resulted in a large increase of officials, so that now the modern town hall is made up almost entirely of office space, and ideas on town hall design have undergone drastic changes.

The competition for the town hall at Hornsey was won in 1933 by R. H. Uren, then a young man in his twenties. The plan of the building is ingenious and interesting, grouped as it is around a courtyard with no considerations of symmetry at all but responsive in every way to its needs. It is built in brick on a steel and concrete frame, and gives a feeling of restful and dignified quiet

in the midst of a busy and noisy suburb. It took two years to build and is still a model of a successful town hall building.

E. Berry Webber won several town hall competitions, Peterborough and Southampton among them. The former has a central portico in the grand classic manner with Corinthian columns, but this architect broke away from the Renaissance manner in his Southampton scheme and in his town hall at Hammersmith, although all his designs show the strong classical influence of Vincent Harris' office, where he spent his early professional years.

The municipal buildings at Norwich were again the result of a competition which was won by C. H. James and Rowland Pierce. To build it many of the old mediaeval buildings near St. Peter Mancroft were swept away, and the impressive civic centre now dominates the old market square which is flanked by the original mediaeval guildhall with its flint-covered walls on one side, and the lovely church of St. Peter Mancroft and the quaint old Sir Garnet Wolseley public house on the other. There was a strong Swedish influence on the more traditional English façades of this time which was echoed by the Norwich Town Hall, in itself a fine structure with its tall clock tower. One cannot help feeling, however, that the scale of the building is far too overpowering for the charming mediaeval buildings in the Market Square, and that it would, to advantage, have been better sited in a newer quarter of the old city or on an unencumbered site outside it.

Worthing Town Hall, by C. Cowles Voysey, is another in the English Renaissance manner. Leeds City Hall, with its two Baroque towers and spires, is a product of Vincent Harris, who has never varied, in his very considerable practice, from the English Renaissance style in some form. He

191

commenced his career by winning a number of important competitions, among which was the design for the row of new government buildings in Whitehall on the site of the old Montague House, although these buildings were not erected until after the last war. His Surrey County Hall at Kingston-on-Thames is also Baroque in style.

The direct effect of the Industrial Revolution on English towns was a fantastic increase in the numbers of people working in the new factories. The value of building land leapt accordingly, and speculative builders threw up thousands upon thousands of small, mean hovels crammed back to back, with the absolute minimum of comfort and amenity, that in a short while deteriorated into the most appalling slums.

Some attempt was made to improve these frightful conditions by the Public Health Acts of 1840, but they were wholly inadequate. Hovels—they cannot be called houses —at a density of fifty to the acre, covered the fields around the big centres of industry, facing mean streets, with the living rooms separated, in countless cases, from open cesspools by a mere covering of rotting wood floor. No running water or sanitation of any kind was provided, a whole street sharing one cold water tap and a communal lavatory.

In time these conditions stirred the more progressive industrialists and social reformers to attempt some betterment in living conditions for the wretches who swarmed in the cholera-ridden courts and rookeries. As this country was the first to industrialise, so also was she to the fore in her Town Planning and Housing Acts which culminated in the garden city movement.

As early as 1818 Robert Owen put forward ideas for villages in his 'Report to the Committee of the Association for the Relief of the Manufacturing and Labouring Poor',

in which he suggested a layout around a square, two storey houses for the inhabitants and a central complex of public kitchen and dining hall and a building for Social and Cultural purposes, the whole village surrounded by 1,000 or 1,500 acres of land. The idea was so revolutionary that it may have been the cause of dissension among the promoters, for it was abandoned after a few years.

James Silk Buckingham in 1849 put forward a plan for a model town in the form of a square, the wealthiest with houses facing on the square, graduating outwards and downwards in the social scale to the industrial zones which bordered the outskirts of the town. The material to be used was iron, thus anticipating the idea of prefabrication which was used to such effect in the construction of the Crystal Palace. Buckingham's plan was limited in size and was to be surrounded by open country, land and buildings were to be in single ownership, and all residents were to have shares in a limited liability stock company. The idea was too communistic to succeed and it was abandoned, although it made a valuable contribution to later developments.

Sir Titus Salt, an enlightened and forward-looking industrialist of a type all too rare in the nineteenth century, was a manufacturer of alpaca cloth, who in 1853 built a large factory on the banks of the river Aire in Yorkshire. Homes for his workpeople were provided, near the factories, of a very much improved design and greatly increased amenity and convenience. He did more. He added a church, a library, public baths and wash-houses, an institute with a museum and lecture hall, and playing fields and a park. It was a tremendous advance. Further industrial estates were built at Bourneville, by the Cadbury chocolate family, and at Port Sunlight, by Lord Lever-hulme, manufacturer of the famous soap, whose company has now developed into the vast Lever Brothers concern.

The Bourneville experiment was built about five miles to the south-west of Birmingham in 1879. The estate was originally intended for employees of Cadbury's, but now it has ceased to belong to the firm and residents from outside are included. The estate is planned on informal lines; every attempt at the picturesque and interesting has been made in order to increase the visual attraction of the layout, and open spaces are liberally provided. Houses, as far as possible, back on to children's playgrounds.

The factory at Port Sunlight was built in 1888 and the surrounding estate has been continually developed on a more formal plan than at Bourneville. Many of the houses have been designed by competent architects such as Sir Ernest George and Charles Reilly. The Classical Art Gallery on the estate is quite out of the ordinary with its famous collection of pictures, left to the estate by the founder of the firm.

Bourneville, Saltaire and Port Sunlight led the way out of the congested, filthy towns to the open fields and country, but these were working-class developments. Now the middle classes, with their increasing prosperity, sought a way out of the town centres to more open and cleaner suburbs that grew, unfortunately, in haphazard manner—but not always. We have mentioned the creation of Bedford Park near Chiswick, designed by Norman Shaw, and later Hampstead Garden Suburb appeared, designed for a variety of income levels but which has now become a prosperous middle-class suburb.

The great local authorities did not come into the picture until the closing years of the nineteenth century, when the Housing of the Working Classes Act of 1890 gave them the necessary powers. The first ex-periment made by the L.C.C. was in Shoreditch, although, in order to rehouse the densely crowded population, the housing authority had to resort to five-storey flats. They were, however, comparatively spaciously sited in contrast to the back-to-back slums that had gone, and other estates followed, until today the standard of houses and flats provided by the L.C.C. has no superior or even equal in the world.

The two garden city experiments of Bourneville and Port Sunlight link the early ideas of Silk and Buckingham with the later development at Letchworth which was conceived by Sir Ebenezer Howard and outlined in his book, *Tomorrow: A Peaceful Path of Real Reform*, published in 1898. The idea behind the suggestion was to draw off the crowds from the already overcrowded centres of population, an idea that anticipated by nearly half a century the present policy of decentralisation by the London County Council.

Good progress was made, and the Garden City Pioneer Company was formed in 1902. Planning of the new town was entrusted to Sir Raymond Unwin and Barry Parker, who laid out the centre on a formal pattern and designed the remainder on picturesque lines in accordance with mediaeval village tradition. Social, educational and amusement centres, trees and lawns have been liberally provided and the town has by now assumed a very attractive appearance, in spite of some indifferent architectural design, in particular in the centre of the town.

Hampstead Garden Suburb is in every way superior in this respect. It was built a few years before the First World War and was planned by Sir Raymond Unwin and Barry Parker. On this occasion, however, they had the assistance of Sir Edwin Lutyens, who designed the two churches which dominate the centre of the project.

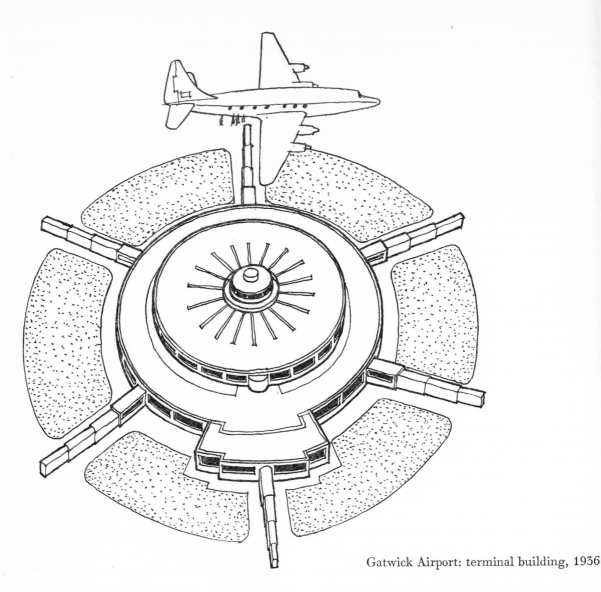

Gatwick Airport: terminal building, 1936

The idea of decentralisation had now obtained a firm grip, although the result was often a mere extension of the built-up area of the city. Based on the garden city idea the modern satellite town was evolved, having its own industries, schools and recreation centres, as a completely 'balanced' town. Those of the present day are planned away from the centres of industry and population.

Many of our great cities, at the close of the nineteenth century, were surrounded by small towns separated from each other by appreciable areas of open country, but with the increase in population and the spread of industry they have gradually grown towards each other and towards the city, on which a big percentage of their inhabitants base their means of livelihood. The result is now, as around London, a vast built-up sprawl some fifty or sixty miles across, building land has rocketed to unprecedented values and the life of the unfortunate inhabitants becomes yearly less comfortable.

Various far-seeing people proposed, after

194

the First World War, a policy of planned dispersal, but were put off by the general insistence on priority for the solution of the housing problem. Finally, a site was acquired with an area of just over 2,300 acres at Welwyn lying to the north of London. The town was very attractively designed by Louis de Soissons, who favoured the English Renaissance manner in his elevations and used the economical cul-de-sac to great effect. (The advantages of the cul-de-sac are, firstly, more houses can be sited around it than on to a through road; secondly, there is no question of through traffic, making for greater safety and quiet, and thirdly, the road can be a lightly constructed service way. The cul-de-sac also lends itself to a far wider variety in the siting of the houses.)

The satellite town, however, remained as merely a dream between the two wars, and piecemeal planning continued. Whereas in Welwyn people who worked there lived near by, in other planned suburbs they had often to journey over considerable distances, sometimes at much inconvenience and discomfort, to reach their factories or offices. Too often, also, the new suburbs were built over good arable and agricultural land.

Middle-class housing between the wars, during which time the population of England arose by two millions, was provided by speculative building, while the bulk of working-class dwellings were built by the local authorities, although nowadays many housing authorities, and notably the London County Council, combine working and middle classes in their estates.

A building which had a significant effect on airport architecture throughout the world was the circular terminal building at Gatwick (1936), by Frank Hoar, Alan Marlow and Benjamin Lovett, which was served by a new railway station so that fast trains from Victoria could run directly to the airport.

The building was of reinforced concrete, with six covered extending corridors to the planes, and contained a restaurant, shops and a control tower. It was connected to the railway station beneath the runways by a spacious underground passage lined with exhibition cases containing the wares of the great London stores. The structure was simple and purely functional, its plan and formation arising directly from its special needs and as such was an outstanding example of the new architecture which owed nothing to traditional forms.

Penrhyn Castle, 1827–40

195

6

The Post-War period

Since the war, it has become increasingly appreciated that the traditional approach to architecture—that it could exist isolated from the fundamental sciences and humanities—can no longer be maintained. Architecture is concerned not only with structure and materials but with function and human requirements. Although much is known of the way a building is made and clothed, far less is known of the social and biological sciences, and their effect on planning and design may be as revolutionary, in the coming years, as that of the engineers' since the passing of the age of revivals.

There is now much active research into the questions of what people want and how they react when exposed to experimental environments; this has added much to our knowledge of the effect of buildings on their inhabitants, and its importance will be seen in the new drive for more hospitals, for example. Nobody will deny that a patient's

chances of recovery are much enhanced by attractive surroundings, or that many of our mental hospitals present positive obstacles to effective treatment.

During the first post-war years the overwhelming need for houses and flats displaced any other form of building. Materials were rigidly controlled and austerity was rigorously applied, so that design was of the simplest, a condition that approximated to what many architects considered as the necessary conditions of good design. Inevitably, it became the opportunity of the local authorities, such as the London County Council, to provide on a large scale the much-needed houses, and the difficulty of carrying on a private practice gave many young architects an opportunity of joining the staffs of such local authorities and initiating the research into new conditions and new materials, which has resulted in the very high standards of domestic and educational buildings, in particular, which have risen throughout the country.

In the designing of new housing estates throughout the country, the architects of the great local authorities have a decided advantage over the private architect. Architecture today has become a subject of much complexity, the combined product of the research and work of sociologists, economists, scientists, town planners and technicians. The style now being evolved is a synthesis of their efforts and demands, and one that has made a complete break from those of the past and is developing in harmony with modern life, an expression of new problems of construction and function. The relationship between architecture and engineering has now been re-established, so that new and unfamiliar forms will inevitably make their appearance.

Comparatively recent discoveries in the use of steel and concrete have widened the scope of modern building to an enormous extent. The techniques of creation have always lagged well behind those of destruction, and the endless and intensive study, for example, of new metals able to withstand the tremendous friction and heat demanded by the modern weapons of annihilation and the fantastic results obtained, are infinitely in advance of the stage so far reached by building research. The old, solid, weight-bearing masses of brick and stone have, however, now been replaced by light, slender supports with a saving of both weight and space. One has only to compare a building of merely a century ago with a corresponding contemporary example to appreciate this fact. Planning has become more flexible and follows the example of the Baroque style, which broke away from the rigid classical formula and led to entirely new forms.

The Festival of Britain and the South Bank Exhibition in 1951 did a great deal to bring the new architecture before the public. Before the war we had tended to lag behind the excellent products of many smaller and poorer countries, and we had also the mistakes of the Wembley Exhibition of 1926 to act as a warning guide.

The effect of the 1951 Exhibition was salutary, with the added benefit of opening up the dreary South Bank to the large-scale development which followed. The Exhibition buildings were cleared away after six months, but one building was left, the Royal Festival Hall, the most important public building erected in England since the war. It contains, in the unanimous opinion of most musicians, the finest concert hall in the world. There have been many criticisms of the elevation to the river front and of the exterior generally, but for the spacious interior, and the concert auditorium itself, there is nothing but praise.

The site, before the war, was part of a semi-derelict industrial area of a very shabby appearance, between County Hall and Waterloo Bridge. The plans for post-war London which were produced by Sir Patrick Abercrombie and J. H. Forshaw, the architect to the London County Council, contained many proposals for the replanning of the area, which in principle are now on the way to completion.

In 1948 it was decided that the concert hall should form one of the main buildings of the Festival of Britain Exhibition proposed for 1951. The technical difficulties were considerable, as two underground railways pass at a depth of 57 feet directly under the site, and the Hungerford Bridge, carrying rail traffic to and from Charing Cross from the south-east of England, borders the area on the west. The concert hall had therefore a double problem: perfection of sound carrying within and insulation from sound

197

without. The ingenious planning of the L.C.C. team of architects headed by Robert Matthew, Dr. Leslie Martin and Edwin Williams, reinforced by Hope Bagenal's immense knowledge of acoustics, solved the problems. The auditorium was given a protecting blanket of insulation in the form of subsidiary accommodation, which includes compartments for B.B.C. commentators and television transmission, the organ chamber, a full sized replica of the concert platform for orchestra rehearsals, artists' rest and refreshment rooms, restaurants, a fine music library, and the resident engineer's penthouse, with its enviable views of London and the Thames.

The auditorium with its unusual acoustically planned boxes measures 170 feet by 100 feet, narrowing to 80 feet at the front, with a seating capacity of 3,165 compared with 3,000 in the Salle Pleyel, Paris.

Owing to competent planning, the web of noisy communications by which the Royal Festival Hall is surrounded, far from being a disadvantage, has proved to be one of its greatest assets, for the Hall is one of the easiest places of entertainment to reach in London.

The auditorium is raised on stilts above the spacious foyers. Clear vistas extend throughout the whole vast area below and around the auditorium, and, looking outward, magnificent views of the river unfold through wide plate glass windows.

The aims of the architects so successfully achieved may best be summed up in their own words: 'We have taken a cube of space roughly 200 feet square and 80 feet high. Within this space we have modelled and sculptured out the shape of the component parts, and as you move through the foyers and promenades, if you are aware of the excitement of its vistas and its continual unfolding of space, we shall not have failed.'

The result is one of the most fascinating building complexes in the country. Postwar rationing of steel determined the construction of the building in reinforced concrete. The outside of the Festival Hall is, however, by no means as happy as the interior; the impression given is that, as it was not possible to express the main idea of the elevated auditorium, the architects' indecision was reflected in a somewhat nondescript exterior. But the very competent planning enables large crowds to circulate with impressive ease, and the design and high quality of the details and materials have done much to raise the prestige of English architecture.

The Dome of Discovery was one of the buildings of the Festival of Britain Exhibition in 1951, and was sited between County Hall and Hungerford Bridge. It was designed as a temporary exhibition structure to house the story of British predominance in exploration and discovery, not only by land and sea, but also into the nature of the living world and the universe.

It was the largest dome in the world, 365 feet in diameter, 93 feet high and 45 feet to the level of the eaves. Three platform levels inside were reached by stairs and escalators.

Speed of erection was all-important. Work was commenced on 1st September 1949, and the building was completed on 15th November 1950.

The appearance of the structure inside was dramatic, bold sweeping lines of the galleries contrasting with the extraordinary lightness of the vast aluminium saucer dome. The cutting of a great inverted aluminium cone at an angle formed a plan of two eccentric circles, the whole design based upon a geometrical conception of part circles, spheres and conic sections.

The dome was entered through a sunken vestibule which emerged well inside the

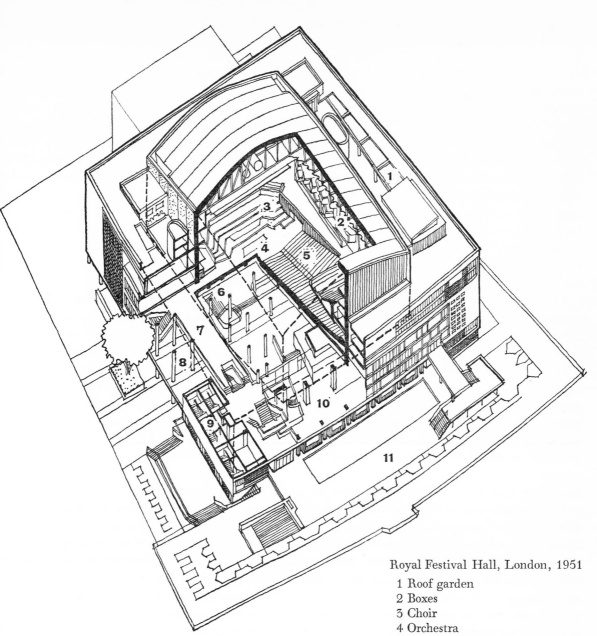

Royal Festival Hall, London, 1951

1 Roof garden
2 Boxes
3 Choir
4 Orchestra
5 Stalls
6 Entrance staircase
7 Side promenade
8 Main foyer
9 Escape stairs
10 Restaurant
11 Terrace facing River Thames

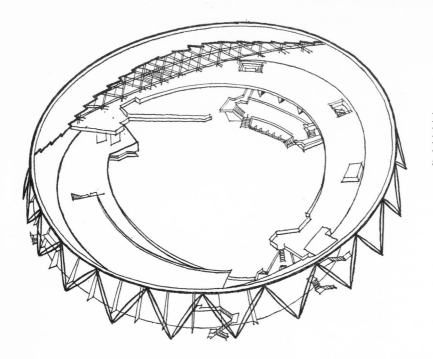

Dome of Discovery,
Festival of Britain Exhibition,
London, 1951:
architect, Ralph Tubbs

structure. The roof structure was of alumini-um alloy built-up ribs, intermediate rafters, purlins and sheeting, the whole dome supported on a welded mild steel circular ring girder, supported 45 feet above ground level on tubular steel diagonal struts. The roof was covered with aluminium sheets riveted together, and the tubular struts supporting the ring girders were formed of three tubes 2 feet 6 inches apart at the centre and joined together at top and bottom to form a cigar shape. These were arranged in a continuous row around the base of the dome in a triangular pattern, and were pin-jointed at top and bottom so that the dome could expand or contract and yet always be held symmetrically against wind pressure.

The problem of housing, after the war, occupied the thoughts of politicians and architects more urgently than any other subject. The losses caused by the war, and the ever-increasing population, demanded a solution that could only be achieved by a large-scale effort. Not only single family

dwellings had to be provided, but high blocks of flats for the denser areas, dwellings for old people, terrace houses and maisonettes, and the incidental buildings for laundries and canteens, nursery schools, crèches and garages, public houses and shops. Designing for a community became a matter of designing part of a town, and when the policy of mixed development was adopted, and estates were created for working-class and middle-class housing, it called for a degree of imagination and competence in the designers that found expression in the best domestic architecture and town planning in the world. There can be nothing but praise for the official architects and town planners who produced these new estates, and their attractiveness, and the way in which natural amenities have been preserved, are in contrast with much of the development by the speculative builder from which we have had to suffer for so long.

Since the responsibility for designing the London County Council estates passed from

200

the Valuer to the Council Architect in 1950, the L.C.C. has created some very significant and invigorating housing. One of the more important is the Alton estate, on a site of 25 acres lying between Putney Heath and Richmond Park, on high ground overlooking the park and providing the tenants with some magnificent views. The development is mixed and includes high blocks of flats, maisonettes and houses, the 'point-block' of eight and eleven storeys being a feature of the design. Another example is the Ackroydon estate of $16\frac{1}{2}$ acres on the east side of Putney Heath, on the site of some of the huge Victorian mansions whose fine old trees have, as far as possible, been retained. This is now the accepted practice in most official schemes, just as their destruction is almost invariable in the case of developments carried out by the small speculative builder, to whom as a rule they represent only an obstacle to the quicker completion of a job.

Many housing sites in London were inevitably designed by private architects. The big Pimlico scheme was won by two young architects, Powell and Moya, who have gone on from there to produce some of the most exciting buildings in the country. Their Skylon feature for the South Bank Exhibition, a cigar-shaped abstraction supported in mid-air by thin wires (which prompted the 'mot' that it represented the future Britain, having no visible signs of support), added further to their reputation. The Spa Green, Finsbury, scheme by Tecton, Lubetkin and Skinner, and the Hallfield, Paddington, scheme by Drake and Lasdun, are among the best of the estates planned by private architects in London.

In 1952 a competition for the Golden Lane Estate, just north of St. Paul's, was won by Chamberlin, Powell and Bon. Other schemes at Boundary Road, St. John's Wood, by Armstrong and MacManus, and Albion Gardens, London, by H. T. Cadbury-Brown, maintain the high standard of post-war domestic building.

Not all speculative building is necessarily poor. The Span Group of companies, who have commissioned Eric Lyons, produce well-designed estates, as at Ham Common and Blackheath. The Lindsay Parkinson Company, with Wells and Hickman, are currently changing the face of Woking to good effect, and Wates, with Kenneth Bland, produce houses and flats of a high order.

In the provinces, Tayler and Green have maintained their good reputation with housing for various Norfolk Councils, and Frederick Gibberd had won fame for his New Town at Harlow long before he won the competition for Liverpool Cathedral. The Lansbury development, which was promoted as part of the Festival of Britain, was conceived as a model neighbourhood development on the lines of the war-time plan for London by Abercrombie and Forshaw, and represents the work of a number of architects.

It is of interest to note that, in spite of the vast amount of research into new materials and methods of building, the old traditional ideas have been found to be more economical in the building of small houses. Just after the war, very rapid methods of house construction and erection were tried out, some of the results of which, the 'pre-fabs', are unfortunately still with us, although they are rapidly being replaced. In no case did they approach the brick-built house either in appearance or in lasting quality, and much of present-day housing continues, fortunately, to be built in the traditional material.

The increase of population in the twentieth century, coupled with the enormous increase in bureaucrats since the Second World War, has led to an alarming monotony in the lives of a large number of citizens which in turn leads to a smothering of individuality, mirrored in much of the architecture of today. Education, biased in favour of the scientific approach, tends to accentuate the importance of the technologist to the detriment of the artist and the craftsman. Hence we have, in the second half of the twentieth century, a deplorable mushroom growth of square boxes, devoid of imagination in the use of materials and design.

Schools, happily, have been built, for the most part, with imagination and economy. The need for vast numbers of new schools after the war was acute. Many had been destroyed, many more were needed in the new housing estates, built to satisfy the demands of a rising population, and the Education Act of 1944, which had raised the school leaving age to fifteen, had further increased the numbers attending school.

Between the wars, the subject had received a great deal of attention. Public interest was focused very largely by the *News Chronicle* which promoted a competition that was won by Denis Clarke Hall. He produced some new and exciting ideas, included the results of much modern research, and planned in a freer and more convenient way. Other good schemes in the same competition brought further ideas, and experiments in light forms of construction and rapid erection were carried out by various local authorities. The Butler Act further stimulated research and design in its re-ordering of the national educational system.

The most successful schools programme by a local authority was carried out by the Hertfordshire County Council under C. H. Aslin, who, with a devoted team of assistants, tackled the problem with conspicuous energy and drive. The difficulty and delays in the delivery of materials, problems of official red tape, and scarcity of labour led,

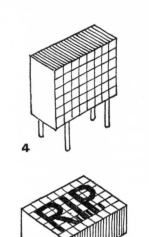

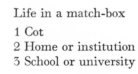

Life in a match-box

1 Cot	4 Office or shop or factory
2 Home or institution	5 Hospital or flats
3 School or university	

in the first instance, to a system of ordering materials in advance; in the second, by the approval of plans in an early stage by the Ministry of Education; and the third, to the use of prefabricated and standardised components. This last led to the adoption of a module, that is, a sort of least common denominator in measurement, which simplified planning and construction.

Two of the best examples of the Hertfordshire schools are the Temple Wood Junior and Infants School (1950) at Pentley Park in Welwyn Garden City, where careful planning secured south sunlight in all the classrooms, and the Summerswood Junior School (1951) at Furzehill Road, Boreham Wood, near Elstree, where walls and ceilings are demountable and can be rearranged to meet changing requirements. Another good example is the Secondary Modern School (1956) at Grove Mill Lane, Langleybury, by James Cubitt and Partners in collaboration with C. H. Aslin.

In London, a newer development is the comprehensive school, with accommodation for up to 2,000 pupils, and the secondary modern school. Private architects are increasingly brought in on these schools to share the work with the local authorities with happy results. One of these is the Woodfield County Secondary School (1954) at Cranford, Middlesex, by Denis Clarke Hall and the County Architect.

Since the lifting of restrictions on materials there has been a tremendous spate of office and commercial building. The planning of individual buildings has given way to the development of larger areas involving many buildings. In the main, this form of development has been carried out by what are known as 'package dealers', that is, big construction firms with adequate financial backing, who submit competitive tenders to owners, usually local authorities, for the reconstruction of large areas. They not only erect the buildings but, having their own architectural offices, they design them in a manner which, it must be admitted, compares favourably with fairly average standards, and in most cases improves considerably on existing conditions.

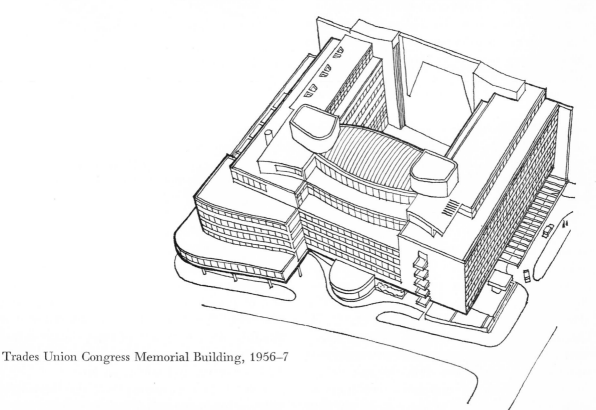

Trades Union Congress Memorial Building, 1956–7

The Era of Experiment

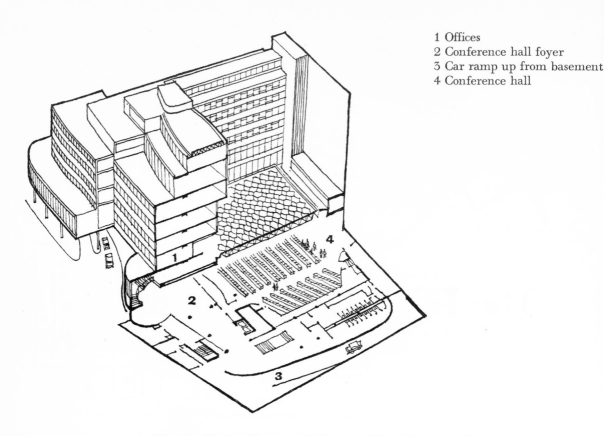

1 Offices
2 Conference hall foyer
3 Car ramp up from basement
4 Conference hall

Trades Union Congress Memorial Building, 1956–7

The design of this building was the subject of an open competition won by David du R. Aberdeen in 1948.

The problem of planning was full of difficulties. The site was very restricted—180 feet by 130 feet—and angles of light and other limitations on height had to be strictly adhered to. The architect had to ensure a smooth and lucid circulation, within and without; he had to achieve a feeling of openness in spite of the restricted site; he had to obtain good natural light and air conditions to the maximum possible office accommodation and bring the sunlight into the very heart of the building. He had also to create a building of elegant simplicity.

All this the young architect (he was only thirty-three) solved in a most competent way. The big open courtyard above the main conference hall permits maximum light to the centre of the building, which is framed in reinforced concrete and covered with thin granite slabs. A great Epstein statue, with a background of green marble, forms the centrepiece of the central area. Cars proceed by ramps to an underground garage.

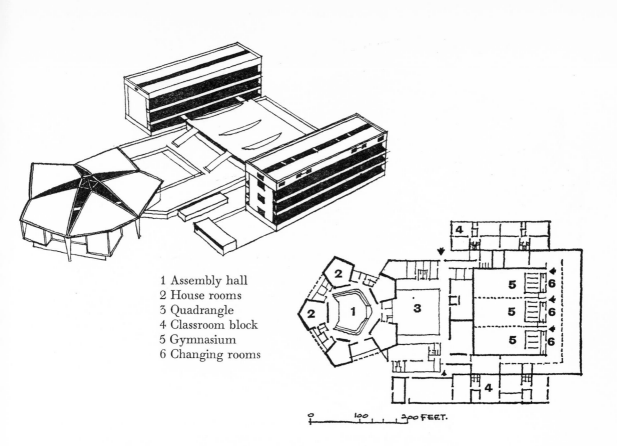

1 Assembly hall
2 House rooms
3 Quadrangle
4 Classroom block
5 Gymnasium
6 Changing rooms

Girls' Comprehensive School, Southwark, 1958

The school was designed by Chamberlin, Powell and Bon, for the London County Council, to accommodate 1,250 girls in a slum clearance area to the north of the Old Kent Road. The school is divided into houses, hence the house rooms around the Assembly Hall.

The shape of the school is unusual and shows imaginative handling by capable designers. There is a four-storey classroom block and another similar practical block, a pentagonal building which contains the assembly hall and house rooms, and three gymnasia, *en suite*, with folding partitions between, with changing rooms.

The staff rooms, library, kitchen and main entrance hall are sited around a central quadrangle. Classrooms in the classroom block are back to back and are served by two staircases, so eliminating a central corridor.

The planning is compact and economical. The school is built of loadbearing brick walls with suspended concrete floors and roofs. The roof of the pentagonal assembly hall is made up of five concrete hyperbolic paraboloids separated by roof lights.

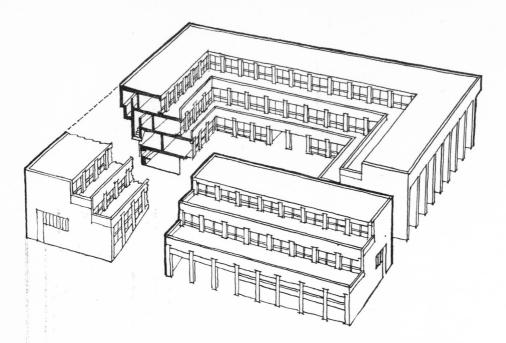

Gonville and Caius College, Cambridge, 1959:
new residential accommodation

The wall of buildings enclosing a courtyard has, since the thirteenth century, identified the college community, bringing into relationship the chapel, hall and residential accommodation for staff and students. This is illustrated by the view of St. John's College, Cambridge, page 101. The courtyard idea had formed the basis of the plans of the earliest Cambridge Colleges—Pembroke, Gonville and Caius, Trinity Hall and the first court of Corpus Christi, built in 1350.

At Jesus College, a monastic rather than a collegiate foundation, the open-ended court already existed, and this type was urged by Dr. Caius when he built the second court at Gonville and Caius College in 1565, with the object of better ventilation, 'lest the air from being confined within a narrow space should become foul'. Wren disliked the closed court and the increasing interest of Renaissance designers in balance and symmetry is shown in William Wilkins' plans for Downing College, and University College, London.

The plan for a residential block for 100 students at Gonville and Caius College, by Sir Leslie Martin and Colin St. J. Wilson, shows a development of the Cambridge College tradition. The rooms open on to terraces facing the courtyard, the staircases serving them are on an enclosed peripheral corridor, and the outward facing elevations take the form of colonnades supporting the upper floors. Each group of rooms around a staircase is planned with its own washing arrangements.

208

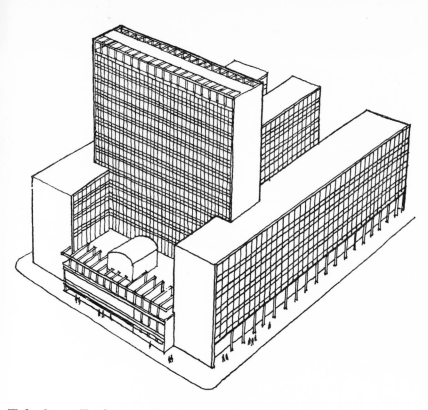

Telephone Exchange, Farringdon Street, London, 1960

The Ministry of Works is responsible for all Post Office building and this telephone exchange in Farringdon Street has a reinforced concrete frame the plan of which was determined by Post Office engineering requirements.

The building accommodates switch rooms, telephone managers' offices, a low-level garage, a large cable chamber at sub-basement level and apparatus and switch rooms from ground to third floors with office accommodation up to the twelfth floor. It is faced externally with Portland stone. Windows are in hardwood frames. The design is competent, if a little dull, but it expresses adequately the purpose for which it is designed.

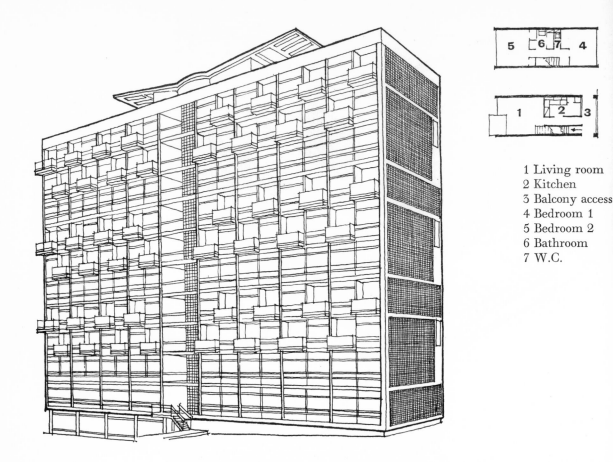

1 Living room
2 Kitchen
3 Balcony access
4 Bedroom 1
5 Bedroom 2
6 Bathroom
7 W.C.

Hillfields, Coventry: ten-storey flats

Coventry was damaged by bombing more severely during the last war than any other British town of its size. The cathedral and town centre were almost completely destroyed, but the new city, which has risen under the direction of the Coventry City architect, is one of the most exciting architectural layouts in Europe.

The building illustrated contains 24 two-bedroom maisonettes, 24 one-bedroom flats and eight bed-sitting room flats. Access to maisonettes is from balconies at second, fifth and eighth floors, and to flats by staircase from each of these levels. The same staircase well is used for the internal stairs of the maisonettes. The feature on the roof contains a lift machine room and water tanks.

The building is constructed of reinforced concrete and end walls have a black aggregate finish between floor slabs. Panels below the windows are of coloured glass. Windows are sliding, and living rooms have electric floor heating. Internal bathrooms and kitchens are mechanically ventilated.

210

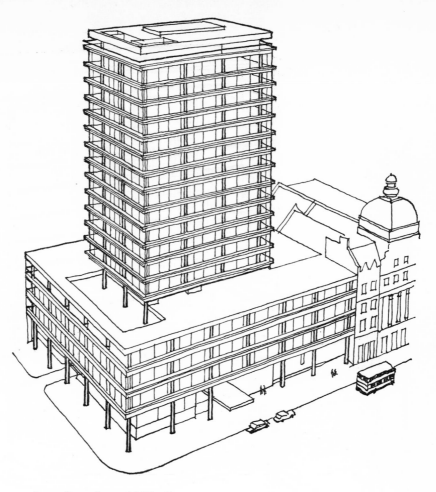

New Zealand House, Haymarket, London, 1961–3

One of London's more graceful office blocks, New Zealand House, by Sir Robert Matthew, is built on the site of the old Carlton Hotel, and will later be extended to cover the site of Her Majesty's Theatre, which adjoins it. This site will, however, not be available until 1970.

The building, the London headquarters of the New Zealand Government, is a reinforced concrete structure which includes a pair of box columns forming the central core of the tower, which rises to a height of 225 feet. Most of the public accommodation is on the ground and mezzanine floors of the lower block, the immigration and other departmental offices on the first and second, and the High Commissioner's suite and external affairs office on the third. This suite has a private terrace overlooking Pall Mall and an open court visible through the building from Pall Mall at second-floor level. In the tower are offices surrounding the central lift shafts, and on top is a pent-house for use of the staff. Another entrance to the building from Royal Opera Arcade gives access to shops and a bank.

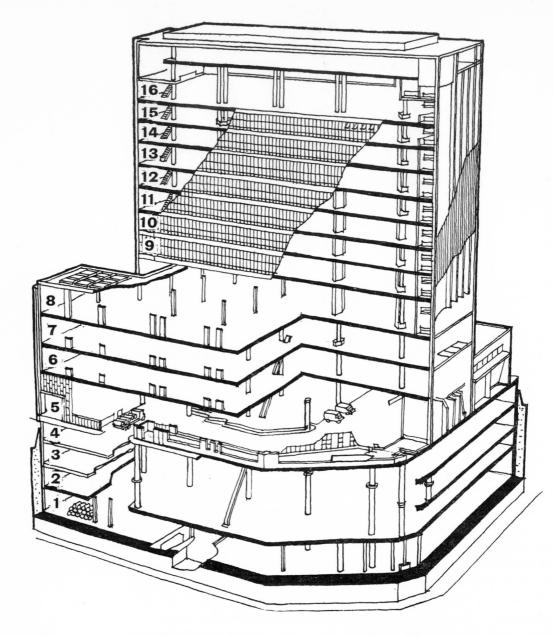

1 Printing presses; paper reel store
2 Printing presses; lower foundry; workshops
3 Ventilating plant; paper reel store
4 Stores; ink tanks; transformer rooms
5 Publishing and despatch—ground level
6 Canteen; telephone; publishing
7 Composing; process engraving; upper foundry
8 Editorial

9 Editorial
10 Circulation; publicity
11 Advertising
12 Production and personnel offices
13 Service departments
14 Directors
15 Accounts
16 Heating and ventilating plant room

Daily Mirror Building, High Holborn, London, 1961

This building in High Holborn was designed by Sir Owen Williams and Anderson, Forster and Wilcox as joint architects and engineers. It is one of the most impressive buildings in reinforced concrete in the country.

The planning problem was difficult. The building had to house highly complex plant, printing machinery, and extensive material stocks, and provide good working amenities for a large number of operatives, together with the most modern facilities for editorial and administrative staff.

The weight of the press lines, the heavy machines which print the newspaper, decided their position on the lowest floor. Each of the five machines weighs 850 tons. Maximum paper storage near the presses had to be provided. Regulations concerning plot ratios and angles of light were vital in the ultimate design of the building.

The load on some of the 20 main columns at lowest basement level is 3,000 tons per column. The erection of the building is of interest. The site had to be excavated eventually to a depth of about 50 feet and surrounded by a retaining wall. The foundations for the main columns, sited at 45 feet centre to centre, were first constructed and the columns built up to the ground floor concrete slab, which is capable of supporting heavy loaded lorries. The erection of the building then proceeded while excavation below ground level still went on.

The height of the building above ground level is 169 feet, and provides, with its vermilion coloured aprons under the windows, one of the most striking features in London. Almost at the top of the building are the Chairman's and the Directors' offices, designed by Hulme Chadwick.

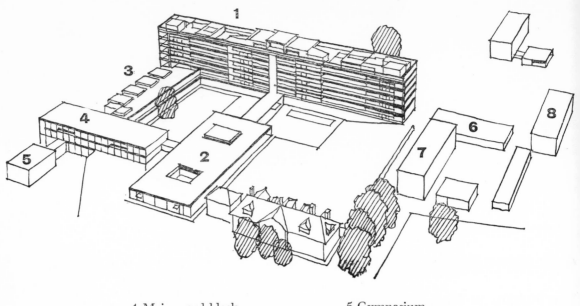

1 Main ward block
2 Out-patients and casualty
3 X-ray and operating theatres
4 Physiotherapy

5 Gymnasium
6 Canteen
7 Maids' home
8 Nurses' home

Kettering General Hospital, 1959

This hospital was designed by Gollins, Melvin, Ward and Partners for the Oxford Regional Hospital Board on the outskirts of Kettering as an extension of the existing nineteenth-century building.

The low two- and three-storey building between the existing hospital and the future ward block includes X-ray, casualty, out-patients', physiotherapy, operating, records and pharmacy departments.

The present dangerous approach from the main road and the levels of the site required a new access leading direct to the new main hospital entrance and the out-patients' and casualty departments. Access from their to the X-ray, records, and pharmacy departments is by ground-floor corridor. These departments must necessarily be easy of approach by the public.

A gymnasium is provided, as well as nurses' and maids' homes with their own recreational rooms and a common canteen.

214

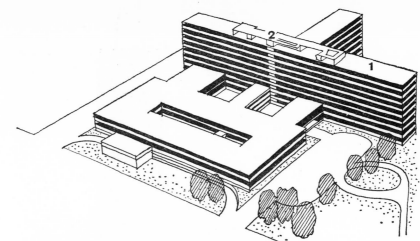

1 Main block
2 Central stairs and lifts

Hillingdon Hospital, Middlesex, 1961

This hospital, also designed by Gollins, Melvin, Ward and Partners, will be built in two stages, the first comprising all the ancillary departments and 210 beds, the second the remaining wards and additional storage.

Each of the 16 wards in the main block contains 30 beds in a modification of the open type Nuffield pattern. The wards are planned in line, two to each floor, with end access from the central staircase and lifts. The remaining wards are in the lower block at the rear and are approached also from the central stairs and lifts. Some of these wards are smaller, and are reserved for special uses. The lower floors of the main block contain the ancillary medical departments, which spread also to the three-storey wings in the front.

Staff cloakrooms, pharmacy and central sterilising departments and stores are on the lower ground floor, the ground floor containing the departments of physio- and occupational therapy, casualty and out-patients' clinics and X-ray rooms. Entrance to the main hospital, adjacent to the administration and the main lift and staircase hall, is at this level, together with the ambulance and walking-case entrances for out-patients and casualties. The greater part of the administration, the operating theatre suite, the pathology department and most of the out-patients' clinics are on the first floor. The kitchens serving both wards and dining rooms are on the lower ground floor to the south of the tall block, an underground passage connecting them to the maternity department. The central boiler house of the existing hospital serves the calorifier chamber on the lower ground floor by steam mains, this chamber feeding the heating and hot water installations. The frame of the building is in reinforced concrete.

215

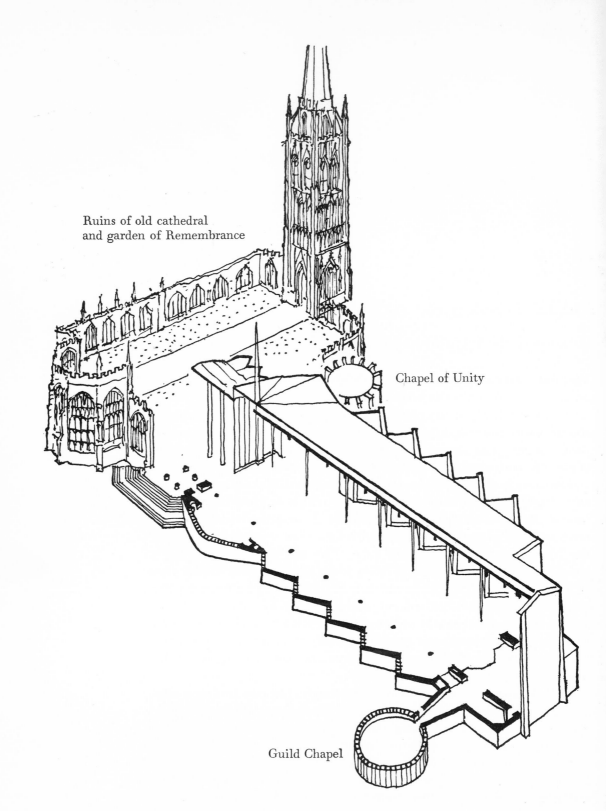

Ruins of old cathedral
and garden of Remembrance

Chapel of Unity

Guild Chapel

Coventry Cathedral, dedicated 1962

The old Cathedral Church of St. Michael was destroyed by bombs during the war, only the walls and spire remaining.

It was decided that the rebuilding of such an important monument should form the subject of an open competition, which was won by Basil Spence, who retained the spire and formed the remaining walls of the old cathedral into part of a garden of remembrance.

The new building is placed at right angles to the old and is joined by a high porch, on the flank wall of which is Epstein's dramatic bronze statue of St. Michael. The porch is separated from the new nave by a tall glass screen etched with figures of saints through which the high altar tapestry can be seen. The tall side windows are so arranged that they cannot be seen from the back but throw their light forward on to the altar which is surmounted by a huge tapestry designed by Graham Sutherland, and woven in France.

The design combines traditional forms with a modern system of construction in reinforced concrete. Exterior walls are of stone, a warm red brown in colour, the roof of reinforced concrete with a copper covering.

The cathedral reduces in width and height towards the high altar, giving an impression of greater length. The use of 'illusion' in building was commonplace during the Baroque period, the outstanding example of deliberate lengthening being the Scala Regia in the Vatican, by Bernini, the staircase leading from the great portal of St. Peter's up to the Vatican buildings. The staircase reduces in length and height towards the top, giving an illusion of far greater length.

217

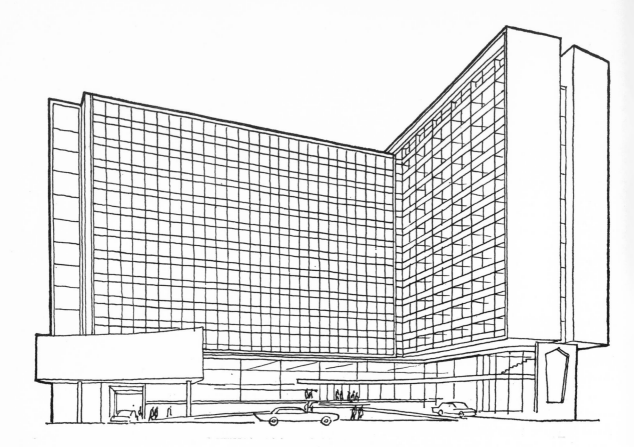

Hotel in Kensington, 1962

This hotel, by R. Seifert and Partners, which is not yet complete, will occupy a site between Kensington Palace Avenue and High Street, with fine views over Hyde Park and Kensington Gardens.

The frame will be of reinforced concrete. Accommodation for nearly 500 bedrooms will be provided, with the usual restaurants, bars and ancillary rooms with an underground car-park. There have been few hotels built in England since the war but increasing numbers of tourists are now an encouragement to build. The Carlton Towers Hotel, by Michael Rosenaur, near Sloane Square, London, the Melbury in Conduit Street, the very successful President in Southampton Row, and the new Hilton Hotel in Park Lane maintain a very high architectural standard.

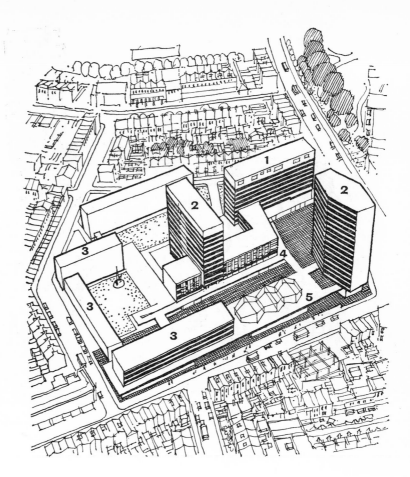

1 Offices and penthouse flats
2 Offices
3 Residential
4 Shops and pedestrians
5 Underground station

Archway Development, Highgate Hill and Junction Road, London

This is an example of a typical commercial development that is taking place throughout the country. It comprises shops, offices and residential buildings sited around a pedestrian area, and is designed in a competent and attractive manner that infinitely enhances, not only the value, but the amenities of the district. The planning is open and airy, pedestrians can shop and children can play in comfort and safety as all traffic proceeds around the perimeter of the site, and underground car-parking is close and convenient. The site is served by buses and the Underground railway, for which a new station will be constructed. The project, designed by Oscar Garry and Partners, is about half-way towards completion.

London County Council Housing in Bermondsey, 1962

This scheme by Hubert Bennett for twenty-one storey blocks and four-storey maisonette blocks is typical of the high standard of London County Council design. The site is 6 acres in area, near the Surrey docks, and comprises 253 dwellings. The high blocks contain 3-room flats with 2-room flats on every fourth floor. 72 maisonettes in four-storey blocks are arranged round a central stair giving balcony access to the upper maisonettes. 36 ground-floor maisonettes have private gardens and 34 garages are provided.

The site, in spite of the high density, is very open; one green space runs into the other, the traffic road running mainly around the site, leaving plenty of safe playing spaces for children. Tenants on the upper floors of the high blocks enjoy impressive views of the river and the shipping.

220

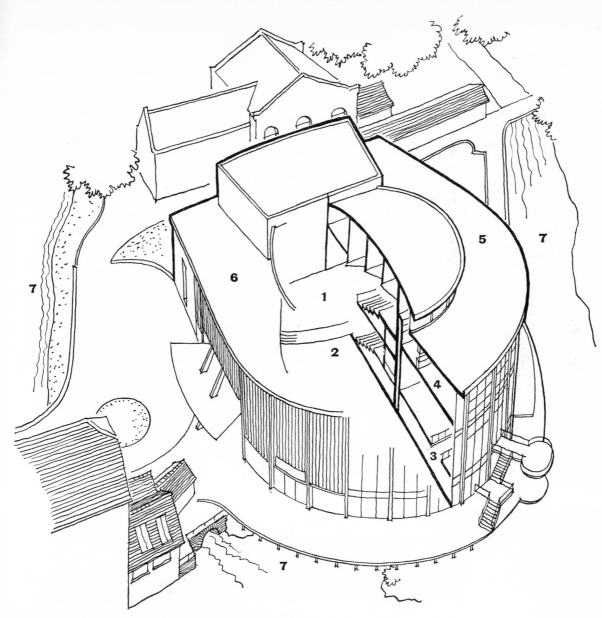

The Yvonne Arnaud Theatre, Guildford

The theatre is about to be built on a picturesque site on the River Wey, at Guildford, and is one of the more attractive designs among contemporary examples. A wide terrace and a spacious restaurant give attractive views of the surrounding waters and the old town, which here retains its charm and its pleasant character, although strenuous efforts are being made to destroy both, with notable success.

Male and female dressing rooms, on separate floors, occupy one side of the building, balanced by a large rehearsal room and offices on the other. Construction is of reinforced concrete.

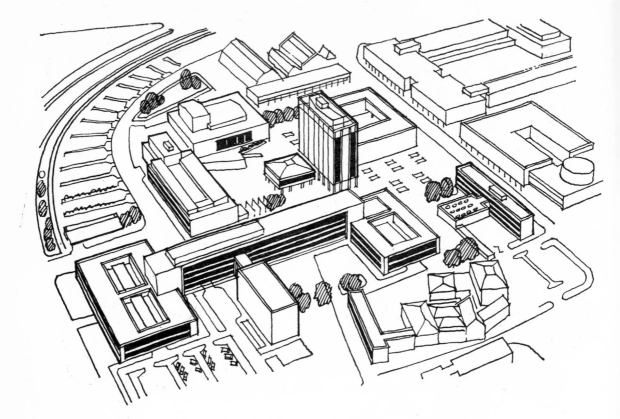

Doncaster Civic Centre, 1962

The replanning of the central area of Doncaster has been regarded as a problem of town design; with its system of inner pedestrian piazzas and car-parking on the periphery it tackles the impact of the motor-car on the inner core.

The city has a lively and prosperous shopping centre, but social and entertainment buildings are scattered and inadequate. The development plan defines an area of 37 acres adjacent to, and south of the existing shopping centre, bounded by a new inner ring or loop road on south and west, on the east by South Parade, a pleasant road lined with trees, and by the shopping centre on the north. The plan provides an over-all master design for the Centre by Frederick Gibberd. Sites for car-parks, a health centre and technical college, and the broad mass of future buildings are defined.

There are about 90,000 people in Doncaster, and motor traffic is heavy. Special regard has been paid to the motor–pedestrian problem, and buildings are grouped to look inwards on to a series of civic closes or precincts where motor vehicles are not permitted. Between the inner peripheral road and the outer ring road are car-parks, with further parks to the north of the site.

Casual motor traffic to the centre can always find a parking place near its point of entry. There will be a service yard or lay-by near each building, and no wheeled traffic at all in the core of the area.

Around the central civic space is the town hall, with technical college and new government offices opposite. The tall office sections of the town hall lend a vertical contrast to the technical college and form the focal point of the area. The office block partially divides the civic open space into a north and a south square which extend into each other. The council chamber is in the south square and committee and other important rooms are situated around a courtyard on the north.

There is an opening at ground level between the civic space and the precinct to the east of the technical college, thus linking it with the proposed art school. The area to the north is being redesigned as a new shopping centre, the main shopping street leading straight into the main civic place, so linking the business and civic zones.

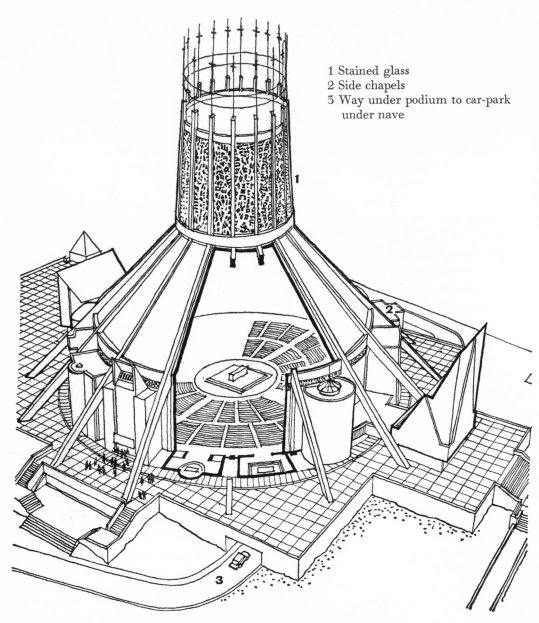

1 Stained glass
2 Side chapels
3 Way under podium to car-park
   under nave

Exterior appearance with three bays removed to show interior planning

Liverpool Roman Catholic Cathedral of Christ the King

The design for the Roman Catholic Cathedral of Christ the King was won in open competition by Frederick Gibberd, already well known for his work at Harlow and London Airport. It is a complete break with the traditional cathedral form.

The building is circular, in which 3,000 people can be seated within 70 feet of a centrally placed sanctuary, with the high altar as the focus of the design. The cathedral is in the form of a cylinder which is developed through a conical roof to a tapering coloured glass tower, in such a way that the most significant internal space and the most expressive external mass occur over the most important place, the tabernacle.

The cathedral stands on the crypt of the cathedral projected by Sir Edwin Lutyens, which was abandoned owing to the enormous cost. The roof of this crypt will be extended to form a podium, on which the cathedral and piazza for open-air services will stand. There will be a car-park under the nave.

The whole concrete structural frame of the cathedral will be faced with white mosaic, as concrete does not weather well. The roof, originally intended to be of aluminium sheeting, may be altered to copper owing to the influence of chemicals in the Liverpool atmosphere, and the external walls will be in Portland stone.

It is hoped to complete the building by 1966.

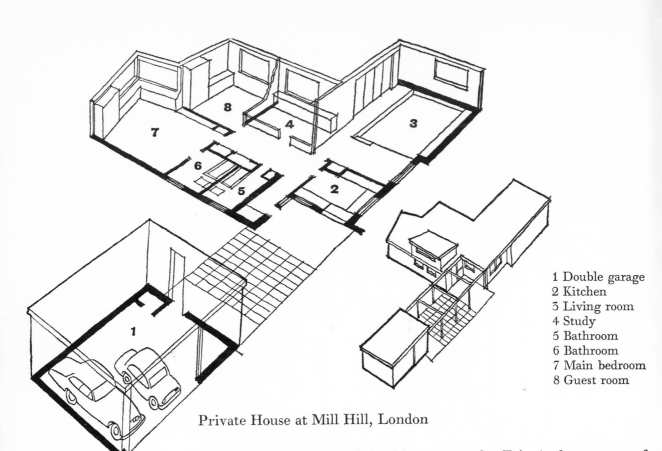

1 Double garage
2 Kitchen
3 Living room
4 Study
5 Bathroom
6 Bathroom
7 Main bedroom
8 Guest room

Private House at Mill Hill, London

The house was designed for his own use by Eric Ambrose, one of the most knowledgable and experienced domestic architects in the country. The exterior brickwork is in dark purple two-inch bricks with dark recessed joints and white bricks under the windows. While the area of double-glazed windows is generous it does not follow the extremes of some contemporary houses. The 'open' plan has been abandoned although the contiguous area of study and large hall can be opened up for entertaining.

A feature of the house is the exceptionally high insulation value for walls, roof, windows and floors. Floors are electrically heated. The rooms are unusually spacious for a small house but the architect was aware that reductions in space do not reduce costs since the basic overheads, such as plumbing and fittings, generally are the expensive items.

For this reason the hall is pushed up through two floors, the bathroom heights kept at a minimum of seven feet, allowing the otherwise waste space of the roof to harbour concealed tanks for water supply and provide an extra room in the form of a minstrel gallery.

The high-level lighting of the hall provides sunshine from early morning until well into the afternoon at all times of the year.

226

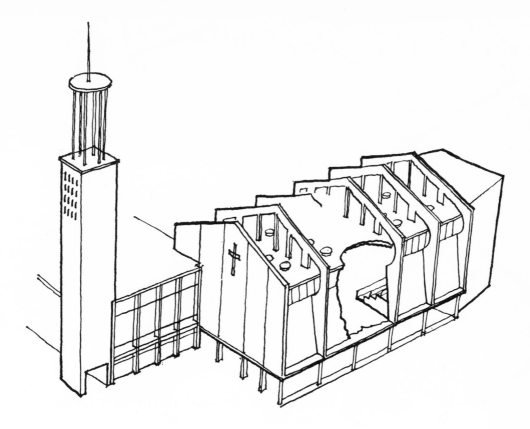

Trinity Congregational Church, Waterloo, London, 1951

The church was built in 1951 during the Festival of Britain Exhibition on London's South Bank at Waterloo, and formed part of the 'Live Architecture' section of the Festival. Designed by Handisyde and Stack, the church seats 400 and with a hall and ancillary rooms provides accommodation for a wide range of secular and religious activities. Most of the light comes from the top as the site is a noisy one. The frame is of reinforced concrete, the inside of the church painted a pale blue, the brickwork is a yellow London Stock and the sloping walls are sheathed externally with copper. Heating is by under-floor panels, radiators and warm air.

227

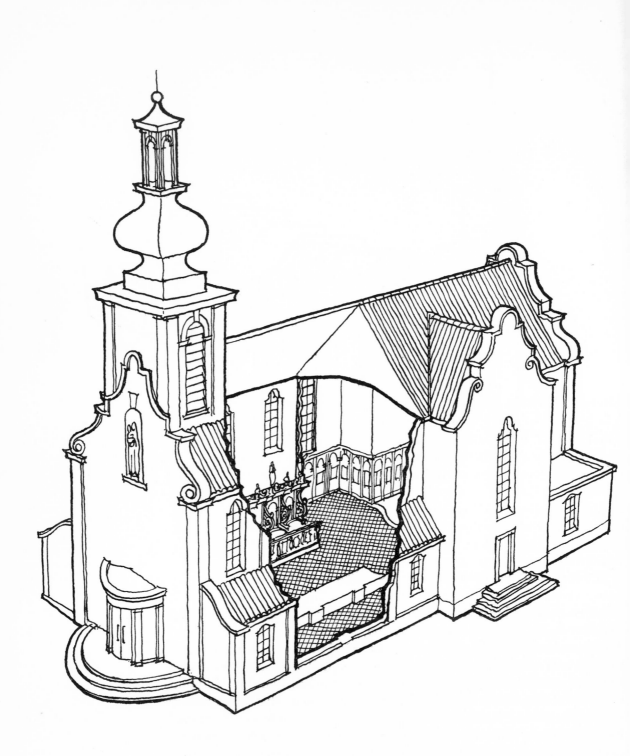

Church at Hythe, Kent, for St. Saviour's Convent, 1963

This church is being built to accommodate some magnificent Bavarian Baroque choir stalls, dated about 1690, from Buxheim in Bavaria, so that more than a hint of the appropriate style was desired by the clients. The interior is simple, the brick walls plastered white inside and out, the decoration restrained so that all attention is focused on the carvings and on the high altar, which is composed of the original carvings. Tiles are a dark brown, the cupola above the tower is copper, which will oxidise in a short while to an emerald green.

Since the setting of the choir stalls was the main consideration, many visits were made to Bavaria by the architect, Frank Hoar, in order to study, at first hand, the architectural surroundings of these splendid works of art, of which there are no finer examples in Europe. The church at Buxheim, from where they came, had been secularised in 1803 and came into the possession of a noble family in the vicinity. Being in straitened financial circumstances the family sold the carvings, in about 1880, to a Governor of the Bank of England who presented them to St. Saviour's Convent in Osnaburgh Street, London. Redevelopment of the site of the Convent necessitated its removal to another site at Hythe and the designing of a new church to house the carvings in more appropriate style.

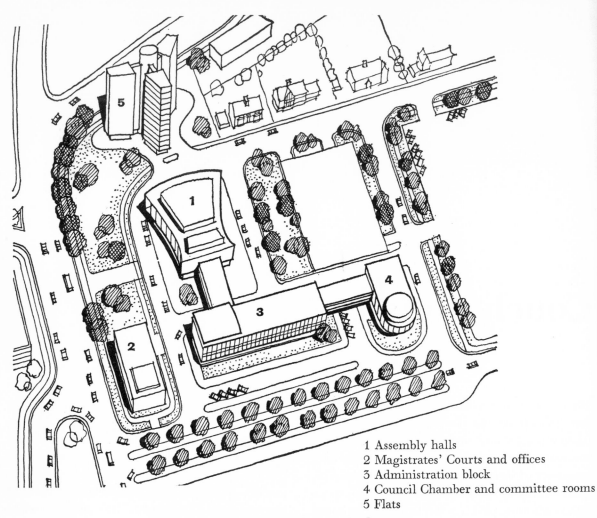

1 Assembly halls
2 Magistrates' Courts and offices
3 Administration block
4 Council Chamber and committee rooms
5 Flats

Project design for Woking Civic Centre

In this scheme by Frank Hoar in association with Anderson, Forster and Wilcox, the main considerations were those of traffic, a convenient approach to the Civic Centre Buildings from a busy traffic artery, and adequate car-parking facilities. Office accommodation for about 200 staff, with a possible extension to 250, was provided. In a separate building two magistrates' courts with ancillary offices were proposed. The Council Chamber, members' rooms and committee rooms were placed in a quieter section of the site, at first-floor level, connecting with the Town Clerk's department. An Assembly Hall, capable of being divided into two separate halls, was also designed. The Council, on this five-acre site, were left with sufficient space for the erection of a block of good class flats, the height of which added dramatically to the horizontal architectural composition.

Conclusion

The factor that will have by far the most forcible effect on the appearance of our future towns and architecture is the ever-increasing problem of communications. The numbers of vehicles in a town of given size, and the future requirements of parking space and roads can, with fair accuracy, be assessed and the necessary provisions planned. Here, however, the planner meets another problem, that of individual ownership, which, outside a communist state or one controlled by a dictator, effectively puts a brake on the planning of large areas.

We have traced the course of English architecture to the present day, when the very existence of the town as we have known it is in question. It is true that vast numbers of people have left the towns for the countryside, but it is also true that such has been the reverse that over eighty per cent of the total population of England lives in urban or suburban areas, while something like one-fifth lives in or around the London area. Economically, it is impossible for the bulk of the population to separate from the towns, and in spite of the speed potential of traffic, in actual fact the ever-increasing density reduces this potential to such a degree that the manual or office worker cannot live at any great distance from his occupation.

We are, as an industrial nation, committed to life in towns and cities and we must, therefore, make the best of the situation by giving our towns a shape and attraction which will make existence in them a profit and a pleasure.

For the last hundred and fifty years the average Englishman has hardly known what it is to live in an attractive city. With the few exceptions of some of our cathedral towns he has lived in growths which sprang from the Industrial Revolution, and he has come to look upon the town as merely a

231

place in which to work, and not, as he should, as a place in which to live as pleasurably and joyously as possible. The urge to escape to the countryside becomes stronger each year, the week-end rush to and from the town ever more chaotic.

The rise in population density, the tendency to settle in the south-east of England, and the resulting shortage of building land will exert very strong pressure to build upward. Indeed, it may in time become the only alternative to a countryside so covered with buildings that open spaces will diminish and eventually disappear.

Certainly we cannot continue to build over good agricultural land as we are now doing at the rate of thousands of acres a year, and the threat by all political parties to provide hundreds of thousands of homes annually conjures up a horrifying vision of a countryside disappearing rapidly under the advancing waves of little dwellings or blocks of flats; of tens of thousands more vehicles on the roads; of exhausted commuters travelling to their distant work, poisoned by petrol fumes, crushed in overcrowded trains, driven to desperation by the constant checks and delays and ageing long before their time with the incessant strain.

Year by year, in this small island, we make futile efforts to cope with the increasing traffic pressure, provide the means to house it and make it flow. All the cumbersome machinery of State, moving slowly and ponderously, provides, here, a few paltry miles of road widening, or there, after years of negotiation, a new by-pass, built at heaven knows what cost in frustration and delay.

To stop and then diminish the ever-widening spread of roads and building in this limited country, to lower the appalling death rate on the roads and the danger to health through fumes and noise, we must

build upwards; vertical travel into the fresh air must take the place of the dangerous horizontal.

The time will come when, for sheer lack of space, a model town of 50,000 inhabitants will be housed in a cluster of tall buildings, occupying little horizontal space, and containing its own industry, shopping centre, offices, schools, entertainment and places of worship hundreds of feet in space, with all the advantages of fresh air, magnificent views, freedom from noise and safety from traffic. The occupants will travel vertically to their offices, their schools, their factories, lessening the pressure on the roads and in complete safety.

Such 'Skytowns', covering only a small space, would take the place of a conglomeration covering thousands of acres, intersected by noisy, dangerous and poisonous traffic roads, all adding to the discomfort of the unfortunate myriads whose homes crowd closely along their borders. Further, the decrease in private traffic would give added freedom to the movement of trade by fast-moving commercial vehicles. Until we are forced to do so, however, the future architectural appearance of our city centres can with fair accuracy be foreseen. The architecture of business will probably retain its rectangular and match-box exterior for many years as being the most economic form of construction, any variety being occasioned by colour and texture of the surface finishings, and, it is hoped, by a more imaginative sense of shape and form. It is possible that the present obsession with large areas of glass will diminish in favour of a design more suitable to this sub-arctic climate, and it is hoped that an increasing use will be made of the work of sculptors and painters to render more attractive the stark outlines of buildings framed in steel and reinforced concrete. Buildings of a more permanent

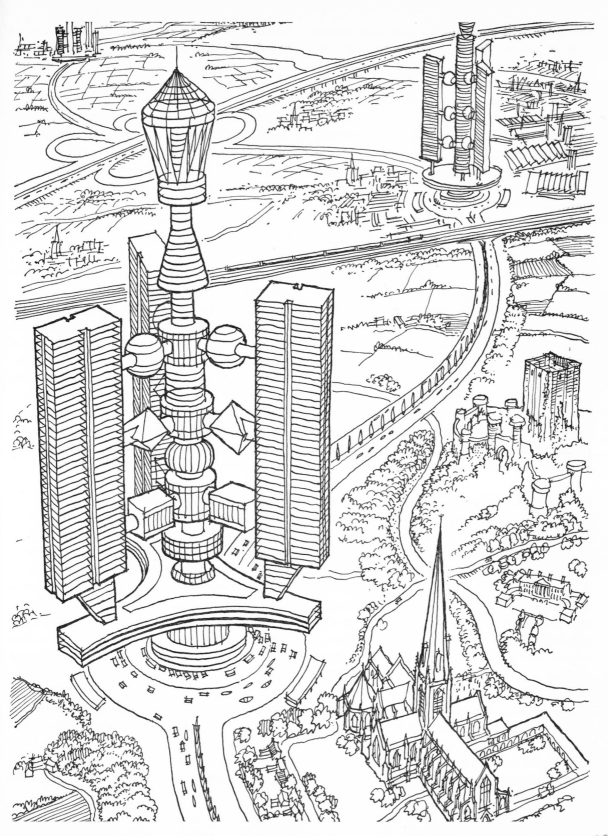

253

character will continue to lend a welcome contrast to the harsher silhouettes of new buildings, and here the City of London, with its variety of domes and church spires, is in a more fortunate position than other towns which are undergoing extensive re-development. The question of silhouette is of great importance. Nothing is more mono-tonous than a townscape of unvaried height, and the post-war appreciation of this fact is shown in the variety of heights of houses and flats on the larger L.C.C. schemes, and the building of church towers and steeples in the new towns. Trees and open spaces, if allowed to remain untouched by the obses-sive craze for car-parks, will play an increasingly important part in the look of a town.

In the residential areas a vast change is taking place. There has been no greater menace to the beauty of the countryside or the appearance of the suburbs than the small speculative builder, almost completely ignorant of good or bad design, usually a despoiler of trees and quite unconcerned with anything but the best possible return on his outlay. His day is fortunately nearly over. Speculative residential development is now being undertaken in increasing measure by large and more enlightened firms who find it profitable to employ either their own architects or to commission a private designer. A house that is architect-designed is a safety factor to many purchasers, who are, surprisingly, willing to pay more for the assurance of a well-built and well-considered home.

The question of what is good or bad in design is no easy one to answer. As far as appearance is concerned the introduction of good manners should be obvious and should play as important a part in building as in society. This is not too often appreciated by planners who seek to impose their own per-sonal ideas. The recent *cause célèbre*, the

Monico building in Piccadilly Circus, is a case in point. Here a building was proposed which, in itself, covered with scintillating electric signs and of no great architectural merit, was refused eventually by the Lon-don County Council. It was a building which would certainly have looked alien in any place but Piccadilly Circus, which is brash, vulgar and noisy, but as essentially a part of the London make-up as the Cockney him-self. No town can follow a preconceived pat-tern; it must in some part be allowed to grow naturally and retain the interest and colour it would otherwise lose if subjected to the dictates of an academic few. The Monico building, in the middle of the enter-tainment centre of London, was in character with its surroundings and offended nobody. The surrender by the L.C.C., which had at first given its consent, was a sorry example of vacillation on the part of a great planning authority.

With the increasing danger and incon-venience of car traffic the centres of towns will inevitably become either closed to traf-fic entirely, or the pedestrian ways will be segregated to ground-floor level with car-riage-ways above. The development of ver-tical flight may see the uppermost levels of buildings used for this purpose, and the improvement in safety devices and the use of new methods of propulsion may promote private travel by air to such an extent that road traffic will fall back to the increasingly subservient position of the railways of today. The town as we know it now may then cease to exist and buildings may spread over the countryside, as today London is begin-ning to sprawl from Cambridge in the north to the coast of the English Channel, inter-spersed by open spaces of varying size and use. There must also, within a compara-tively short time, be an improvement in the traditional methods of building. In the use of brick, for instance, no advance has been made in the last five hundred years, and in comparison with, for example, the techniques of the motor-car industry the building industry lags hopelessly behind. Houses produced on an assembly line will naturally raise the same problems of good and bad design, and imagination falters at the fantastic possibilities of houses made from plastics or similar materials.

Looking back on the course of English building since the war it must be admitted that, by and large, the work of the great official bodies such as the L.C.C. holds a marked advantage over that of the private architect. They are certainly more favourably placed in that their financial resources are not so limited, and the areas they deal with far greater, thus simplifying their planning problems. There is no doubt that the best modern English official architecture has no equal in the world, and the standard of design of our better architects holds its own with that of any other country. The increasing tendency, however, on the part of a so-called 'advanced' section among our architects towards the purely functional and technological contains a danger of its own: that architecture may in time become indistinguishable from engineering and the architect will find himself supplanted by the engineer and out of a job. This country has never held the artist in any great esteem. It will be a disaster when conditions become so impossible that he cannot even exist.

We may expect to see many new towns designed entirely by official architects, such as the L.C.C. is doing at Hook in Hampshire. In the work of these official bodies lies practically the only hope of the sculptor or the designer in mosaics and coloured materials, and we may yet see, as in the age of Baroque, buildings created by architects, sculptors and painters working on equal terms. The landscape architect, who disappeared from the English scene with the close of the eighteenth century, is again coming into his own, employed in the main by the great official bodies who have replaced, with their patronage, the wealthy and cultured aristocracy of the age of taste.

We may expect to see also a vast improvement in the slum areas of our industrial towns. The recently announced drive to supplant these dreary wastes with housing of fresh design and new materials should result in some astonishing alterations in the appearance of our less beautiful cities.

A comparison of the architecture of England since the war with that of the other great English-speaking countries is not without interest. Their climates vary from the arctic to the tropical, but where modern architecture goes up the conditions are not so very different from those of Europe. Apart from the greater cities of the United States, those with over a million inhabitants in the Commonwealth are Sydney, Melbourne and Montreal, and it is here we must look for the most significant advances.

By 1930 only a very few buildings in England had stemmed from the architectural revolution in Europe, and in the United States hardly any. Le Corbusier influenced the first Canadian house in the new style by Robert Blatter at Sillery, Quebec, which was built in 1932. In Australia, Roy Grounds built his own house at Mount Eliza, Victoria, and in New Zealand an Austrian emigrant architect, Plishke, built one in 1939. In England Connell, Ward and Lucas were in the architectural van with their 'High and Over' house at Amersham and others of a similar style.

In the main the United States and the Commonwealth countries are devoted to free enterprise, with the speculative builder given free rein, too often with disastrous results in the almost total absence of planning. New Zealand leads in official architecture which, however, cannot compare with this country. The bungalow is in most general use, widely spaced in prosperous districts, crammed desperately together in poorer. Toronto has some high blocks of flats of good standard but there is nothing like the vertical contrasts in large estates that make those of England so interesting. The problem of associating modern forms with conditions of climate appears, on the whole, to have been ill-considered, and the air-conditioning of America serves as the unsatisfactory solution.

England as a source of architectural inspiration has certainly been eclipsed by America, which is thousands of miles nearer to the Dominions, although many of the Professors in their great architectural schools have been trained in England. All these countries, however, can show buildings that equal and better those in the older European countries, and the extraordinary Opera House in Sydney Harbour, won in competition by Joern Utzon in 1957, is a work of genius.

The headquarters of Unilever in Sydney, and the I.C.I. building in Melbourne, are good and sober examples of great office buildings. The Music Bowl at Melbourne has a domed roof in shell concrete of most imaginative design, and individual houses such as that at Turramurra in New South Wales are of high quality.

New Zealand is only one-thirtieth the size of Australia, but Christchurch airport, the dental training school at Christchurch, the offices at Wellington facing Lambton Quay and many small private houses show a very good standard of design.

The influence of the United States on Canadian architecture is of course paramount, and the fact that many Canadian enterprises are American owned has strengthened this influence. The great American architectural firm of Skidmore, Owings and Merrill has an enormous following in Canada and the west-coast towns show also a certain Asiatic quality in their buildings. There are now signs of revolt against the stereotyped curtain wall of glass and steel which has hitherto been the answer to most commercial building problems, as it has been in England, but the arctic conditions of the northern territories, with their rich industrial opportunities, may evolve an entirely Canadian form of architecture owing little to other influences. British influence is confined rather to the Vancouver area but finds its expression more in the way of life there than in the architecture. Outstanding buildings which may be mentioned are the B.C. Electrical Board offices in Vancouver, and the new scheme for the Toronto Civic Centre, but there are plenty of others, too numerous to be mentioned here, of outstanding quality.

The English firm of James Cubitt and Partners has operated to good effect in Ghana, in the College of Technology at Kumasi. The high office building at Ibadan in Nigeria, by Fry, Drake, Drew and Lasdun, for the Co-operative Bank of Western Nigeria, and their University College, Ibadan, demonstrate the imaginative qualities of an English firm designing for tropical conditions. This firm was associated also with Le Corbusier at Chandigarh, the capital of the Punjab, a tremendous compliment to English architects.

The Aga Khan hospital at Nairobi is a recent design of Amyas Connell, who led the English *avant garde* before the war. His Crown Law Offices, also in Nairobi, owe nothing to tradition and are uncompromisingly but gracefully modern. English architects operate also throughout the Caribbean,

Malaya, in Hong Kong and throughout the Pacific, producing a balanced and unsensational form of architecture whose inspiration derives from the spirit of the mother country.

While it cannot be said that modern English architecture has had any significant influence at all on the architecture of the United States, there is without doubt a regard for the English way of life in the Eastern States that is not without its effect, but generally speaking the building problems of that huge country are on a far vaster scale than in England, and while America has much to learn from this country in its educational buildings and in its official housing, of which there is very little, she will solve these problems in her own way.

During the last two centuries our lives have become more and more absorbed by the processes of mechanisation. In the remote parts of Bavaria the family still, on Sunday evenings, sits around the table and sings folk songs. Samuel Pepys, in the seventeenth century, would choose his maids as much for their clear singing voices as for their industry, so that they could join the family in their evening recitals. Nowadays, the transistor radio provides the mechanical, and too often the irritating, solution to the need for song.

The worship of the machine commenced in the nineteenth century. With the advance of techniques a new environment with a highly organised routine of life satisfied the need to live in an orderly world. Building techniques, however, on the whole tend to lag behind those of other industries, and the lead in this direction has often been taken by the engineers. The Festival Hall in Chianciano, Italy, with a dome composed of simple prefabricated elements which can be assembled in a new and fantastic way, was designed by Pier Luigi Nervi. The French engineer Freyssinet built the locomotive sheds at Bagneux, near Paris, with reinforced concrete slabs that can be bent almost like cardboard. In Maillart's parabolic vault for the Cement Hall in the Swiss National Exhibition of 1939, the thickness was only two inches. The dome of the Crystal Pavilion in the Exhibition of the German Werkbund, in Cologne in 1914, was built up on the principle of a wickerwork construction without the use of supports, anticipating the later forms of construction in laminated wood.

The main form of development in steel construction is in welding, with its greater strength, cleaner design and continuity of construction, and in tubular steelwork. The new high-tensile steels make possible a lighter form of construction, thus decreasing the load on foundations and facilitating a higher building.

In concrete the chief advances have been in the composition of mixes and in reinforcement, in particular in shell construction and pre-stressing, again with a strong tendency to a lighter form of construction. In the technique of timber construction the progress has been greater than in that of any other material by the new selective process of stress grading and by lamination, by improved methods of jointing by modern adhesives and by metal connectors. Timber construction in this country can never reach any great proportions as we have no large home-grown supply.

Foam glass and fibre glass have been developed as insulators in walls and floors, and new types of glass are coming continually on to the market. Double glazing, which is of standard use in Switzerland and U.S.A., is being used here in increasing amounts.

Reinforced brickwork, hollow clay blocks, prefabrication applied to brick wall construction, and new types of plant which speed up bricklaying by the traditional methods, all encourage the continued use of this well-tried material. Light metal alloys are still costly and are used only for special purposes where lightness and resistance to corrosion are needed, although the inevitable increase in their use will undoubtedly decrease their cost.

New additions to building techniques wil widen the technical scope of the architect although this will depend largely on hi imagination and skill, and here the responsi bility to train the budding designer rest heavily on our schools of architecture.

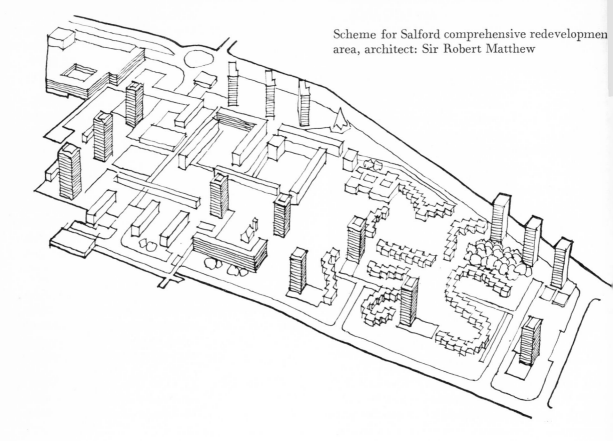

Scheme for Salford comprehensive redevelopmen area, architect: Sir Robert Matthew

Glossary of Architectural terms

ABACUS In Classic architecture the flat top of the capital of a column usually supporting an Entablature.

ABBEY A community of monks or nuns under an Abbot or Abbess. An Abbey is usually larger than a Priory.

ABUTMENT The mass of solid masonry on a pier or wall supporting an arch.

ACADEMY A cultural institution which sometimes included a School of Architecture. Examples are found in the main cities throughout Europe.

ACANTHUS A plant whose leaves, treated conventionally, form the decoration of Greek, Roman and Renaissance capitals, usually on the Corinthian order.

ACROPOLIS The citadel of an ancient Greek city, built on an elevated site and overlooking it. The most famous example, which includes the Parthenon, is at Athens.

ADOBE Walling of clay or mud bricks, used extensively in Southern and Central America.

AGORA The forum or market-place of a Greek city, used for public assembly, usually surrounded by public buildings and colonnades.

AISLES The lateral spaces parallel to the nave in a church or basilica. Very large churches may have double aisles, as at Cologne Cathedral.

ALCOVE A vaulted recess in a wall or hedge, or opening out of a room.

ALMERY or AMBURY Sometimes an alms box in a church. Occasionally a cupboard in a church for the storage of sacred vessels.

AMBULATORY An open or covered arcade. In large-aisled churches it is usually the walk behind the altar. There is a famous example in Chartres Cathedral.

AMPHITHEATRE A Roman oval or elliptical building used for sports or gladiatorial combats. An arena surrounded by tiers of seats. The most famous example is the Colosseum in Rome.

'ANCIENT LIGHTS' Existing windows constituting an obstruction to a person wishing to erect an adjoining building in such a way as to interfere with the light enjoyed.

ANTEFIX or ANTEFIXA An ornamental block fixed vertically along the lower edge of a roof to protect the end of the tile.

'ANTIQUE, THE' A term associated mainly with sculpture, used to describe the art of the Greeks and Romans.

APSE The circular end of a church sanctuary most commonly used on the Continent. It contrasts with the square end of English Gothic buildings. There are fine examples at Notre Dame, Paris, at Bourges, Rheims and Amiens.

AQUEDUCT An artificial channel conveying water from its source to its destination. Nine of these, some of many miles in length, and carried on high piers, were used to supply Imperial Rome.

ARABESQUE Light surface decoration in fanciful continuations of lines used by Arabian artists. They were interwoven with flowers, fruit and figures.

ARCADE Either a series of arches supporting a roof, a roadway under a continued series of arches, or, in modern usage, a covered walk between shops.

ARCADING In Romanesque architecture a series of small arches forming arcades, used for decoration.

ARCH A structure supporting itself and capable of carrying a load over an opening, composed of bricks or stone blocks, wedge-shaped to prevent slipping.

239

ARCH, TRIUMPHAL	A monumental arch built by the Roman Emperors to commemorate a victory, often decorated with reliefs depicting scenes of battle. Famous examples are in Rome and Orange. Napoleon built the Arc de Triomphe in Paris after his victories.
ARCHITECT	Someone who is qualified to design and supervise the erection of buildings.
ARCHITRAVE	In the Roman and Greek 'Orders', the lowest division of the entablature which stretches from column to column.
ARCUATED	An erection in which the structure is built on arches.
ARENA	In an amphitheatre the open oval space on which gladiatorial sports and games took place.
ARSENAL	A building in which are stored military weapons, also a manufacturing place of munitions. There is a sixteenth-century example in Venice.
ART NOUVEAU	A movement in European architecture which began in the 1880's but hardly affected English architecture. This form of decoration consisted chiefly of flowing ornament based on plant shapes.
ASHLAR	Masonry consisting of smooth, accurately cut stones laid in regular courses.
ASYMMETRY	The lack of balance either in the façade or plan of a building. The opposite of symmetry.
ATRIUM	The open central hall or court of a Greek or Roman house. Also the forecourt of an Early Christian church.
ATTIC	The storey or floor above the principal storeys in a classical building, often hidden behind a parapet. In modern times a room partly or wholly built in the roof of a house and lit by dormers or a skylight.
AUDITORIUM	The space in any large building used for seating an audience or congregation.

BAILEY	The space or court enclosed by one of the external walls of a mediaeval castle. Later there were two courts, an inner and outer bailey.
BALCONY	A raised platform, usually protected by railings, projecting in front of a building, outside the windows.
BALDAQUIN or BALDACHIN	A structure within a building in the form of a canopy supported by columns. It may be placed over portals, thrones or altars. The most notable example, designed by Bernini, is in St. Peter's, Rome.
BALISTRARIA	The opening in a fortified wall, usually of cruciform shape, through which a crossbow could be fired.
BALL-FLOWER	The circular three-lobed flower carved at intervals along a hollow moulding, used in English Decorated Gothic architecture.
BALUSTER	A carved column or pillar supporting a handrail. A series of such balusters forms a balustrade.
BAPTISTERY	A building used for the baptismal rite and containing a font. Sometimes merely a bay or chapel reserved for baptisms. Probably the most famous example is at Pisa.
BARBICAN	An outwork of a mediaeval castle sometimes with a tower, the object of which was to protect the drawbridge.
BARN	A building used for the storing of hay and corn. Famous examples include the great barn at Bradford-on-Avon, Wiltshire.
BAROQUE ARCHITECTURE	An extremely decorated form of Renaissance architecture which originated in Italy but which culminated in Bavaria.
BASE	The lowest portion of masonry in any building. It may also mean the part of the pedestal of a column between the shaft and the plinth.

BASEMENT	The lowest storey of a building; also applied to the lowest storey beneath the Orders in classical buildings. It may be rusticated to give an impression of strength.
BASILICA	Either a hall for the administration of justice in a Roman city, or an Early Christian church resembling the former in its plan.
BASTION	Normally a strong semi-circular projection placed at intervals along the main wall of a town or fortress to protect the intervening stretches of wall from the besiegers.
BATTER	A term applied to the slight tilt of a wall from the base upwards, usually for the purpose of strengthening the base.
BATTLEMENT	A type of parapet having indentations through which archers could discharge their crossbows.
BAY	A term used to describe a projecting window or one of the compartments into which the nave of a church or other building is divided.
BAZAAR	A Persian word meaning a market-place lined with booths.
BEAK-HEAD	In Norman architecture a carved ornament vaguely resembling a bird's head with a beak.
BEAM	Originally a tree trunk which has been carved in a square shape. Normally any horizontal roof timber in a building.
BEAUX ARTS, ÉCOLE DES	The most famous and the oldest school of architecture in the world, situated on the Quai Malaquais in Paris.
BED MOULDING	The series of mouldings immediately beneath the cornice of a building.
BEE-HIVE HOUSE	A primitive Irish dwelling of hemispherical form built on a circular foundation, found also, built of stone, in Southern Italy.
BELFRY	A word normally applied to the stage or floor in a tower in which the bells are hung. It may also mean a bell-tower or campanile.
BELVEDERE	A structure, usually found in Italy, erected on the roof of a house and commanding a fine view. It is roofed and open on three sides.
BENCH END	The carved end of a pew in a church. Some beautiful examples of these are to be found in English Decorated and also Baroque churches.
BLIND STORY	An alternative description of the triforium in the nave of a Gothic church as opposed to the Clerestory (Clear Story) which has many windows.
BOLECTION MOULDING	In wood panelling a moulding projecting beyond the face of the framing. It was especially used in panelling by Wren.
BOSS	A projecting ornament at the intersection of ribs in a vaulted roof, found also at the intersection of wooden beams.
BRACE	In timber framing, a diagonal member placed over the angle of the horizontal and vertical members as a stiffening.
BRACKET	A support projecting from a wall usually bearing the weight of a cornice or window-sill. In these cases it is sometimes called a Modillion or Console. In modern times it is called a cantilever.
BRATTICE	A temporary wooden gallery constructed on the top of a wall or tower in mediaeval times for use in a siege.
BRISE-SOLEIL	An adjustable form of screen to diminish the glare of the sun upon windows. Venetian blinds are used for the same purpose.
BROACH SPIRE	An octagonal spire rising from the tower without a parapet, with pyramidal 'broaches' at the angles.
BUTTRESS	A vertical support at intervals on the wall of a building to resist the outward pressure of a vaulted roof, sometimes used merely to strengthen a wall. It is a most important feature of Gothic churches.

CABLE MOULDING — In Norman and Romanesque architecture an enriched moulding resembling a twisted rope.

CALDARIUM or CALIDARIUM — A chamber with hot baths in a Roman bathing establishment.

CAMBER — The slightly curved rise of an otherwise horizontal structure to avoid the appearance of sagging. In road construction, the slight fall from the centre to throw off water.

CAMPANILE — A detached bell-tower usually found in Italy. A famous example is the 'leaning tower' at Pisa.

CANOPY — A roofed covering usually found over a niche or window. A form of baldaquin over an altar.

CAPITAL — The moulded or carved crowning feature of a column. The capitals used in the Greek and Roman Orders are in themselves distinctive examples of each style.

CASINO — A small pavilion or summer house of which the most famous is the 'Casino' near Dublin by Sir W. Chambers. It may also be a public gaming house.

CASTELLATION — The fortification or crenellation of a building by means of battlements.

CENOTAPH — A tomb or monument erected in honour of a person buried elsewhere, the most famous being the Cenotaph in Whitehall, London, commemorating the British dead of the First World War.

CHANCEL — The portion of a church facing east which is reserved for the clergy and choir. It is raised from the level of the nave by several steps.

CHANTRY — A small chapel in the church where masses were sung for the soul of the donor. The word originally meant the donation itself.

CHAPEL — Originally a sanctuary for relics, later a place of worship inside a church in honour of a particular saint.

CHAPTER-HOUSE — The assembly place of the governing body of a monastery or cathedral for the discussion of business. It was usually many-sided, the vaulting supported on a central column.

CHARNEL-HOUSE — A room or series of rooms used for the storage of human bones, especially those found during the digging of new graves.

CHEVET — The circular or polygonal east end of a church, containing chapels off the ambulatory.

CHEVRON — A zig-zag moulding in Norman architecture used especially around arches and doors.

CLASSICAL — The architecture of Ancient Greece and Rome, revived in the Renaissance in Europe and elsewhere.

CLOISTERS — In a monastery, the covered arcade around four sides of a square open space, connecting the church with other important parts such as the chapter-house and refectory.

COLUMN — A vertical support consisting of a base, cylindrical shaft and capital. It may also mean a detached column standing alone, e.g. Trajan's Column in Rome.

CORNICE — In Classic and Renaissance architecture, the projecting upper part of an entablature.

CRENELLATION — An indentation in the upper part of a parapet. In mediaeval England royal permission had first to be obtained before crenellating could commence.

CRUCKS — A pair of timbers or tree trunks arched and joined at the top to provide a timber frame at each end of a building, used in primitive house construction.

CRYPT — A subterranean chamber under a church sometimes provided with altars of worship.

CURTAIN WALL In mediaeval military architecture, the length of wall surrounding a courtyard, with towers at intervals.

CUSP The projection carved on the underside of an arch in Gothic architecture. Cusps divide the arch into ornamental foils.

DAIS A slightly raised platform, at the end of a mediaeval hall, where the lord of the manor and his family ate on a higher level than his retainers.

DECORATED The term applied to the prevalent Gothic architecture in England in the fourteenth century. It was at this time that 'tracery' took the place of 'lancet' windows.

DOG-TOOTH An ornament found in Early English architecture consisting of a row of tooth-like projections each carved into four leaves.

DORIC The simplest of the three 'Orders' of Greek Classic architecture.

DORMER A roofed window projecting from the roof of a building for the purpose of letting light into attic rooms.

DOVECOT A round or sometimes many-sided building for the nesting of doves and pigeons. Some famous examples in England have nests of over a thousand birds.

DRESSINGS Smooth stones used at the corners, and around door and window frames, of a building made of rough material.

DRIPSTONE In Gothic architecture the projecting stone, often carved, placed over the heads of doorways and windows to throw off the rain.

DRUM The vertical and cylindrical lower portion of a dome or cupola in which windows might be placed to introduce light into the central part of a building.

EARLY ENGLISH The thirteenth-century phase of English Gothic architecture distinguished by its use of simple lancet windows. Tracery had not yet been introduced.

ELIZABETHAN The term applied to English Early Renaissance architecture during the reign of Queen Elizabeth (1558–1603).

EMBRASURE On battlements the space between two merlons through which arrows were fired. It may also refer to the splaying inward of a window or door.

ENTABLATURE In Classic architecture the division from above the columns of a temple to the rafters, comprising the architrave, frieze and cornice.

ENTASIS The slightly convex tapering of a column used in order to counteract the optical illusion of curving slightly inwards.

FAÇADE The face, elevation or principal front of a building.

FANLIGHT An oblong or semi-circular piece of glass, placed over the door, decorated with copper, brass or iron. In the eighteenth century the glazing bars spread outwards from the centre like a fan.

FAN-VAULTING A form of vaulting of the Perpendicular period in which all the ribs have identical curvature resembling a fan. Most famous are the vaulting at King's College Chapel, Cambridge, and Henry VII's Chapel, Westminster.

FASCIA In Classic architecture, a portion of the architrave in the Ionic and Corinthian Orders. It is most commonly used to describe the strip of wood placed over the ends of the rafters on a tiled roof.

FLAMBOYANT	Term applied to the latest phase of French Gothic architecture. Its counterpart in England in the fourteenth century was called Flowing Decoration in which the stonework forms long flowing divisions.
FLUTING	The narrow concave channels cut vertically on columns and pilasters.
FOIL	One of the small, arc-shaped openings between the cusps in tracery. The number of foils is known by the terms trefoil, quatrefoil, etc.
FORMWORK	The moulding of concrete in wooden casing when wet. The casing is designed for easy removal from the concrete when set.
FORUM	One of the main public squares in a Roman town, used for civic and market purposes.
FRESCO	A form of wall-painting originated by the Romans executed while the plaster is still wet. It is also applied to any form of wall-painting not in oils.
FRET	In Classic or Renaissance architecture an ornament made up of many small bands or fillets interlacing at right angles.
FRIEZE	In Classic architecture the centre division of the entablature usually ornamented with figures or other carved work.
FRIGIDARIUM	The cooling room in a Roman public bath equipped with a large cold water bath.
GABLE	The triangular-shaped section of a wall of a building enclosed on two sides by the roof from the eaves to the apex. German mediaeval gables were often richly ornamented.
GALLERY	A long room serving as a communication between others, usually hung with pictures. The raised storey at the back of a church used for seating.
GARGOYLE	A spout, often grotesquely carved, for the dispersion of rainwater on mediaeval buildings.
GEORGIAN	The term applied to English Renaissance architecture from the time of George I to George IV (1714–1830).
GOTHIC	The term applied to the pointed architecture of England from the thirteenth to fifteenth centuries.
GOTHIC REVIVAL	A manifestation of the mediaeval Gothic, prevalent in England during the late eighteenth and nineteenth centuries.
GREEK REVIVAL	The revival of Greek Classical architecture beginning in the late eighteenth century, abreast with the Gothic Revival but terminating about 1840.
GROIN	In vaulting, the angular curve formed by the intersection of two arches.
GUTTAE	Small cone-like ornaments found under the triglyphs and mutules of the entablature of the Doric Order.
GYMNASIUM	In ancient Greece a building used for running and physical training.
HALF-TIMBER BUILDING	A building framed in timber, the spaces between being filled with bricks or clay, usually found in the more wooded parts of England.
HALL CHURCH	A church in which the aisles are approximately the same height as the nave.
HAMMER-BEAM ROOF	A roof truss having no tie-beam, arched by means of short cantilevers, or hammer-beams.
HERMES	A bust of a person on a pedestal used decoratively in Classical and Renaissance times. The name of a Greek deity.
HIPPODROME	The Greek equivalent of the ancient Roman circus, used for chariot racing. The Piazza Navona in Rome is built on one such.

HYPOCAUST	A method of heating in which heat from an oven, outside the building, was directed inside the house under the floor, which was raised on pillars.
HYPOSTYLE	A large hall of a temple in which the roof rested on columns. These are mostly to be found in Egypt.
IONIC	The second of the Orders of Greek architecture.
JACOBEAN	The term applied to English Renaissance architecture during the reign of James I (1603–1625).
KEEP	The main inner tower of a fortress. It was the strongest point in the structure and was the place of last resistance by the defenders.
KEYSTONE	The centre wedge-shaped stone of an arch, sometimes carved.
KING-POST	An upright timber extending from the ridge to the tie-beam of a roof-truss.
LANCET ARCH	An acutely-angled thirteenth-century Early English arch resembling a lancet.
LANTERN	A glazed construction usually on the top of a dome or at the crossing of the transepts of a church.
LIERNE	A supporting rib between two main ribs in Gothic vaulting.
LINENFOLD	A carved wooden ornament resembling the folds of linen, found on panelling of the fifteenth and sixteenth centuries.
LINTEL	A horizontal support of wood or stone laid across an opening. Also known as the architrave.
LOGGIA	The roofed portico or gallery behind an open arcade.
LOUVRE	A downward slatted ventilator admitting air without rain. It may be in the form of a turret.
LOZENGE	A figure in the shape of a diamond.
LUNETTE	A semi-circular aperture in a dome or vaulted ceiling.
LYCH GATE	A roofed wooden gateway to a churchyard affording a resting place for the coffin pending the arrival of the priest.
MACHICOLATION	In mediaeval military architecture, a row of openings below the projecting parapet of a barbican or wall, through which boiling lead or stones could be poured on the enemy.
MANNERISM	A term applied to the relaxed Classic architecture of the Italian Renaissance during the time c. 1530–c. 1600. This was the origin of the Baroque.
MANSARD ROOF	A characteristically French roof with steep sides and flatter upper portion allowing space for rooms.
MARQUISE	A projecting glass canopy, sheltering from the weather the entrance to a building.
MASTABA	An ancient Egyptian tomb with sloping sides and flat roof. It preceded the pyramid as a royal burial-place.
MEDIAEVAL	The term applied to architecture in England during the Middle Ages.
MERLON	On a parapet of a fortress the upstanding portion between two 'embrasures' or 'crenels'.
METOPE	The space between two triglyphs on the 'frieze' of the Doric Order.
MISERICHORD	The small projection, often carved, on the back of a hinged seat, enabling a person to rest while standing during a long service.
MITRE	In joinery, the diagonal joint or angle formed by two mouldings meeting at right angles.
MODULE	One half the diameter of a column at its base. It is divided into thirty 'minutes' or parts. The term is used also as a standard of measurement.

MOSAIC | A picture formed by many small cubes of coloured stone or glass, used to decorate floors, walls or ceilings. The churches at Ravenna are famed for this form of decoration.

MOTTE | The artificial mound in a mediaeval castle on which the keep stood, joined to a fenced courtyard or 'bailey' by a drawbridge.

MOULDINGS | The ornamental curves carved on projections. They may be plain or elaborately carved.

MULLIONS | Vertical bars of wood or stone dividing a glass window into many lights.

NARTHEX | A hall or large porch forming the entrance to a basilican church.

NAVE | The central and highest aisle or body of a church. It does not include the transepts or chancel.

NECROPOLIS | A burial ground, literally, a city of the dead.

NEWEL | The central shaft around which the stairs of a circular or 'spiral' staircase climb.

NICHE | A rounded recess in a wall for the display of an ornament, usually a statue.

NORMAN | The term given to describe the eleventh and twelfth-century architecture in England equivalent to the 'Romanesque' on the Continent.

OBELISK | A very tall squared pillar tapering upwards and ending in a point. It was usually monolithic and of granite.

ODEION | A building for musical contests similar to a Greek theatre.

OGEE | An arch or moulding with a convex and concave curve. It was used in late Gothic architecture but originated in Muslim architecture.

ORDER | There are mainly three Classic forms of column—the Doric, Ionic and Corinthian. The 'Order' includes the column, its base, capital and entablature.

ORIEL | A window projecting from the face of a building and sometimes supported by corbelling.

PALLADIAN MOTIF | In Classic architecture an arched opening with two rectangular openings on either side.

PARAPET | Usually the topmost battlemented wall of a fortress, also the low wall built on the top of a wall of a building to hide the roof.

PATIO | In Spanish architecture a courtyard with colonnades for protection from the heat.

PEDESTAL | The base supporting a statue or column.

PEDIMENT | In Classic architecture the three-cornered low gable above the entablature. In Renaissance architecture it may also be broken or curved.

PENDENTIVE | The triangular-shaped overhanging support used to carry a dome over the angles of a square opening.

PERPENDICULAR | The word applied to the latest phase of Gothic architecture in England, coming after the 'Decorated' period, in the late fifteenth and early sixteenth centuries.

PIAZZA | An Italian open space or square surrounded by buildings.

PICTURESQUE | The term used to describe an informal phase of building and landscape gardening of the late eighteenth and early nineteenth centuries.

PIER | The masonry on which an arch is built in a colonnade or bridge.

PILASTER | A shallow, projecting column of the same design as the Order with which it is used.

PISCINA | The stone basin near an altar which receives the water with which the priest has washed the sacred vessels.

246

PLAN	A drawing or representation on a flat surface of the ground plot of a building.
PODIUM	The enclosing wall of an arena. Also a continuous pedestal.
PORTCULLIS	In the barbican or gateway to a mediaeval castle, the iron gate which is raised and lowered vertically, the bars of which are sharpened at the bottom.
PORTICO	A porch or vestibule, usually pedimented, supported on at least one side by columns.
PRIORY	A small monastery presided over by a prior. It was usually attached to an abbey.
QUADRIGA	Monument on a triumphal arch, usually of horses, driver and chariot.
QUATREFOIL	In Gothic tracery an opening carved into four leaf-like mouldings or 'foils'.
QUIRK	A sharp V-shaped groove between two other mouldings.
QUOIN	The dressed stone placed at the corners of a wall of rubble. Sometimes applied to the angle itself.
RAMPART	A defensive bank of earth surrounding a fortress or fortified city, sometimes surmounted by a stone parapet.
REBATE	A channel or groove cut in a piece of wood to receive another.
REFECTORY	The eating hall of a monastery, now applied also to colleges.
RENAISSANCE	The European revival of Classic architecture in the fifteenth and sixteenth centuries, originating in Florence and Rome.
REREDOS	The carved screen rising behind the altar.
RETABLE	A long shelf behind the altar to hold vases or candles.
RIB	A projecting band on a vault. Also one of the plaster bands in Jacobean ceilings.
ROCOCO	A later lavish form of Baroque decoration in which fantastic shell-like forms are used.
ROMANESQUE	Early church architecture founded on Roman architecture, prevalent in Europe from the ninth to the twelfth centuries.
ROSTRUM	The raised platform in a Roman forum, decorated with prows of ships, from which orators spoke. It is now applied to any orator's platform.
RUSTICATION	A Renaissance method of using large, rough stones on the basement floor of a building to give an impression of strength. A fine example is the Pitti Palace in Florence.
SCREEN	The partition separating the nave from the choir. It was often carved.
SECTION	The representation of a building cut by a vertical line in order to show its construction.
SEDILIA	Stone seats of masonry for the priests in the south aisle of a church.
SHAFT	The part of a column between its base and its capital.
SPANDREL	The triangular space between the curves of two adjacent arches and the horizontal moulding above them.
STALLS	Situated in the choir of a church the wooden seats with arms often elaborately carved. They are sometimes surmounted by a canopy, also richly carved.
STILTED-ARCH	An arch in which the springing line is higher than the impost instead of being at the same height.
STUART	The term applied to the period of English architecture between 1625 and 1702.
STUCCO	A fine plaster much used in Renaissance decoration in low relief.
TABERNACLE	A small cupboard above an altar for the Eucharistic Host.
TEMPIETTO	Literally a small, usually ornamental, temple in the park of a Renaissance mansion.

TERRA-COTTA	Baked earth for use as decoration, usually moulded. It is a harder substance than brick.
TIE-BAR	The iron rod holding parts of a building together, mostly found in Gothic churches to resist the outward pressure of vaults. It is a feature of Florentine Renaissance buildings.
TRACERY	The ornamental stonework in the upper part of a Gothic window, usually made up of combinations of geometrical figures.
TRANSEPTS	In a cruciform church the rectangular projections representing the cross-bar of the cross.
TRANSOMS	The horizontal cross-bars of a window.
TRIFORIUM	The raised arcaded corridor on top of the main arches of the nave of a Gothic church.
TUDOR	The term applied to the phase of English architecture from 1485 to 1558.
TURRET	A small circular tower containing a spiral staircase, used in mediaeval architecture.
TYMPANUM	The flat triangular surface in between the three cornices of a pediment. Also the flat surface between the base and cornice of a pedestal or the segmental space between the lintel and the arch of a mediaeval doorway.
UNDERCROFT	In a mediaeval monastery, the low vaulted rooms upon which the main rooms are raised.
VAULT	A continuous arch of brick or stone over any building. It is self-supporting.
VELARIUM	A large awning used in Roman theatres to protect the audience from the sun.
VESTIBULE	In Roman architecture a hall, but now an ante-chamber into a larger room.
VOLUTE	The spiral scroll occurring in Ionic, Corinthian and Composite capitals.
VOUSSOIR	One of the wedge-shaped stones forming an arch.
WEATHERING	A slope on a wall or buttress to throw off rain-water.
WINDOW-TAX	A tax levied upon all windows of a house after the sixth window.
ZIGGURAT	A Mesopotamian pyramidal temple with stages to the summit. There was a sacred upper temple at the top. The Assyrian version, instead of stages, had a continuous ramp to the top.

Index

In view of the length of this index, a certain number of cross reference have been omitted and entries have been classified under the headings Buildings, Bridges, Castles and Royal Residences, Cathedrals and Abbeys Churches, Houses (Residential), Schools, University Colleges. Reference to illustrations are indicated by bold type.

251

254